SINISTER RESONANCE

SINISTER RESONANCE

The Mediumship of the Listener

David Toop

continuum

2010

The Continuum International Publishing Group Inc
80 Maiden Lane, New York, NY 10038

The Continuum International Publishing Group Ltd
The Tower Building, 11 York Road, London SE1 7NX

www.continuumbooks.com

Library of Congress Cataloging-in-Publication Data
Toop, David.
Sinister resonance : the mediumship of the listener / by David Toop.
    p. cm.
Includes bibliographical references and index.
ISBN-13: 978-1-4411-4972-5 (hardcover : alk. paper)
ISBN-10: 1-4411-4972-4 (hardcover : alk. paper) 1. Music—Physiological effect. 2. Auditory perception. 3. Musical perception. I. Title.

    ML3820.T66 2010
    781'.1—dc22   2009047734

ISBN: 978-1-4411-4972-5

Typeset by Pindar NZ, Auckland, New Zealand
Printed in the United States of America

Contents

For Paul Burwell (1949–2007)
drumming in some smoke-filled region —
'And then the sea was closed again, above us' —
and Doris Toop (1912–2008)

Prelude: Distant Music
(on the contemplation of listening)

Out of deep dreamless sleep I was woken, startled by a hollow resonance, a sudden impact of wood on wood. Was the sound an isolated auditory event within my consciousness — a moment of dream without narrative or duration — or was it a real sound from the physical world? The reverberation time was too long for the sound to have emanated from the bedroom. This would imply a sound coming from somewhere else in the house, an echoing space, mysterious and distant. If that was the case, then I could only assume the presence of an intruder, unlikely as a possibility. The sound came from nowhere, belonged nowhere, so had no place in the world except through my description.

Words fly away; the written letter remains. Sound is absence, beguiling; out of sight, out of reach. What made the sound? Who is there? Sound is void, fear and wonder. Listening, as if to the dead, like a medium who deals only in history and what is lost, the ear attunes itself to distant signals, eavesdropping on ghosts and their chatter. Unable to write a solid history, the listener accedes to the slippage of time.

This possibility — that sound is nothing — is characteristic of sound, perplexing, disturbing, yet dangerously seductive. Distant sounds of unknown origin are enshrined in myths, such as the Swedish legend of the Näcken — naked male water sprites living in rivers and lakes who lure children to their deaths with songs and the sounds of musical instruments. They have no reality as physical beings yet their sound, just beyond reach, is a deadly lure. Sound is a present absence; silence is an absent present. Or perhaps the reverse is better: sound is an absent presence; silence is a

present absence? In this sense, sound is a sinister resonance   an association with irrationality and inexplicability, that which we both desire
and dread. Listening, then, is a specimen of mediumship, a question of
discerning and engaging with what lies beyond the world of forms. When
sound, silence and other modalities of auditory phenomena are represented
through 'silent' media, this association of mediumship becomes more acute.
Dwelling in every written text there are voices; within images there is
some suggestion of acoustic space. Sound surrounds, yet our relation to its
enveloping, intrusive, fleeting nature is fragile (a game of Chinese whispers)
rather than decisive.

As a boy I read James Fenimore Cooper's nineteenth-century novel,
The Last of the Mohicans, and became fixated on preternatural hearing, a
recurring theme of the book, No footfall is safe from the cracking of a
dry stick, no rustling of leaf free from suspicion: night trembles with calls
and whispers that demand perpetual vigilance. The name of the central
character is Hawk-eye, the scout with raptor vision, yet what I recall, and
a rereading confirms this, is the importance of hearing to survival in the
forest. Hawk-eye's companion, Chingachgook, is always alert, head turned
aside, 'as though he listened to some distant and distrusted sounds.' Cooper
wrote frequently of a 'breathing silence' through which the harried protagonists must pass, often in darkness or concealment from their French
or Iroquois enemies. Though the narrative becomes laborious and barely
credible, Cooper maintains interest with vivid descriptions of an intense
engagement with a sublime yet dangerous environment. Sight is prioritized
— the naming of this engagement falls by default to the eye — but some
of the most strikingly affective incidents of the story are auditory. When
the fugitives led by Hawk-eye shelter in a cave, the comically pious singer,
David Gamut, is interrupted in his impromptu recital of psalmody by a cry,
'neither human, nor earthly'.

In this context, the cave functions as a vernacular church in which the
sonorous tones of Christianity resonate in natural acoustics. Wilderness is
reclaimed by holy texts that stir the emotions and raise the morale of the
listeners, only to be pulled back into inexplicability by an external sound so
strange that even the scout is inclined momentarily to consider unearthly
origins. 'If 'twere only a battle,' he says, 'it would be a thing understood
by us all, and easily managed, but I have heard that when such shrieks are
atween heaven and 'arth, it betokens another sort of warfare!' Though
the sound is understood eventually as the screams of terrified horses, its

capacity to unnerve and confound is so powerful that only supernatural origins seem adequate as an explanation.

In *The Haunting*, Robert Wise's 1963 film adaptation of Shirley Jackson's psychological ghost story, a harp sounds without any sign of human activation, a sinister resonance. I don't believe in ghosts, at least not the kind hunted in television programmes like *Most Haunted* — wan creatures draped in white, clanking knights and headless horsemen that nobody actually sees. But I am fascinated by the spectral qualities of sound, disturbing noises, eerie silences and the enchantments of music. Distant music is the perfect poetic expression for such qualities (another debt we owe to James Joyce), a reaching back into the lost places of the past, the slippages and mirages of memory, history reaching forward in the intangible form of sound to reconfigure the present and future.

All of us, or should I say those of us equipped from the beginning with the faculty of hearing, begin as eavesdroppers in darkness, hearing muffled sounds from an external world into which we have yet to be born. The film editor and sound recordist who invented the term 'sound design', Walter Murch, was intrigued by the paradox of hearing. Four and a half months after conception we begin to hear. This is the first of our senses to function: hearing dominates amniotic life and yet after birth its importance is overtaken by seeing. As a revolutionary sound designer for films such as *The Conversation, THX-1138, American Graffiti* and *Apocalypse Now*, Murch wondered why this should be so. 'The reasons, no doubt, go far back into our evolutionary past,' he wrote in an essay called 'Sound Design: The Dancing Shadow', 'but I suspect it has something to do with the child's discovery of causality. Sound, which had been absolute and causeless in the womb, becomes something understood to happen as the result of. The enjoyment a child takes in banging things together is the enjoyment of this discovery: first there is no sound, and then — bang! — there is.' If Murch is right, then sound without apparent source will always return us at some unconscious level to our pre-birth state, but with the added anxiety of awareness, of knowing that sounds should have a cause. If they lack a cause, then our need is to invent one.

'We are faced with the immense difficulty, if not the impossibility of verifying the past.' Harold Pinter once said. Places are saturated with unverifiable atmospheres and memory and these are derived as much from sound as any other sensation. 'How beautiful a London street is then,' Virginia Woolf wrote in her essay, 'Street Haunting: A London Adventure', 'with its islands of light, and its long groves of darkness, and on one side of it perhaps some tree-sprinkled, grass-grown space where night is folding herself to sleep naturally and, as one passes the iron railing, one hears those little cracklings and stirrings of leaf and twig which seem to suppose the silence of fields all around them, an owl hooting, and far away the rattle of a train in the valley.'

Although this book is more about listening than it is about music, in the first section I list sounds and recordings of music that connect me with that presentiment of reaching back or forward over hidden far distance to hear echoes of an unverifiable past. Some of these recordings have never been released in digital formats, so I listen to them on vinyl. When the stylus connects with the surface of the record the crackle of this contact ushers in a ghost of time, even before music has begun. Like the cracklings and stirrings of leaf and twig heard by Virginia Woolf, this is a transformative sound, a sound that dispels for a moment the visual, tactile reality of the present. Inspired by Jacques Derrida's neologism, hauntology, a cabal of research, ideas and auditory practice has grown around such experiences, dedicated to exploring the ghostly and nostalgic affect of music. I will leave it to others to unpick the hauntological labyrinth of Derrida's *Specters of Marx*, but this haunted aspect of sound is fundamental to my earliest encounters with sound. In the amniotic ocean, all of us are unified by the furtive yet helpless condition of eavesdropping, unable to identify what we hear when its operation is enacted in another space, entirely beyond our experience as unborn beings.

Am I hearing things? Is there anybody there? I began a new phase of enquiry by asking such hypothetical questions. Why, for example, are the various modalities of sound — from silence to noise — associated so frequently with disquiet, uncertainty and fear, with childhood terrors and a horror of the unknown? At the same time, many people seem to be oblivious to noise and resistant to silence. The two positions seem contradictory, but are they inextricably linked?

'To listen is an effort,' Igor Stravinsky once said, 'and just to hear is no merit. A duck hears also.' Quite why a duck should be singled out as a symbol of unthinking sensory input is unclear (perhaps a misunderstanding over a viaduct and a chicken, though this is a conundrum only a Marx Brothers scholar could untangle). Stravinsky's point is that auditory discernment demands a certain attentive skill, but never mind the duck, the rest of his terminology could be questioned. Is listening more attentive than hearing, or is it the other way around? Both possess an active sense; neither can be consigned entirely to passivity: 'listen to your heartbeat'; 'she's just hearing things'. Listening may be executed with effort yet result in nothing being heard, whereas hearing may begin as instinct and end in *Le Sacre du Printemps*. The point is that all hearing individuals are open to sounds at all times. There is shuteye, but no shutear. Our reasons for deciding to listen, or learning to hear, may range from survival to poetry, from sexual desire to jealous desperation, from curiosity to snooping with malice. Developing our listening abilities in order to gain a deeper understanding of complex passages of sound from the entire auditory world — this is a decision that involves a rejection of cultural norms.

I had been thinking more deeply about sound and silence, attempting to separate out the experience of hearing everyday sounds from the act of listening to music. Listening more intently to those microscopic sounds, atmospheres and minimal acoustic environments that we call silence, led me to examine more closely the subtle perceptual entwinement of our senses. I kept notes in a journal, according to ordinary events. In detail, at an emotional as well as a perceptual level, what was I hearing as I walked the dog in local woodland, or listened to the nocturnal murmurs of our house? A pleasurable intensity of sensation grew out of this practice. For example, as a late-night reader, I became more alert to the importance of sound in literature, not only for innovative twentieth-century authors such as James Joyce, Virginia Woolf, Franz Kafka, William Faulkner and Samuel Beckett, but in the supernatural fiction and ghost stories of writers like Edgar Alan Poe, Algernon Blackwood, Shirley Jackson, Arthur Machen, Bram Stoker and Wilkie Collins.

I revisited John Berger's *Ways of Seeing* (asking myself why there was no equivalent *Ways of Hearing*) and found myself questioning aspects of his emphasis on seeing, particularly his belief that seeing establishes our place in the surrounding world. Yet from Berger's inspired reading of time and silence within the physical surface of *Woman Pouring Milk* by Vermeer it was possible to imagine a sound world within 'mute things', as Nicolas Poussin once described his profession of painting. For some years I had been conscious that my own ways of seeing had atrophied. I wanted to look again, with the same attention to detail that came naturally when I was an art student in my teens, before music and sound took over.

Then I visited the Wallace Collection in London, finding there a hushed atmosphere underscored by the gentle roar of air conditioning, the ticking

PRELUDE

of ornate eighteenth-century French clocks, and a quiet but insistent background note of chimes emanating from a sound installation by Leora Brook and Tiffany Black (otherwise known as brook & black). As I walked through the galleries, paced by time and broken time, floorboards creaked and echoed under the pressure of my footsteps. I had been there before, yet already there was a prickle of anticipation, a feeling described by Freud as 'the uncanny' in his 1919 essay of the same name.

One particular work in the collection began to link all these disparate threads. The painting was called *The Eavesdropper*, by Nicolaes Maes, a seventeenth-century Dutch artist who had joined Rembrandt's studio in his teens, then later became a highly successful portrait painter. *The Eavesdropper* is one of his early genre scenes, one of a series of six works on the same theme. What all of them show is a moment of surreptitious listening, a prolonged instant of collusion between the central figure within the painting and the person looking at the painting. Both of these protagonists silence themselves in order to hear sound from another space within the painting's frame. This led me to consider sounds as phenomena that are difficult to control or subdue, signals that may seem to come from nowhere, or an unknown source, then fade and die. In many circumstances, sound and silence are uncanny. That may be because we live in a visuocentric culture, so sound seems disturbingly intangible, indescribable or inexplicable by comparison with what we can see, touch and hold. It may also be a reaction to noise pollution, through which the rarity and unfamiliarity of clear listening environments can attach strange associations to quiet places or odd sounds.

On the day I finished revising the first draft of this book I read an interview with an American band, Animal Collective. One of the members recounted an epiphany, experienced when he first saw Stanley Kubrick's film, *The Shining*. In particular, the peculiarly conservative avant-gardism of Wendy Carlos's electronic music score was a revelation. 'It's strange,' he said, 'how abstract, non-musical sounds can have a really intense effect on you emotionally.' Kubrick's use of music and sound in *The Shining* was exemplary in this respect. For cinema of such reach and ambition, it was revolutionary. The alien atmosphere of Carlos's synthesized sounds heightens the eldritch power of Krzysztof Penderecki's *De Natura Sonoris No. 1*, the eerie suspended tension of Gyorgy Ligeti's *Lontano*, the crunching of snow, the bounce of a ball, the noise of Danny's small car as he races over the hotel's various floor coverings, or the distant echoes of old music by Henry

Hall, Ray Noble and Jack Hylton that may be seeping through solid air to be heard by a disintegrating mind, or simply the sinister resonance of a ghost. Their cumulative emotional effect is overwhelming; the question of whether one or other of them is music, noise, ambient sound, real music or good music is hardly an issue.

A line was cast into the dark, a search for similar memories of this emotional affect from my own childhood, particularly my acute fear of strange sounds heard within eerie silences, those things that go bump in the night. Looking at Dutch paintings of the early modern period stirred a realization: many of these painters were representing sounds, noise, silences and moments of listening through visual means. In other words, they were using one of the only means available to record auditory events for future centuries to decode. From that point I began to listen more closely to visual media from all periods. In many cases I heard nothing, but in artists as diverse as Juan Muñoz, Georges Seurat, Marcel Duchamp and Ad Reinhardt, I encountered rich soundworlds. This unexpected sensation of clairaudience of hearing inaudible sounds, either from remote history or recent times, struck me as uncanny, as if I could suddenly hear the grass growing or listen to the inner thoughts of a stranger.

The thought is not so strange. In *The Invention of Solitude*, Paul Auster describes something similar in relation to the crystalline silence of Vermeer's *Woman in Blue*: 'A. stares hard at the woman's face, and as time passes he almost begins to hear the voice inside the woman's head as she reads the letter in her hands.' Samuel Beckett wrote about looking at a painting by Emil Nolde, wanting to replay it over and over as you would a recording of music. All of these paintings in the Wallace Collection were silent recordings of auditory events, some more silent than others. Sound haunts their silence as a spectre of history that can never be heard in full, yet its presence is buried within their creation.

Sound and silence have become the recent focus of a rapid expansion of interest. As if now worn out, the century of cinema, television, photography and audio records relinquishes control to less tangible sensations of a new time. But this sudden growth suggests that the phenomenon of sound in itself, distinct from music and speech, has been neglected in the past. I hope to show that sound — and by sound I mean the entire continuum of the audible and inaudible spectrum, including silence, noise, quiet, implicit and imagined sound — can be identified as a sub-text, a hidden if uncertain history within otherwise silent media. It's not so much that sound has been neglected. A profound engagement with sound runs though all aspects of human culture and yet in many cases that engagement goes unrecognized. Neglect invariably engenders a counter movement, so sound and silence (and even noise) can be idealized as the most pure and positive of all sensory impressions. This, it seems to me, reduces the fullness of sound, ignoring its darker attributes as trespasser, invader of territory, agent of instability, unreliable witness. 'I confess my predilection for the silent arts,' wrote Eugene Delacroix in his journal, 'for those mute things of which Poussin made profession, as he said. Words are indiscreet; they break in on your tranquillity, solicit your attention and arouse discussion.' Exactly these irritants may be the reasons why sound is valued — Delacroix also claimed to prefer the society of things to that of men. 'Silence is always impressive,' he wrote, 'even fools look respectable when they are silent.' But surging beneath this respectability there are the problematic properties of silence as chaos, lacuna, intangible presence. Sound is energy unleashed, yet also the perpetual emerging and vanishing, growth and decay of life and death — the perfect metaphor for a ghost.

Freud's description of the uncanny as eerie or frightening, the unhomely sensations arising from that which is unfamiliar and uncertain, particularly when they are once familiar feelings that have become secret or repressed, extended to the uncanny nature of silence and darkness. Inconclusively, at the end of his famous essay, he attributed this to infantile anxieties that none of us fully overcome. Such fears may be childish, but they are rooted in very deep memories of unknown sounds and eerie silences overheard in the dark. Perhaps this returns us once again to the womb, floating in darkness, eavesdropping on mysterious sounds from the unknown world outside. These anxieties are not easily overcome, so when a writer or director needs to evoke atmospheres, administer shocks or summon the uncanny, sound is powerful in its capacity to disturb, to unsettle and install dread.

Just as a silent reader is implicitly a containment of sounds, so the letter itself, the silent speaker, can become a listener. 'The door was shut; and to suppose that wood, when it creaks, transmits anything save that rats are busy and wood dry is childish', wrote Virginia Woolf in *Jacob's Room*. And yet, a letter, personified as Jacob's mother, sits waiting on the hall table, eavesdropping on the faint sounds of her son (his unthinkable sexuality), 'stretched with Florinda,' on the other side of the bedroom door. 'But if the pale blue envelope lying by the biscuit-box had the feelings of a mother, the heart was torn by the little creak, the sudden stir. Behind the door was the obscene thing, the alarming presence, and terror would come over her as at death, or the birth of a child.' Sounds, along with silences, are invoked frequently as signs of the uncanny. Writing about his drawings, Odilon Redon said that they place us, as does music, 'in the world of the ambiguous and the indeterminate.' This is not dissimilar to ideas expressed by Walter Murch, who believed that contemporary cinema is diminished by its technical capacity to show everything imaginable under the sun.

What comes together through sound is emergent and passing time — a sense of duration, the field of memory, a fullness of space that lies beyond touch and out of sight, hidden from vision. Sound must be trusted, cannot be trusted, so has power. When sound that should be present seems to be absent, this is frightening. Through silence we come face to face with ourselves, but into silence sound may enter, intruder again, a question directed at tangible, visible reality. 'One can look at seeing;' wrote Marcel Duchamp, 'one can't hear hearing.' Through that strange anomaly of the senses, the way we perceive the world and the ways in which we represent those perceptions, we strain to hear what can never be there.

Sinister Resonance begins with the premise that sound is a haunting, a ghost, a presence whose location in space is ambiguous and whose existence in time is transitory. The intangibility of sound is uncanny — a phenomenal presence both in the head, at its point of source and all around — so never entirely distinct from auditory hallucinations. The close listener is like a medium who draws out substance from that which is not entirely there. Listening, after all, is always a form of eavesdropping

Because sound vanishes into air and past time, the history of listening must be constructed from the narratives of myth and fiction, 'silent' arts such as painting, the resonance of architecture, auditory artefacts and nature. In such contexts, sound often functions as a metaphor for mystical revelation, instability, forbidden desires, disorder, formlessness, the supernatural, for the breaking of social taboos, the unknown, unconscious and extra-human.

PART I

Aeriel — Notes Toward a History of Listening

1   Drowned by voices

'For beauty is nothing but the beginning of terror . . .'

— RAINER MARIA RILKE

Ishmael is ruminating on Narcissus, in the Loomings section of *Moby Dick*. Narcissus could not grasp the 'tormenting, mild' reflection of himself he saw mirrored in water, so plunged and drowned. 'But that same image we ourselves see in all rivers and oceans', Melville wrote. 'It is the image of the ungraspable phantom of life; and this is the key to it all.'

Through sound heard in darkness, this ungraspable phantom comes to haunt the crew of the Pequod:

At last, when the ship drew near to the outskirts, as it were, of the Equatorial fishing grounds, and in the deep darkness that goes before the dawn, was sailing by a cluster of rocky islets; the watch — then headed by Flask — was startled by a cry so plaintively wild and unearthly — like half-articulated wailings of all the ghosts of all Herod's murdered Innocents — that one and all, they started from their reveries, and for the space of some moments stood, or sat, or leaned all transfixedly listening, like the carved Roman slave, while that wild cry remained within hearing. The Christian or civilized part of the crew said it was mermaids, and shuddered; but the pagan harpooners remained unappalled. Yet the grey Manxman — the oldest mariner of all — declared that the wild thrilling sounds that were heard, were the voices of newly drowned men in the sea.

3

For sailors, the sound of haunting voices heard at sea is a mystery solved by recalling the story of Ulysses in *The Odyssey*, the ears of his crew stuffed with wax to shield their hearing from the death lure of siren song: 'And a call, pure, long and throbbing', wrote James Joyce in the Sirens section of *Ulysses*. 'Long in dying call.' But from Ahab, a man in obsessive pursuit of the white whale, the void, Moby Dick, they learn the truth. The sound they hear is made by seals that have lost their cubs, but according to Ahab, this eerie sound of distress is not the only cause of superstition among sailors. 'Under certain circumstances,' he tells them, 'seals have more than once been mistaken for men.'

DUMBED BY THE CHARM

In *The Voyage of Maildun's Boat* (*Immram curaig Maíle Dúin*), an ancient Irish tale first written down in the early eighth century, a curragh, a boat of wood lath and animal skins, carries Maildun and more than sixty other men from southern Ireland over a boundless ocean. Number is important. Maildun, also known as Maeldune or Maelduin, was cautioned by a man of divination and spirits that he should embark on his mission of revenge with no more nor less than sixty companions. In fact, the exactitude of the wizard is not matched by translators of the story, as in some versions there are seventeen rather than sixty and this seems more likely for a boat of skins. Whatever the numbers, this condition of travel was compromised from the outset by the misplaced goodwill of his foster-brothers. We join your voyage or drown, they say, plunging into the sea. Exceeding its sacred quota the craft is diverted from violent purpose by a magical storm, then forced to accede either to the will of God or chance, depending on one's beliefs.

Drifting and wandering where the wind and currents pull them, through haunted weather and transparent seas, Maildun and his followers encounter a series of wonders. Each of these is confined to its own island — deserts in the ocean — as if the world were a body, a map of disease and pathology, within which all entities, plagues and humours could be located and isolated precisely. There is an isle of giant ants; an isle of red-hot animals; an isle of cannibalistic quadrupeds; a monster who rotates himself within his own skin; an isle populated by people of black skin and clothing, all weeping as they walk; an isle split in two halves of black and white; an isle of laughing that transforms one of their company into this state of permanent joy.

Sound is the precursor to some of these strange adventures, an early warning of what will be. In others, sound is a charm, a binding of spells. There is the small island on which they find a fortress. The door of this fortress is connected to the land by a glass bridge. According to the Celtic scholars who published translations of the story between 1879 and 1906, details of the door differ slightly. In P. W. Joyce's translation, the door is festooned with a copper chain and silver bells; in the translations of Lady Gregory and Whitley Stokes,the door is brass, with brass fittings. A woman comes with a pail, lifts a slab of glass from the bridge and fills her pail with water from the well. She acknowledges Maildun and leaves. 'After this they were striking the brazen fastenings and the brazen net that was before them,' wrote Whitley Stokes, 'and then the sound which they made was a sweet and soothing music, which sent them to sleep till the morrow morning.' For three nights they try to gain entry to the door in the same way, but the metal music entrances them. At the conclusion, their waking brings the evaporation of a dream. No sign can be seen of a fortress, a woman, or even an island.

On the first island appearing out of the great endless ocean, they discover the men who murdered Maildun's father. Eavesdropping outside their forts, they hear the warrior who committed the murder boasting. The scene is mirrored at the end of the tale, when they eavesdrop again at the same spot and realize that the vengeful motive that drove them has melted in the heat of their initiatory trials and revelations. They hear the murmur of surf through darkness, a sign that land is close. Then at night, after their somniferous experience on the island that vanishes, they hear on the air, from a distant north-easterly direction, a low confusion of voices, as if many people are singing psalms. Following the sound until noon the next day, they arrive finally at the Isle of Speaking Birds, black, brown and speckled, all shouting and singing with human voices.

SINGING FROM THE DEEP WATERS

Over the years I have imagined this sound as an unearthly composite of some of what I like, or partially like: those birds prone to harsh volubility, such as rooks, magpies and jays; the shifting, sliding manner, water flowing over water, in which a congregation negotiates Gaelic psalms on the Scottish island of Lewis; vocal polyphony from Corsica, Sardinia, Bulgaria; antiphonal choirs of Georgia; the elaborate melisma and falsetto of Korean Buddhist pomp'ae hossori chanting; one-voice chording of Tantric Buddhist rites of Tibet; chants of Ethiopian Coptic debteras; the updraft and eddies of air suggested by Poul Rovsing's Olsen's 1975 recording of a Sufi group of 25 men, worshipping in the Khalif's mosque in Baghdad; Morton Feldman's *Rothko Chapel*; the Scratch Orchestra singing 'Paragraph 7' of Cornelius Cardew's *Great Learning*; Krzysztof Penderecki's *Canticum canticorum salomonis*; György Ligeti's *Lux aeterna*; 'Search For Delicious' by Panda Bear; the Beach Boys at their most blissed, bootlegged and outré; Björk's 'Pleasure Is All Mine' and 'An Echo, A Stain'; Tim Buckley's 'Starsailor'; *The Bird Song* by Muhal Richard Abrams; songs by Guillaume de Machaut and Gesualdo da Venosa; *The Country of the Stars* by Elisabeth Lutyens; Gustav Holst's *Choral Hymns from the Rig Veda*; the 4th movement of Giacinto Scelsi's 1966 work for ondes Martenot, chorus, percussionists and small orchestra — *Uaxuctum; The Legend of the Mayan City which they themselves destroyed for religious reasons*; Olivier Messiaen's *Oraison* for ondes martenot ensemble; Miya Masaoka's a cappella choral work, *While I was walking, I heard a sound*; Salvatore Sciarrino's *La Bocca, I Piedi, Il Suono* for 4 saxophone soloists and 100 saxophones in movement; John Zorn's *The Clavicle of Solomon*; Alan Lamb's recordings of wind humming through long telegraph wires in rural Australia; Max Eastley's aeolian wind flutes; the whistling of strong winds through John Butcher's soprano saxophone, recorded near Stenness, in the Orkney Islands; the dream chord (as La Monte Young described it) of Japanese gagaku court music; sacred flute music from Papua New Guinea; potoos and howler monkeys from South America; lemurs and aye-ayes from Madagascar; the umbrella of noise formed by gangs of starlings massing in the treetops of my local wood and in Scotland's north-western highlands, blubbersome gobbets of foetid moaning wind snorted out by seals over the mercury shimmer of Loch Linnhe into thin silver air.

In Beijing I heard the eerie cloud-chord of pigeon flocks flying overhead, each bird fitted with a globular multi-pitch whistle made from a lacquered gourd. As the flock wheeled through the sky in mysterious patterns so the strange unbounded sound of their whistles followed in a vapour trail like finely perfumed smoke. *Ko-tze*, these eight note whistles are called, and their practical function is to deter birds of prey. The one on my desk, a six-centimeter mottled brown globe given to me by an old man in the hutongs of Beijing, feather-light in the palm and face-on like a cross between an African mask and an alien spaceship, looks little different to the *ko-tze* collected prior to 1890 and photographed for a postcard published by the Pitt-Rivers Museum in Oxford. The otherworldly formlessness of their sound serves as a symbol of paradise and its freedoms in Frank Capra's 1937 film of *Lost Horizon*.

'You know, every time I see you I hear that music,' Conway the diplomat says to Sondra, the woman he meets in Shangri-La. 'What is it?'

'You mean my pigeons,' she says.

'Was this your idea?' he asks. No, there are at least 13 examples from the nineteenth century housed in the collection of the Metropolitan Museum of Art in New York, is the answer she should have given, though of course she says yes. Dimitri Tiomkins's soundtrack cue is persuasively unearthly at this point. Orchestrated by the African-American composer William Grant Still, whose piano works, notably *Bells: Phantom Chapel* and *Seven Traceries: Mystic Pool* and *Out of the Silence*, are hauntological evocations of place and moment, Sondra's pigeon music is a blurred cascade of harp arpeggios, dissonant see-sawing strings and what might be a held organ chord, anticipating minimal and ambient music nearly three decades before its birth.

I also recall a murmur of speaking and singing voices heard many years ago at night, as I lay half awake in a room directly above the mill race of a barn in Devon. These apparitional voices were picked out from the white noise complexity of a rushing stream diverted through resonant interior space below. They gave the impression of communicating in an unknown tongue bridging music and human speech, and even though it made no sense to me I felt a strong compulsion to decipher the language. Like the interwoven streaming inner voices of Virginia Woolf's *The Waves*, such secrets present themselves as a potentiality of meaning to the attentive eavesdropper: 'One must have patience and infinite care and let the light sound, whether of spiders' delicate feet on a leaf or the chuckle of water in some irrelevant drainpipe, unfold too.' Others have noted similar ethereal musics:

T. S. Eliot's 'voices singing out of empty cisterns and exhausted wells', Thomas Hardy's 'wind oozing thin through the thorn from norward/And the woman calling', and the strangely wounded children, the White Order of the Innocents in Arthur Machen's short story, 'The Happy Children'. Heard by the narrator, they sing 'from the deep waters' an old tune, whose 'modulations were such as I had never heard before.' Composer John

Ireland experienced a momentary vision of phantom children during a picnic on the Sussex Downs, at a spot haunted by relics of a prehistoric fort, Neolithic flint mines, and a medieval lepers' colony and church. They danced around him in silence, dressed in archaic clothes. He wrote to Machen, recounting his vision. Machen replied, by postcard, with a blithe, 'Oh, you've seen them too.' Ireland's deeply romantic, nostalgic *Legend*, written in 1930 for piano and orchestra, was dedicated to Arthur Machen.

Less romantically, strange distant singing by children is heard by K., the land surveyor, in Kafka's *The Castle*. Mladen Dolar quotes the passage in his book, *The Voice and Nothing More*. K. uses the telephone, a recent invention, to clear up what he believes to be a misunderstanding about his need for a permit to stay in the area of the castle: 'The receiver gave out a buzz of a kind that K. had never before heard on a telephone. It was like the hum of countless children's voices — but yet not a hum, the echo rather of voices singing at an infinite distance — blended by sheer impossibility into one high but resonant sound that vibrated on the ear as if it were trying to penetrate beyond mere hearing.' For Dolar, voices are subject to constant change. They are fleeting and unverifiable. K. only wishes to verify the law, but he is connected to indeterminate voices. 'The letter of the law is hidden in some inaccessible place and may not exist at all,' writes Dolar, 'it is a matter of presumption, and we have only voices in its place.' Dolar also scrutinizes the perplexing displacement of the voice, its detachment from the body as the acousmatic voice (the Pythagorean term used by Michel Chion to describe sounds whose origin cannot be seen), and its equally tenuous relationship to the body, even when attached. 'We can immediately see that the voice without a body is inherently uncanny,' Dolar writes, 'and that the body to which it is assigned does not dissipate its haunting effect.'

If I were writing this sixty years ago I might have imagined the Isle of Speaking Birds as Debussy's *Sirènes*, from the three *Nocturnes*, completed in 1899. *Trois scènes au crépescule*, a lost work mentioned in 1892 by Debussy and commonly assumed to be the precursor of *Nocturnes*, was a setting of poet Henri de Régnier's *Poèmes anciens et romanesques*. A familiar visitor to those salons of Mallarmé also frequented by Debussy, de Régnier had written of a 'wan choir'. But Debussy's sirenic choir now sounds too close to kitsch to evoke an island of souls, having been pulped by an excess of imitative swirling climaxes, wild seascapes and tempestuous emotions in too many films of the 1930s. The ethereal female sirens and their wordlessness, 'the collective and impersonal voice, an instrumental timbre,' as Vladimir Jankélévitch put it, have travelled far from the original Greek sirens: birds with human heads, male or female, funerary muses who lured the living to their deaths, then consoled their souls with music in the afterlife. Their ancestor may be the harpy, or snatcher, the winged death-spirit seen in William Blake's watercolour, pen and ink illustration of Dante — *The Wood of the Self-Murderers: The Harpies and the Suicides*. Grotesque beaked creatures squat and screech in trees whose branches drip with blood. Blake's vision captures the spirit of Dante's chilling lines from *Inferno XIII*:

> Wide winged they are, with human necks and faces,
> their feet are clawed, their bellies fat and feathered;
> perched in the trees they shriek their strange laments.

DEAD VOICES

Voix Mortes, the title of a little book dedicated to Debussy by his friend, Victor Segalen, is closer to this conception, but Debussy, like many writers and artists of the late nineteenth and early twentieth century, was also beguiled by fauns and satyrs, and by Pan, the Classical god of sensuality, languor and animate nature. Pan pursued Syrinx to the edge of the river Ladon. Desperate to keep her chastity, she called for help from the river nymphs, so they transformed her into reeds. Pan fashioned himself a flute from these hollow reeds cut to different lengths. According to Golding's sixteenth-century translation of Ovid's *Metamorphoses*, Pan's sighs pass over the open endings of the reeds (an end-blown flute without air ducts, according to organologists) to produce a sound that was still, sweet, strange, feeble and mournful: death and transfiguration were acknowledged then, but a more significant death to Pan was his loss of a conquest, lust in the dust. Pan's breath passed over the open endings of the reeds and airy music materialized, but the 'instrument' was Syrinx herself, known for the beauty of her voice. In James Merrill's poem, 'Syrinx', the sacrificial, erotic surrender of this embodiment within an instrument is conceded: 'I tremble, still / A thinking reed. Who puts his mouth to me / Draws out the scale of love and dread'. Complex influences contribute to this mythical music: The origins of Pan's instrument and his hybrid nature as goat-god — half human-image, half animal — locate his music somewhere within a triangulation of forces. He behaves as a god, operating outside human morality and structures, yet we can recognize human passions and desires. The instrument itself suggests the supposedly random actions of nature, the latter rediscovered for twentieth-century music by composers such as John Cage and Tōru Takemitsu, and by sound artists such as Christina Kubisch, Annea Lockwood, Max Eastley, Jem Finer, Felix Hess and Akio Suzuki.

Other sonic and acoustic ingredients lurk within Pan's lineage of wildness. In some versions of his ancestry, his mother was the oak tree woodpecker nymph Dryope, whose drumming echoes through woodlands. According to Robert Graves in *The White Goddess*, not always the most reliable source, the Latin god Faunus was the equivalent of Pan: 'Faunus is worshipped in sacred groves, where he gives oracles; chiefly by voices heard in sleep while the visitant lies on a sacred fleece.' Another nymph to lose her human form to Pan was Echo, dismembered by his followers to leave only her voice, echoing the sounds made by others. The primal scene of *Music*, painted by Henri Matisse in 1910, could be an illustration of these origin myths, in which the first articulations of musical form are found in ecstatic vision, sexual desire and tragedy. *Music* was a companion piece to *Dance*, murals commissioned by the Russian industrialist Sergey Shchukin for his Trubetskoy Palace in Moscow. Both paintings magnified scenes visible in an earlier work, *Le Bonheur de Vivre* — which portrayed a ring of dancers, inspired by the Sardana, a folk dance that Matisse had witnessed during a sojourn in Collioure, southern France. A female aulos (the double-reed pipe of shepherds) player lies with other naked figures at the front of the picture, and in a woodland grove, an androgynous shepherd plays a single reed pipe. In *Music*, this golden Edenic age has regressed further into primeval time, long before the Fall. Against a depthless blue sky, Matisse shows five naked figures, all of them dry blood-red, deep as the ochre of Australian desert. Two musicians play at the left of the picture. One stands, bowing a tiny violin (despite the self-conscious primitivism of the painting, the violin is too modern to support the idea that this depicts the first music). The other musician sits, blowing an aulos, which is also played by some depictions of Pan. To their right, three figures sit on the ground, knees drawn up as if cold and vulnerable. Their mouths gape wide open, emitting a continuous wail; they could be sacrificial victims, lamenting as they await their fate. The inflated cheeks of the piper's circular breathing would allow a continuous drone with variations — a musical equivalent of the ritual ring dance, circling perpetually like seasons, life cycles, planets orbiting the sun, an astringent harmony of naked voices, reeds and strings. This strand of musical myth may be ethereal, partially Aeolian, oscillating between nature and culture, but in the lower depths it smoulders with eroticism, bestiality and cruelty. Retold through Mallarmé's 'L'Après-Midi d'un Faune', the myth of Pan and Syrinx radiates out from a drowsier aura of dream, heat and sound:

Through the motionless, lazy swoon suffocating with heat the cool morning if it struggles, there murmurs no water not poured by my flute on the thicket sprinkled with melody; and the only wind, quick to breathe itself forth out of the two pipes, before it scatters the sound in an arid rain, is, on the horizon unmoved by any wrinkle, the visible, calm and artificial breath of inspiration returning to the sky.

Debussy gave sound to these images in *Prélude à L'Après-Midi d'un Faune*, *La Flûte de Pan*, from *Chansons de Bilitis*, and a solo flute piece, originally titled *Flûte de Pan* but later renamed *Syrinx*. Many writers of the period struggled with the limitations of words in attempting to describe distant ethereal or elfin music. These sounds, a seduction, a siren song, drew the receptive listener toward an experience of bliss: erotic reverie or a mystical union with nature. Arthur Machen's *The Hill of Dreams* begins with a fictionalized self-portrait of the author as tortured young aesthete, drawn to the remains of a Roman fort in the countryside of his home in Wales. Hearing 'the faint echo of a high-pitched voice singing through the air as on a wire', he lies on the grass. Disinhibited by hypnagogic trance and the lingering occult atmosphere of place, he sheds his clothes and daydreams of merging with the mosses, bark and tree roots, 'the gleaming bodily vision of a strayed faun.' Machen's invocations of Pan — in *The Hill of Dreams*, *The Ceremony*, *The Rose Garden*, and *The Great God Pan* — were as suggestively sexual as mainstream publishing of the time allowed. 'Faint stirring sounds from the fringe of reeds' are heard by the unnamed woman who is the subject of *The Rose Garden*, as she looks at the centre of a lake to see a carved white pedestal of a boy holding a double-flute to his lips (at this point, the doughty organologist might query a discrepancy between Pan's original end-blown tubes of reed, 'with wax together knit' according to Ovid, and more sophisticated double duct flutes and reeds, such as the ancient Greek aulos, the instrument of madness played by the satyr Marsyas and by Dionysus's Maenads in the Temple of Apollo at Delphi). An unnamed man,

11

the stranger, murmurs rich unknown words that 'sounded as the echo of far music.' For these diffuse murmurings she is happy to annihilate her former self, her likes and dislikes, feelings and emotions: 'He had shown her that bodily rapture might be the ritual and expression of the ineffable mysteries, of the world beyond sense, that must be entered by way of sense; and now she believed.' The old world of daylight, built upon parental influences, is abandoned for nocturne, the irrational, sybaritic and sensual life.

Though loosely associated with such decadence through his contributions to *The Yellow Book*, Kenneth Grahame was disinclined to admit Pan's essential nature as predatory seducer. Pan's reputation, portrayed through art and poetry, was incorrigible: the leering, voyeuristic goat-gods of Bacchanal, painted by Rubens; the debauchery of Poussin's *Bacchanal* before a statue of Pan; and Pan's rapacious lunge depicted by Boucher in *Pan and Syrinx*. Study Boucher for too long and even the landscape rewrites itself into pornographic code: labial rocks; phallic trees and pubic river grasses through which Pan thrusts forward into the vulva shape formed by two young nymphs, pink and fleshy as lips. One of these nymphs supports herself on a large pot, its opening facing the viewer. Water flows around them in a landscape that is obsessively and onanistically all orifices and liquidity, lapping and resonance. Occultists of the early twentieth century also found Pan serviceable as a malleable symbol of various transgressions against the laws and prejudices of their time: Austin Osman Spare's drawings of inventively priapic satyrs, Victor Neuberg's homosexual and bisexual poem, 'The Triumph of Pan', and Aleister Crowley's 'Hymn To Pan' — 'And I rave; and I rape and I rip and I rend' — the latter typically excessive in both sentiment and alliteration. 'When Crowley and Neuberg speak of Pan, the imagery is redolent with heat and violence,' Alex Owen writes in *The Place of Enchantment: British Occultism and the Culture of the Modern*, 'a god, half man, half beast, who rapes and ravishes men and women alike.'

Equally remote from Grahame's dilution of Pan is E. M. Forster's surreptitious politicization of the metaphor. 'The Story of a Panic' was Forster's first story, written before the First World War. An oppressively bourgeois group of English tourists picnic in the chestnut woods above Ravenna. During a visitation of panic, a member of their company, a young man named Eustace, is transformed suddenly from an idle, unmanly 14-year-old boy to a creature tormented by elemental forces. First there is a silence, as if reality has been stilled. The boughs of two chestnut trees grind together, then Eustace blows an 'excruciating noise' on the whistle he has made from a piece of wood. 'I had never heard any instrument give forth so ear-splitting and discordant a sound,' says the priggish, xenophobic narrator. Stone through glass, the reed shatters their complacency. The marks of goat hooves are found; dog-like, Eustace rolls in their imprint. On their return to the hotel, he forms a mysterious understanding with the stop-gap waiter, 'a clumsy, impertinent fisher-lad.' At the conclusion of the story, Eustace disappears joyously into the trees, shouting and singing, and the waiter falls dead. As in so much of Forster's writing, landscape, particularly those sites imprinted with occult memory of a pagan past, confronts the refined, hypocritical world of manners that enforced its silence on Forster's homosexuality.

Grahame, on the other hand, preferred to believe that woodlands and riverbanks were 'clean of the clash of sex.' Speaking of his most famous creation, *Wind In the Willows*, that is what he told his devoted fan from America, Theodore Roosevelt, with the implicit suggestion that sex for him was more conflict than pleasure. Accounts of his life bear this out, and his writing is suffused with powerful nostalgia for a prelapsarian world, a childhood of dreamy days spent escaping from the emotional complexity of adulthood. 'The Rural Pan', one of a collection of essays published as *Pagan Papers* in 1893, shows Mercury and Apollo in ascendance within the city while Pan hides from sight and hearing. His presence can only be felt once civilized society is left behind: 'In solitudes such as these Pan sits and dabbles, and all the air is full of the music of his piping.'

Quiet anxiety drives these thoughts, the fear that Pan will be driven into permanent exile by 'the growing tyranny' of forces Grahame identifies as commercialism, fashion and chatter. But cute Pan was more susceptible to commercialism than an amoral, animalistic seducer. J. M. Barrie's *Peter Pan in Kensington Gardens* depicted Peter, half-bird and half-human in origin, making a pipe of reeds: '. . . and he used to sit by the shore of the island of an evening, practicing the sough of the wind and the ripple of the water.' Arthur Rackham's original illustration for the book — captioned *Peter Pan is the fairies' orchestra* — showed a plump, naked baby sitting on a toadstool, blowing at pan pipes. Peter has preternatural sensory capacities. He can see grass grow and hear insects walking about in tree trunks — both his human component and his music are so finely tuned to natural sounds because he has crossed the threshold that supposedly separates humans from animals. Even birds are deceived by the ambiguity, unable to distinguish between Peter Pan's reed pipe and the sound of fish leaping in the water; in 1912, this interspecies scene was fixed as a tableau in Kensington Gardens by Sir George Frampton's statue of Peter Pan, the boy who would not grow up, one hand lifted as if to gather about him all species, the other holding an improbable tricorn pipe (more hunting horn than panpipe, so perhaps not the most suitable instrument for a pagan Halfling). Stoic in the ultra-human constancy of this animistic flute, cormorants stand in line on the wooden stakes that cross the Long Water, grave and black as undertakers. At its most banal, this nostalgic image of the idle piper by a riverbank found its nadir in a 1970s fashion for insipid panpipe music by George Zamfir and Los Incas, both precursors to a 'lifestyle' choice of new age, world music and other suitably innocuous dinner party backgrounds. Animal nature, the goat half of the god, was tranquilized. Panic, pandemonium and the terror sparked by unknown noises in dark woods were mastered, though given the nature of (and within) human beings, can the mastery ever be permanent?

A more faithful rendition of Pan as havoc (even though anthropologi-cally dubious), and his resuscitation through the goat-god Boujeloud, father of fear, can be found in Brion Gysin's novel, *The Process*, and various writings by William Burroughs. For Burroughs, the rhaita (oboe), flute and drum music of Jajouka, in Morocco's Atlas Mountains, became shorthand for a control mechanism, a soft machine for altering time and space: 'From siren towers the twanging tones of fear — Pan God of Panic piping blue notes through empty streets as the berserk time machine twisted a tornado of years and centuries,' he wrote in *The Soft Machine*. In the 'Chinese Laundry' section of *Nova Express*, the narrator plays back hallucinatory tape montages of Moroccan music: 'The music shifted to Pan Pipes and I moved away to remote mountain villages where blue mist swirled through the slate houses — Place of the vine people under moonlight.'

AIR AND EAR

In Cy Twombly's sculpture, *Untitled 1953*, the allusion to panpipes is inescap-able. Eleven strips of wood are bound together, painted white and bound in fabric and wax. Nails protrude from two of the strips; they are not hollowed. Their lengths are irregular, as if this is a flute that emits music of illogical intervals. Two years later, Twombly produced another *Untitled*, this one five slats of wood standing vertically on a single pole. Four of the slats are wrapped in cloth and all five are bound with twine. The piece could be an ancient bellows disinterred, its air constrained. For a third sculpture from this period, *Untitled (Funerary Box for a Lime Green Python) 1954*, he fixed palm leaves to two upright sticks and mounted these on a box. Again: white. Air is implicit in all these works, but the air is stilled, palm leaves like fans fixed solidly in the snake coffin; withheld from the compressed bellows; blocked off in the panpipe.

'The Piper at the Gates of Dawn', an anomalous ethereal reverie of far-off heavenly music implanted within adventures that are otherwise reassuringly four-footed (if a toad who drives a car can be described as four-footed) gave *The Wind in the Willows* its psychedelic credentials in the 1960s, more than 60 years after first publication. Like Maildun and his men, Mole and Rat are rowing between the hours of dusk and dawn, and the elusive music they hear, delicately picked out from the heightened sounds of night and water and described as intoxicating, beautiful, strange and new, a song-dream, 'a sudden clear call from an articulate voice', draws them to an island. Unlike Maildun, however, they put up their oars and go on land; their reward is to tremble in the presence of Pan himself. 'Such music I never dreamed of,' says Rat, 'and the call in it is stronger even than the music is sweet.'

Grahame's anthropomorphic fantasy is very pleased with itself: vulgarity is repulsed, the unruly working classes are put back in their place, and the landowner learns responsibility to the peasants, but the sensory acuity described in 'The Piper at the Gates of Dawn' chapter deepens and unsettles the atmosphere of this otherwise complacent tale. The book is not the only published example of his sensitivity to sound. In 1895 his short essay — 'The Inner Ear' — was included in that quarterly bible of fin-de-siècle decadence and aestheticism, *The Yellow Book*. The title chimed with another contribution, Rosamund Marriott-Watson's poem, 'The Isle of Voices', so the two were printed facing each other. The metaphor of her poem, the siren song of lost youth and memory and its potential to shipwreck those seduced by its call, illustrates the modish appeal of this theme, speaking of a wind 'strange with the sounds and scents of long ago . . . word from a lost world.' 'The Inner Ear' anticipates ideas relevant to the current environmental crisis. Grahame writes about a dulling of senses, the consequence of urban life. A Sunday excursion out of town has the opposite effect, of bombarding the listener with unnatural silence. 'The clamorous ocean of sound has ebbed to an infinite distance', he wrote, 'in its place this other sea of fullest silence comes crawling up, whelming and flooding us.' Gradually, the silence is itself displaced by a revivification of listening:

Silence, indeed! Why as the inner ear awakes and develops, the solid bulk of this sound-in-stillness becomes in its turn overpowering, terrifying. Let the development only continue, one thinks, but a little longer, and the very rush of sap, the thrust and foison of germination, will join in the din, and go far to deafen us.

This is similar to the narrator's crisis in E. M. Forster's short story, 'The Curate's Friend'. During a picnic (a surprisingly dangerous activity in Forster's fiction) a dull curate is befriended by a Faun, visible and audible only to him: 'Already in the wood I was troubled by a multitude of voices — the voices of the hill beneath me, of the trees over my head, of the very insects in the bark of the tree. I could even hear the stream licking little pieces out of the meadows and the meadows dreamily protesting.' His Christian duties are now compromised, not unhappily, by this pagan secret.

Grahame's innocent precognition of psychedelic visions is striking. In an earlier passage from 'The Inner Ear' he refers to the fairy tale in which a man's hearing is so sensitive that he can hear the grass grow. A precursor of The Move's acid-pop classic of 1967, 'I Can Hear the Grass Grow', this ability to perceive microscopic levels of biological activity is a reminder of Peter Pan, who escapes his bedroom to become a child of nature. As Grahame infers, there is a prospect of nightmare in this hypersensitivity to the minutiae of living processes, though only so long as human attributes are preserved. Many fictional transformations into unearthly creatures such as werewolves and vampires are marked by preternatural sensory capabilities, manifesting during the transition from human to bestial. This becoming-animal is implicit in any intensification of perception, but in transfiguration the qualities acquired come from creatures whose sight is a lesser sense: the so-called 'blind' bat, or the wolf, whose geography of scent and hearing extends, respectively, for nearly two miles, and between six and ten miles according to terrain. Dr Jekyll notes this sensory acuity of himself as he becomes Mr Hyde: 'I have more than once observed that, in my second character, my faculties seemed sharpened to a point and my spirits more tensely elastic.' At a further stage in the dissolution and transformation of human into compost and plant life, a different language becomes intelligible. There are intimations of this level of extra-human communication in Ezra Pound's *Canto XLVII*:

> By prong have I entered these hills:
> That the grass grow from my body
> That I hear the roots speaking together.

As Thom Gunn writes, in a commentary on the poem: 'The god enters the earth, the man enters the woman, Odysseus enters the porch of the underworld, we all enter the ground in our death, and in doing so make it fertile.' In David Lynch's film, *Blue Velvet*, the homely surface of Lumberton is penetrated by sudden burrowing, through an audible layer of grass into what crawling horror lies beneath. Soon after this Mole-like entry into the underworld, a severed ear is found, hidden in the grass, and within the ear, descending from the sound bowl of the auricle, the scapha and the concha, down into the auditory canal to the chthonic roaring of its black chambers, lies Lynch's other universe, in which sex and death, decomposition and growth, writhe together like snakes.

Grahame, Barrie (and Lynch) may have been thinking of Fine Ear, one of the seven attendants of Fortunio. In Grimm's version of this fairy tale, 'The Six Servants', a young Prince is faced with an apparently impossible task. During his journey he forms a company of six men endowed with what we would now call superpowers. He encounters one of them with his ear pressed to the ground and asks him what he is doing. The Listener, as he comes to be known, replies: 'I am listening to everything that is going on in the earth; nothing escapes my ears; I can even hear the grass growing.' But the central argument of *The Inner Ear* is that intensive listening of this kind is humbling. Grahame's contention was that humans are superfluous to the workings of the world: we should make ourselves as small as we can and interfere as little as possible with other species. That was, of course, the opposite of what happened subsequently. In fiction's reinvention of the Pan myth, sound materializes out of nowhere as a visitation from nature, an uncanny reminder that humans ('an invention of recent date' as Foucault wrote) have less control or superiority over their environment than they like to believe. Like a biblical plague, the enigmatic rattle of acorns falling on the cabin roof in Lars von Trier's 2009 film, *Antichrist*, is a certain prediction that sciences of the mind will not repel the chaos forces of nature soon to be violently unleashed.

Pan's laughter taunts complacency, as in Bruno Schulz's story, 'Pan', in which a dishevelled, despairing Pan, like a tramp or drunkard, is discovered in the darkest corner of an inaccessible garden of the imagination, hiding among the 'bestially liberated' cabbage heads of burs:

> Deeply shaken, I saw how, still roaring with laughter, he slowly lifted himself up from his crouching position and, hunched like a gorilla, his hands in the torn pockets of his ragged trousers, began to run, cutting in great leaps and bounds through the rustling tinfoil of the burs — a Pan without a pipe, retreating in flight to his familiar haunts.

Sound gathers like an electrical field around the peculiarly self-destructive hunter Thomas Glahn, central character and narrator of Knut Hamsun's *Pan*, first published in 1894. Living in a hut detached from a remote community in the north of Norway, he experiences acute, if self-induced, loneliness. Enfolded in silence, he rattles coins together to break the isolation. At night, he asks himself if Pan is abroad, sitting in a tree, watching him, shaking with silent laughter. 'There was a rustling everywhere in the woods,' Hamsun wrote, 'beasts sniffing, birds calling one to another; their signals filled the air. And it was flying year for the Maybug; its humming mingled with the buzz of the night moths, sounded like a whispering here and a whispering there, all about in the woods. So much there was to hear! For three nights I did not sleep.'

There is another link between the Isle of Speaking Birds and the music of Pan. The death of Pan is a story reported during the reign of the Roman Emperor Tiberius. Attributed to Epitherses, it was retold in Plutarch's *de Defectu Oraculorum*, and again in the sixteenth century by Rabelais in *Gargantua and Pantagruel*. Epitherses was sailing from Greece to Italy. One evening, a disembodied voice called out to the ship as it came near to the island of Paxos. The voice cried loudly once, twice. 'No one replied,' wrote Rabelais, 'but all stood silent and trembling. Then the voice was heard a third time, more terrible than before.' This time, the pilot of the boat, an Egyptian named Thamus, answered, what do you want from me? The voice commanded him to set a course for the island of Palodes and on arrival to announce that the Great God Pan is dead. Close to Palodes, the wind dropped, the ship was becalmed, and silence fell upon the scene. Reluctantly, Thamus climbed on to the prow and shouted the message: Pan is dead. 'Immediately there arose from the forest a great lamentation which resounded through the peaceful evening sky,' wrote W. R. Irwin, in his essay, 'The Survival of Pan'. 'But the shore itself was empty; no wailing devotees could be seen.'

In his lecture, 'The Great God Pan: the survival of an image', Classics scholar John Boardman interpreted this as a recurring theme of nature sorrowing at the death of pagan gods. He quotes Milton, from *Paradise Lost*:

> Nature . . .
> Sighing through all her works, gave signs of woe
> That all was lost

Pan's demise as a force of nature was not always lamented. An amusing allegory of sacred and profane love painted by David Teniers the Younger, copied from a now lost original by Annibale Carracci, shows an undignified scrap between Pan and Cupid. Cupid has laid his bow and arrows to one side; Pan has thrown down his staff and panpipes. The contest between a virile goat-god and a fleshy baby encumbered by wings would seem unequal, but Cupid is on top, one little fist pounding at Pan's face, the other pulling his pointy ear, while the right knee aims for his groin. Unsurprisingly, given this ignominious defeat, Pan's expression is a picture of panic.

BARKLESS DOGS — SONGLESS LARKS

Of course, there is no way to hear the island choir of Maildun's voyage, no magic radio tuned to ancient poetry, lost voices and faded memory. Thomas Hardy's poem of 1917, 'In a Museum', from *Moments of Vision and Miscellaneous Verses*, nevertheless speculated on such possibilities. In Exeter museum he sees the 'mould of a musical bird long passed from light,' and blends its imagined 'coo' with the contralto voice he heard the previous night. Time is a dream, Hardy says; ultimately, their mix of sounds from different periods of history will join all other sounds 'in the full-fugued song of the universe unending.'

Personal interpretations, based as they are on an absence of information, take the liberty of re-imagining any music possessing the characteristic that Freud, in *Civilisation and its Discontents*, described with some scepticism as 'oceanic'. He was responding to a letter sent to him in 1927 by a friend,

Romain Rolland. The letter supported Freud's assessment of religion as an illusion but deplored his failure to appreciate the source of religious feeling. 'It is a feeling,' wrote Freud, 'which he would like to call a sensation of "eternity", a feeling as of something limitless, unbounded — as it were, "oceanic".' Freud considers this argument but finds it unconvincing. He concludes that the oceanic is more likely to represent an early phase of development, of infantile helplessness before the ego detaches itself from the external world, and argues that this stage can survive, crocodile in a modern world, alongside mature feelings. Sensations of bliss that revisit the experience of a child in the womb, floating in dark liquidity and undifferentiated sound, may not be religious, but they are entirely comprehensible.

Perhaps it was a choir not to the liking of Maildun and his men, or perhaps the paradox of unbounded music encircled by the finite shores of an island was too close to reality, for they choose not to land. Instead they move on to another island close by, inhabited by an ancient hermit and many birds. These birds that cover the island's trees, the hermit tells them, are the souls of his dead children and descendants. Together they wait for judgement day.

Where translators Lady Gregory, P. W. Joyce and Whitley Stokes stayed fairly close to earlier sources in their retelling of the story, taken from the *Book of the Dun Cow*, a twelfth-century manuscript of Gaelic literature, Alfred Lord Tennyson took Joyce's account of the navigations, published in *Old Celtic Romances* in 1879, and set off on his own romantic voyage. Some of Tennyson's elaborations in his poem of 1880, 'The Voyage of Maeldune', built upon the theme of hearing and sound. He wrote, for example, of the Silent Isle, a place of barkless dogs and songless larks where 'a silent ocean always broke on a silent shore.' Maeldune and his men abhor this paradise, quiet as death, where streams, waterfalls and birds may be viewed in all their beauty but not heard. Their voices, usually manly and warlike, become 'thinner and fainter than any flittermouse-shriek.'

'[D]umb'd by the charm', the heroes are flustered by feminisation, this transposition into falsetto, hysteria and insubstantiality, this fade to grey. 'They almost fell on each other; but after we sail'd away', Tennyson wrote. Is there a suspicion that this emasculating silence might encourage another form of physical contact, a prospect that can only be averted by fight or flight?

Silence is there to be broken, a caesura, a tensile, fragile state capable of breeding fear in certain people. These men fit a contemporary tendency identified by John M. Picker in *Victorian Soundscapes*: 'Victorians also were beginning to endorse gendered conceptions of levels of sound. Women were increasingly "socialised as the quieter if not silent sex," while "bravura noise-making was an essential signal of masculine identity for much of this era."'

As for the isle of speaking or shouting birds, this was a seductive sound, according to Joyce. The question of what manner of beings might constitute such a spectral heterophonic choir motivates the sailors to row for many hours, from the faint edges of a sonic territory to its core. Their curiosity satisfied, they sail on, as if merely perplexed. Tennyson, on the other hand, moves from one extreme to another, amplifying the shouting of these wild birds to weapons level. Once every hour the birds cry out in human tongue, and at the noise-clock's striking, men and cattle fall dead, buildings collapse and catch fire, crops wither. Coming so quickly after the silent waterfalls, one might expect noise to be of some relief, but Maeldune's men are infected and inflamed by its destructive force. Shout leads to shout and before long they are seizing and slaying all over again.

Maildun's voyage, in particular his hallucinatory encounter with the Isle of Speaking Birds, has haunted me for decades. By inference, this is an island of lost souls, all crying out for salvation but lacking the central figure of a hermit patriarch to console them in their long wait. Can their music resolve itself? There are implications here: society's need for a patriarch composer, a representative of Christianity's God. The birds shout, presumably to attract the attention of any wanderer who might share their burden, but metamorphosis counts against them. Is Maildun a superstitious traveller, who refuses to stop and pass the time of day with magical birds that speak with human voices, or does he refuse to consider the possibility of trans-species communication, even in this narrative of miracles?

Does Maildun abandon beliefs and laws?

The symbolic significance of birds in human culture seems clear: birds connect the earth with the sky; for humans their effortless flight from solid land up to the boundless heavens embodies a yearning desire for some form of freedom, whether our corporeal prison, the limits of human consciousness, or earthly tedium and bondage. But what is it really like to be a bird (to paraphrase Thomas Nagel's famous question: what is it like to be a bat?)? Birdsong can be attractively melodious, close in certain qualities to human music, yet intensive listening reveals the otherness of birds, the difference of their world to ours. 'The fly, the dragonfly, and the bee that we observe flying next to us on a sunny day do not move in the same world as the one in which we observe them,' writes Giorgio Agamben in *The Open: Man and Animal*, 'nor do they share with us — or with each other — the same time and the same space.' The rapidity of a bird's perceptions is reflected by a complex tumbling and pouring of clear melodic sequences, but these are interrupted and augmented by elements that in much human music would be considered illogical: unpredictable, leaping pitch intervals; irregular rhythms and insistent repetitions; lengthy silent pauses; tones with no front attack (impossible to copy on a piano); interventions of enharmonic noises; percussive, microtonal gradations; multiphonic trilling; sliding, bent tones and stratospheric flights into frequency ranges too high for us to hear. Then there is movement, sudden, quick, constant, and the spatial displacement of the song caused by flight and environmental masking. These are the elements that composers inspired by birdsong — Respighi, Purcell, Daquin, Vivaldi, Mozart, and even Olivier Messiaen — were too civilized to acknowledge. Like A. M. Jones's transcriptions of African music in the 1950s, such projects can be only partially successful: not only are the specifics of sound ignored; notation also flattens out subtle variations in pitch and rhythm to fit the standardisation of tempered tuning and the division of time between bar lines. Essentials of difference are eradicated.

Intense, beguiling, misanthropic, J. A. Baker's book, *The Peregrine*, showed little interest in domesticating bird song. He wrote of the 'rich dungeon notes' of the crow, the drumming of a snipe as 'an ominous sound, as though an oracle was about to speak from the sky.' Of a cock bullfinch, quietly snapping buds from a larch twig, he wrote this: 'Beauty is vapour from the pit of death.' Seamus Heaney writes of human beings discovering death for the first time, seeing their souls in birds, a flock at twilight, 'Cawing and headed back for the same old roosts.'

'Death', Heaney says, 'would be like a night spent in the wood.'

In his classic work, *Shamanism: Archaic Techniques of Ecstacy*, Mircea Eliade considered the universal motif of magical flight and the mythical image of the soul embodied within the form of a bird.

What concerns us in this instance, is the fact that sorcerers and shamans are able, here on earth and as often as they wish, to accomplish 'coming out of the body,' that is, the death that alone has power to transform the rest of mankind into 'birds'; shamans and sorcerers can enjoy the condition of 'souls,' of 'discarnate beings,' which is accessible to the profane only when they die. Magical flight is the expression both of the soul's autonomy and of ecstasy.

UNSEEN, UNKNOWN, UNCANNY

Yet from what Maildun witnesses, the island birds are flightless: half-human, half-avian. Entrapped in their sonic limbo, they enact eternal penance. This leitmotif can be found in other early Irish tales. The children of Ler are forced to bathe in the waters of Loch Dairbhreach by their jealous stepmother. She strikes them with a wand and transforms them into swans, but then suffers an attack of remorse. With no powers to reverse the spell, she tells them that they will be swans for 900 years. 'The birds however retain their human speech and reason', wrote Anne Ross in *Pagan Celtic Britain*. 'They have the gift of making music so beautiful that everyone falls asleep on account of it. Sleep-music is a constant feature of supernatural birds in the Celtic world.'

A distant murmuring mass of birds, at closer quarters found to be loud human shouting, saying nothing intelligible, speaks for the seductive difficulties of sound: where does it come from; who or what is producing it; what are its boundaries; what can it be communicating? In stories like this, the floating vessel — sailing boat or rowing boat — is an island itself, a temporary home passing through liquidity and air, though not full light. A microcosm of human society, the boat navigates uncharted, chaotic boundlessness in order to discover forms, as if discovering the diverse possibilities of musical structure within the ocean of sound. A number of possible interpretations of these episodes — birth and rebirth, for example — are tempting, but what interests me is their role as metaphors for the act of hearing, and how listening is an act that brings us closer to what we are not, the parallel worlds of the extra-human.

Then there is the revelation that comes twice to Maildun through the morally dubious method of eavesdropping on sounds not intended for his ears. Finally, Tennyson presents us with a paradox: a disturbing silence, which ends, only to be replaced by maddening noise. This paradox is increasingly familiar in the contemporary world. Quiet is felt as disquiet, silence as unnatural, a seal to be broken, yet noise levels are rising inexorably across the globe, so sound is an irritant, a headache, inescapable, a physical assault on the senses, a threat to well-being, health and longevity.

The two phenomena are linked, since dread emptiness will be filled by whatever noise comes to hand, yet they contradict each other and in their antagonism search for a reduced condition, an ignorable neutrality in which non-functional sound is relegated to the far edges of perception. The motif of eavesdropping is familiar, also, since surveillance of various kinds — for military purposes, social control, crime prevention, terrorism and anti-terrorism, snooping, blackmail, espionage, pornography, the use of webcams and 'reality' entertainment — has been so augmented in potential by technological developments that in Britain, where I write, ways of thinking about privacy and public space have congealed into a concoction of profound anxiety, suspicion, paranoia, voyeurism and mass prurience.

AERIOS

The aerial (or ariel) nature of sound, and by extension — music — always implies some degree of insubstantiality and uncertainty, some potential for illusion or deception, some ambiguity of absence or presence, full or empty, enchantment or transgression. Through sound, the boundaries of the physical world are questioned, even threatened or undone by instability. Does sound rise out of solid life, or is it hallucination, a lack, this charm? 'Where should this music be?' asks Ferdinand, Prince of Naples, as he follows the singing of invisible Ariel in *The Tempest*. 'I' th' air or th' earth?' Sound is uncanny.

Maildun's story, and most literary invocations of Pan, are set during the hours of night, before sunlight dispels illusion, or in dream states and sleep. Emanating from far away, over the horizon and out of sight, the ethereal music is easily confused with the sound of wind, or breezes whistling in the reeds. Even those who are susceptible must strain to listen; even for them, there is no certainty, no permanence. Walter de la Mare wrote of his improvised song of enchantment, sung low, turning in widdershins, 'Just as the words came up to me', under the wild wood tree:

> But the music is lost and the words are gone
> Of the song I sang as I sat alone,
> Ages and ages have fallen on me —
> On the wood and the pool and the elder tree.

Both sound and silence are ambiguous, both elusive in their meaning and persuasive: a charm. Prescient, anticipating the sonic power of dictators like Hitler, the senseless rhetoric of so many politicians, Joseph Conrad wrote, 'The power of sound has always been greater than the power of sense.' Perhaps in its persistent fading, even on recordings, sound short-circuits rationalism, seducing in the same way that moments of perfect weather or the flowering of certain plants tantalize us with loss, passing, the decay of all things.

Music was a reminder of the transience of life in the didactic vanitas genre of seventeenth-century Dutch still life paintings. In Edwaert Collier's *Vanitas Still Life* of 1664 we see open books, a snuff box, globes, an hourglass, a lute, violin and flute; Adriaen Coorte's *Vanitas Still Life in a Niche* of 1688 shows a glass half-filled with wine, pipe and tobacco, dice, a watch, playing cards, an oil lamp with smouldering wick, an empty shell, a pochette (a small bowed string instrument also known as a kit) and a music book. A skull serves as paperweight; upper teeth clamped on the cover of the book, whose dog-eared corners artfully rise to beguile scholars of the future with glimpsed fragments of notes on staves. Even the pneuma of music, transient yet so easily resuscitated through notation, is destined for the silence of the tomb. Though imbued with sufficient vitality to overpower such inherent morbidity, music, along with silence, is uncomfortably close to death — a shocking and shaping of the air, then suddenly gone. Sound may not excel in certainty until shaped with precision in certain forms of music, but both possess, in their different ways, sublime attributes as metaphors or representations of all that is not solid: emotions, atmosphere, sensuality, passions of all kinds, the passage of time, abstract mathematics, memory, loss and mourning, nostalgia, the metaphysical, supernatural, spectral, unseen, unknown and uncanny.

Earlier navigations — Homer's *The Odyssey* and Virgil's *The Aeneid* — resound with passages in which sound breaks through the membrane separating living from dead, a tangible force, acting in the world of humans and objects for those who are disembodied. Odysseus travels the River of Ocean into Hades' Kingdom of Decay, where he opens a wound in the earth to unleash the 'eerie clamour' of the souls of the dead from Erebus. Guided by doves to the golden bough, Aeneas follows the instructions of the Sibyl at the cave of Aornos, a place where no bird can survive the rank breath pouring from its black throat. There he sacrifices a black-fleeced lamb to Night, the mother of the Furies. In trance, the Sibyl walks with him into the world of spirits, silent shades, Chaos, dark and silent wastes. At dawn, earth bellows underfoot and dogs howl in darkness, signalling the arrival of the goddess. Dead silence resonates in this subterranean clamour — Ajax's embittered refusal to speak, his turning away to join the souls of the other dead, and Dido's silent rejection of Aeneas.

In a reversal of Maildun's vision of the birds that shout in human tongues, Aeneas sees 'numberless races and tribes of men, like bees in a meadow on a clear summer day, settling on all the many-coloured flowers and crowding round the gleaming white lilies while the whole plain is loud with their buzzing.'

Shuddering at the scene, Aeneas asks his father, Anichises, who they are, these noisy, humming human-bees?

'These are the souls to whom Fate owes a second body,' Anichises replies.

THIS MUSIC CREPT BY ME UPON THE WATERS

Blind under darkness, Maildun and his crew row their curragh for hours, charmed by the magnetism of an indistinct murmur audible in the far distance. Yet when they arrive into light, the balance of what they see against what they hear is irreconcilable. This world is ungraspable phantom, quite beyond their control or understanding. These flightless birds of diverse colour have no route of escape from their island; their sound is inchoate, a heavenly but also earthly music drifting out over water, a limbo of human language, creature tongues, the songs of the dead — a formless meteorological sound like mist, 'voices in the wind's singing, more distant and more solemn than a fading star,' eternally repeated through the constancy of those who are condemned to do nothing else. The music is without beginning or end, remote from human culture yet haunted by its signs. 'Quick air singing in the boat's tight wires', wrote Robert MacFarlane in *The Wild Places*, mistaking the keening noise he was hearing in the dying light of dusk for Aeolian voices, then realising that hundreds of seals pulled out on the rocks of the bay were singing an eerie heterophonic chorale. 'They were giving off noise without seeming to, as bees do, or water.'

Long in dying call, far from family, home, fireside — dogged, restless, uncomprehending but curious — Maildun and his fellow sailors continue on their way through the flux of ocean, in search of stillness, silence.

2   Each echoing opening; each muffled closure

In 1972 John Berger opened his book, *Ways of Seeing*, with an unconditional statement: 'Seeing comes before words. The child looks and recognizes before it can speak.'

The statement is printed on the front cover of the current edition, just to ensure that further reading is encouraged and then informed by its cast-iron authority. All insight and understanding stemming from this important, influential book must follow, though as Geoff Dyer remarks in *Ways of Telling*, 'This has all the resonance of the genuinely empty claim.'

So far, so good. Interpreting these two sentences according to their intended meaning leads to an incontrovertible conclusion: words follow looking — they name and describe what has already been seen, only after the acquisition of language. Babies can't hold a verbal conversation with mother, midwife or paediatrician, as soon as they are born, or for some time after. But Berger goes further, extending the primacy of seeing over words to a more generalized primacy of seeing over all other senses. 'It is seeing which establishes our place in the surrounding world;' he wrote, 'we explain that world with words, but words can never undo the fact that we are surrounded by it.' Whether generalisation or empty claim, this demands closer examination. Seeing may be, by consensus, the most valued filter through which the majority of modern humans engage with their environment, yet Berger's claim is more exclusive than that. He talks about the surrounding world, yet seeing is the least effective of the senses in grasping this sense of surrounding. Listening, smelling, touching, ther-moception, proprioception (even taste in certain cases) can supply feedback that is specific, enveloping, immersive. Seeing, however, gives us what is in front of our eyes.

Whatever the case for adult life, his binary division of the world into vision and word is not a full reflection of the experience of a small child, born or unborn. During a conference on sound and anthropology, held at the University of St. Andrews in 2006, I watched Professor Colwyn Trevarthen's video of premature babies, so tiny that their physical place in the world seems under perpetual threat. With remarkable precision, using pitched and rhythmic vocal sounds and small finger movements, they communicate with the adult who cradles them. This brings us closer to the sensory environment of infants.

A baby in the womb hears sound and responds. Any parent-to-be can discover the short-term response for themselves without an expert. Go out to hear some loud music and the kicking will start. Mothers talk and sing to children not yet born. Some are primed for life as a future genius by a background of 'improving' music by Mozart or J. S. Bach, though the sight of Dr. Hannibal Lecter in incarcerated reverie, finger conducting to Bach's *Goldberg Variations* in *The Silence of the Lambs*, could make one question the efficacy of such subliminal culture coaching. True to form, Hannah Merker, author of *Listening: Ways of Hearing in a Silent World*, played Mozart and Chopin to the children she was carrying. She also read them stories related to her research into horror in children's literature. This was not a wish for a genius brood, though horror and violence at a formative stage of development can help matters turn out that way. 'I wanted my children, once they got here,' she writes, 'to allow themselves to be affected by alternate realms of feeling.' From where do the stories, the voices, the music emanate? By the time the child learns the answer to this question, involuntary hearing, the uncertain, obscure nature of sound and the eavesdropping mode of listening are established. This is more strange than we allow: present but unseen, the unborn child involuntarily eavesdrops on people it does not yet know, overhearing sound from a world of which it has no knowledge or experience.

Overhearing is an excess of hearing. 'The studies that suggest the foetus can hear the world beyond the womb mortify me,' wrote Jenny Diski, in her account of stillness and silence, *On Trying to Keep Still*.

I chose to believe that I managed to ignore the disruptive sounds of the world (my father groaned, my mother wept) and lived only with a background rhythm of two beating syncopated hearts, one fast, one slow, like the tocking of old clocks in an empty house, and the gentle babbling and gurgling of digestive juices.

Anna Karpf explores the audio responsiveness of unborn infants in her book, *The Human Voice*. Not only can a foetus react to some sounds from as early as 14 weeks — it can distinguish between male and female voices, and from within a group of people can recognize its mother speaking and so be soothed or excited by her voice and its relationship to breathing, heart rate, muscular tension and movements of the diaphragm. This emotional, auditory and tactile bond then endures for at least four years until, according to the official version, a comprehensive employment of the senses is displaced gradually by a growing predominance of the visual. Therapists and sound artists may feel differently about these auditory origins, in the manner through which the masked echo of the maternal voice or its simulacrum may be a presence of problematic diversity and subterfuge through childhood into adulthood, even to death, or through mysterious preferences for noise that is filtered, immersive, physically overwhelming, rhythmic or in some other way, via distant memory, intra-uterine.

As Karpf points out, the mother's voice is conducted both through air and through the body of the mother, passing from abdominal tissues into amniotic fluid, via her spine and pelvic arch. Newborn babies prefer filtered voices that continue the muffled conditions in which they have developed and of which they have been a part, two heartbeats (or more) but a single place of sound. She refers to the studies of a psychoanalyst, William Niederland, who believed that 'the foetus experiences sound as contact, possibly because sound waves from a person's voice create tiny yet distinct impressions on the eardrum and skin, so that vibrations are felt as well as heard.' Karpf's conclusion is this: 'When mothers speak, therefore, they are engaged in a body-to-body experience with the baby in their womb, and aren't just producing some localized vocal or auditory experience.' As she speculates, the relationship between hearing and touch is closer than we realize, and this has, as she writes, 'huge psychological implications, and might go some way to explaining the intimate connection between maternal voice and secure attachment.'

Awareness and the difficulties of the self in the social world begin, then, with an immersion in sound, coming from within, without and inside, all at once, and this sound not so much heard but felt and not entirely emanating from a separate consciousness, but also not belonging to specific identifiable places or the recipient. This phase ends with a shock of light and noise, the small eyes screwed tightly shut, gripped by hands or surgical instruments shaking the sudden expansion of air space and sensations with cries. So noise is the first means of meeting this world. Too lengthy a silence from the newborn child, on the other hand, raises concern, and perhaps the anxious associations of this silence contribute to a more general unease in the presence of silence.

Life is no less complicated after birth. 'An eight month old child is aware of noise, particularly animal and human noises, in the next room,' wrote Yi-Fu Tuan in *Space and Place: The Perspective of Experience*. 'He attends to them; his sphere of influence expands beyond what is visible and of pressing concern. However, his behavioural space remains small.' In other words, sound is a medium that outreaches the known and negotiable world, but remains beyond comprehension at this stage of development.

A WHISTLING BREATH

As I write this, my mother is dying, slowly, painfully. When I speak to her and hear her voice I can deduce the fluctuations and crisis of her state: a cracked, hoarse voice, barely present and collapsing under the crushing implosion of extreme old age; a faint, childlike voice, vulnerable and helpless; a confused, questioning voice that struggles to find sense in what I say; a sharp, angry voice, frustrated by continuing to be alive; a fading voice that speaks only because she can still hear the demands of others, only because the world is still there, insisting that she continue to speak. Never particularly good at listening, she is now unable to hear very much of anything, partly because of deafness, partly because her brain functioning seems much reduced, now limited to three or four subjects unless a miniature of precise memory from the beginning of the last century surfaces like a miraculous once-extinct creature from the depths. Conversation is exhausting, so only the voice can carry the weight of who this person once was and who she has become. There is very little of her, a diminishing bird-like frame. Her mobility vanished long ago, her environmental stimulus has narrowed drastically, her sight and hearing have deteriorated, the food she once loved to cook and eat is no longer appealing. The world contracts to a thin thread of voice and little else other than presence. The behavioural space becomes small once more, but then expands again after death. In the silence at the end of her funeral, as curtains closed on the theatre of cremation, the whistling breath of an elderly woman seated across the aisle from me swishes the suspended air.

Then my own voice, affected for some weeks after her death, caught somewhere between throat and external air, a frail self, refusing to project or occupy its full spectrum: a dying echo; the words died on his lips.

SILENCE, TIME, THE TRAIL OF THE BRUSH

A profound ambiguity within the sensorium highlights our problem, the problem exaggerated unwittingly by Berger in his attempt to school a mass audience in looking and seeing in the age of mass media, rampant visual communication and the projection of power though images. The senses are curiously entwined. There are no clear boundaries. As a writer of great insight, John Berger is sensitive to sensory confluence. In *Ways of Seeing* he wrote the following:

> Original paintings are silent and still in a sense that information never is. Even a reproduction hung on a wall is not comparable in this respect for in the original the silence and stillness permeate the actual material, the paint, in which one follows the traces of the painter's immediate gestures. This has the effect of closing the distance in time between the painting of the picture and one's own act of looking at it.

This passage is illustrated by a monochrome reproduction of Johannes Vermeer's *Woman Pouring Milk*. As I read Berger, I recalled my own past experiences in the National Gallery in London, absorbing the deeply sub-jective quality of silence and stillness in Piero della Francesca's *The Baptism of Christ*, Giovanni Bellini's *The Agony in the Garden* and Vermeer's *A Young Woman standing at a Virginal*. At the time this may have seemed to me like looking at pictures, or a brief respite from all that was outside, in the city; now they figure more clearly as deeper and durable acts of replenish-ment, beginning with seeing but leading on to the implication of sound. A sound-world inhabits and emanates from certain paintings. Despite their actual silence, that sound-world accumulates as the scene, the space of the scene, the activity within the scene, and the world beyond the scene all gather force. There is sound as the servant pours milk, and that sound is heard through invocation within various forms of silence and space. Piero's *The Baptism of Christ* is dynamic in its composition and colour yet infused with stillness. Bernard Berenson, in his classic study, *Italian Painters of the Renaissance*, spoke of his light effects, their 'subduing and soothing qualities,' and of his impersonality, 'the quality whereby he holds us spellbound.' Echoing the shape of clouds in the distance, a dove hovers above Christ's head, the three faces to his right are placid, the left foot of St. John is raised with elegance. One sound resonates in this stillness, a thin trickle of water clearly depicted, a silvered ghost falling from the fifteenth century.

What Berger says about Vermeer — 'silence, time, the trail of the brush' — gains in significance by comparison with Peter Webber's film of Tracy Chevalier's novel, *Girl with a Pearl Earring*, in which a literal enactment of precious little available historical material brings all-too specific sounds, movement, external ambience, fictional narrative and other properties, spurious or otherwise, to Vermeer's work. The film may be beguiling, yet its telescoping of time between the works and the act of experiencing the works can only be banal by comparison. Berger is more interested in deeper complexities of silence. In his preface to Timothy O'Grady's novel of Irish exile and displacement, *I Could Read the Sky*, he dwells on the silences of writing, their timing and the hiding of silences so that the reader falls into them, those barely noticed silences at head and foot of page, dividing sentences, air between lines, inside sentences, the unsaid. 'The silence of the unsaid is always working surreptitiously with another silence,' he writes, 'which is that of the unsayable.'

In a more recent book, *The Shape of a Pocket*, John Berger attempts to explain why more and more people visit art museums and find themselves satisfied with the experience. 'In art museums,' he says, 'we come upon the visible of other periods and it offers us company.' Work of other periods can also repel our company and mock modern sensibilities, but Berger's observation reminds us, rather poignantly, that this exact experience is not possible with sound. Prior to the 1870s, sound could only be captured and preserved for posterity through representation in another medium: notation, written description, or the visual arts, as in a painting such as *The Nativity* by Piero della Francesca, in which baby Jesus hears, in his first moments, a braying donkey and a quintet of angel musicians. *The Nativity* is a curious example of this representation. The open mouth of the donkey brays in line with the five angels, two singing, two plucking lutes and the one in the middle bowing a viol. The fact that they are so obviously lined up, with the donkey almost at the centre of the painting, suggests that Piero considered their implicit sound — a strange inter-species harmony of highest heaven and lowest earth — as an element of the work. Not all species are party to the exaltation, however. On the roof above the heads of this choir a magpie sits, still as carving. For once, its raucous chatter is silenced.

Notions of authenticity are built on such partial source material, but the transposition is awkward. Ways of hearing are notoriously subjective. We have mechanisms for comparing sounds by scientific testing and anecdotal evidence, but no way of knowing exactly what another person is hearing at any given moment. Each person's brain adapts auditory input to a template particular to the individual, so if one person were to suddenly inhabit the body of another, what they heard would be quite unfamiliar. The further back in time we travel, the less certainty can be ascribed to the way people once listened, what it was they heard, and what it was they believed they heard. By speaking through a fictionalized version of Thomas Edison, the nineteenth-century writer and impoverished aristocrat, Villiers de l'Isle-Adam, was free to question the limitations of recording technology, as if from within the inventor's mind. His science-fiction novel, *L'Eve Future* (translated as *Tomorrow's Eve*, published in 1886), imagined Edison in Menlo Park, cataloguing all the historical events he might have recorded, had he been one of the first-born of humanity and so ensured phonographic documents of the chants of the Sibyls, the trumpets of Jericho, the bellow of Phalaris' bull, the laughter of the augurs and so on. Provoked to sarcasm by the crude jokes aimed at his phonograph, he considers those sounds that are beyond the capabilities of a mechanical device:

For example, I would have complained that while the phonograph was reproducing sounds, it was unable to represent the sound, say, of the fall of the Roman Empire. It can't record an eloquent silence, or the sound of rumours. In fact, as far as voices go, it is helpless to represent the voice of conscience. Can it record the voice of the blood? Or all those splendid sayings that are attributed to great men? It's helpless before the swan song, before unspoken innuendoes; can it record the song of the Milky Way?

ACOUSTEMOLOGY

Virginia Woolf (whose extravagant vowels can now be heard on a British Library compilation of the recorded speaking voices of British authors) was half-convinced that this problem of the vanished auditory past would be resolved in time, by a technological invention of even greater sensitivity than the phonograph. 'Instead of remembering there a scene and there a sound,' she wrote, 'I shall fit a plug into the wall; and listen in to the past. I shall turn up August 1890. I feel that strong emotion must leave its trace . . .' As if to resuscitate eccentric notions such as Charles Babbage's Victorian-era theory that the air is a vast library, inscribed with the sonic impressions of every sound ever uttered, or Guglielmo Marconi's conviction that sounds enjoy eternal if ever-diminishing life in the earth's atmosphere, a growing number of academic studies address the problem of sonic history through detective work, a verbal reconstruction by auscultation of the lost sound embedded within a wide variety of sources. In these fields of auditory archaeology and historical acoustemology there is Bruce R. Smith's *The Acoustic World of Early Modern England*, for example, along with Wes Folkerth's *The Sound of Shakespeare*, John M. Picker's *Victorian Soundscapes*, Christopher L. Witmore's *Vision, Media, Noise and the Percolation of Time*, Sean Shesgreen's *Images of the Outcast: The Urban Poor in the Cries of London*, Mark Michael Smith's *Hearing History*, Richard Cullen Rath's *How Early America Sounded*, David Garrioch's *Sounds of the City: The Soundscape of Early Modern European Towns*, Emily Cockayne's *Hubbub: Filth, Noise and Stench in England* and Frank Harrison's *Time, Place and Music*. Predating the other examples by some three decades, the latter is an anthology of texts, dating from somewhere between 1550 and 1800 and predominantly written by Christian missionaries, colonists, diplomats and explorers who attempted to describe unfamiliar music heard in places such as Paraguay, China, Persia and southern Africa.

The images suggested by Babbage and Marconi are of sound floating upwards or through the air, either writing itself into the outer reaches of the human environment or thinning into unimaginably insubstantial states of materiality: thin, thinner, thinnest yet never quite nothing. Sound unearthed through written memory and other forms of inscription, on the other hand, is closer to metaphors of sediment, a collecting of dissipating earthly stuff: silt, dust and partial objects that must be sifted, as if by an archaeological dig, from other impacted matter underfoot. The problem, as we realize from examining the ways in which sound is understood, is that sound is described through a fog of confusion.

Being predominantly literary historical studies, these texts sit alongside extensive analysis of Virginia Woolf's modernist preoccupation with sound, listening and atmosphere in the context of the age of mechanical repro-duction, in studies by Melba Cuddy Keane, Kate Flint, Emma Sutton and Michele Pridmore-Brown. Almost all of them are informed by R. Murray Shafer's inspirational, if problematic, invention of soundscape studies and the concept of the soundmark in the late 1960s. Sound, previously condemned to a relatively short life cycle not unconnected to its own transience, is added to an overpopulated gallery of phenomena and objects subject to the haunted emotions of anxiety, nostalgia and conservation. Can this bring us into closer accord with John Berger and his implicit suspicion of words, talk, discussion and the formidable wealth of analysis aimed at the history of art? The description of a sound, or the visual depiction of a sound, pulls sound into the world of things, the world of text. For writers this is a difficult and sometimes painful contradiction. When words describe sounds, do we think we hear those sounds? Villiers de l'Isle-Adam's fictional Edison surmised that if sounds could be retrieved from the past and transmitted to the present, they would be dead on arrival: 'They would be, in a word, sounds completely different from what they actually were, and from what their phonographic labels pretended they were — since it's in ourselves that the killing silence exists.' In a prescient thought for the nineteenth century, he concludes that phonographic mastery of sonic events, hubbubs as he calls them, robs them of their interest: 'No man has a right to regret their loss,' he says, then concludes that he might as well lie like the idler Tityrus under the shade of a beech tree, apply an ear to the receiver of his freshly invented microphone and listen to the grass grow.

Considering sound in its relationship to vision and objects, we should remember that the objectification of sound was an overwhelmingly suc-cessful twentieth-century project. Some optimists believe that the less tangible products of digital distribution will reverse this trend and send all of us back to communal music making. Whether that happens in the long term remains to be seen. Some new sound work certainly attempts to reposition sound as an elusive element — somewhat like the weather — an immersive, temporal condition that can redefine spaces, or ques-tion states of being and their time base, without becoming the object that we describe as a track, a record, a CD, a video clip, an MP3 or any other form of retrieved audio or audio-visual file. As the established economic structures of the music business implode, built as they are on the ownership and trading of material objects (from sheet music to CD), so there is a remembering, however faint, of the impermanence of sound and how that poignancy of loss, even in moments of overwhelming pleasure, adds depth to the experience of audition.

AN IMMERSION

Sound is a medium that can be shaped to precision, as in many forms of music and speech. Its relation to a source can be unequivocal. A smash: the glass is broken, nothing doubted. 'Train drivers can recognize places on their route, and detect differences in speed of travel, from tape recordings of the sound,' wrote Dr. Helen E. Ross in *Behaviour and Perception in Strange Environments*. Sound is a highly significant component of the mental map — matching memory to the delicate overlapping of perceptions, memories and a shifting, predictive sense of where, and how, and how long. On the other hand, sound's boundaries lack clarity, spreading in the air as they do or arriving from hidden places, and its significance potentially vague, closer to perfume or smoke than the solidity of touching another person, understanding a conversation, or eating a meal. This relative lack of form creates perplexing relationships between the properties of states: inside and outside, material and immaterial, the way thoughts become sound through speech, and external sounds become sensory impressions that may be thoughts as they pass through the ears and outer membrane into awareness. A sound may not be connected to the conscious formation of a thought, yet may reflect feelings that are hidden from self-awareness, and do so in an instant transmission of their secrets to the air beyond the body. Think of the times when your stomach has rumbled and groaned at inappropriate moments: in that dreadful silence during a funeral, or the quietly frantic concentration of an exam room. Why am I hungry now? But this is not hunger; the body is registering the tension of the situation, emitting sound as a message to a mind still lost in the enormity of significance.

Just to dwell in unfamiliar silence reveals all those sounds that are obscured in normal circumstances by the noise of life. Sounds such as clicking, grating, popping and ringing, not so much 'in the head' but from within the bones, can be generated by a wide range of problems, ranging from teeth, jaw and chewing muscles to anxiety and stress. Anybody who can hear is exposed to the effects of sound all the time, even in sleep. Much of it is subliminal, or peripheral to immediate needs, though such sounds can influence mood and attention as effectively as a shot of strong coffee, a sharp word, or an unwelcome torrent of rain. If I walk through a succession of rooms and corridors, some high-ceilinged and marble-hard, some claustrophobic and stuffy with carpets and fug, my sense of how I feel, where I am, and what is going on, changes dramatically. I may be lost in thought, not looking at anything in particular, certainly not listening to the resonance of these rooms, but my senses fluctuate in synchronisation with each echoing opening, each muffled closure. This is not so much listening to sound, but a becoming aware of sound, space and movement in combination.

Although combinatory senses are the means by which the world is negotiated, most studies tend to separate them by specialising in one or other. As a reflection of its perceived value, the literature on visual culture, in particular, is vast. Music studies are numerous, of course, but audio culture is a diminutive interloper, a newcomer adding contextual breadth and perspective through its concentration on aspects of auditory experimentation (in all fields of music), so-called sound art, the voice, environmental sound work, the phenomenology and philosophy of listening and so on. Anthropologist Tim Ingold has welcomed the new flourishing of sound studies, but with certain reservations. He argues that the term 'soundscape', coined by R. Murray Schafer for educational purposes in the 1960s and now in common usage, is flawed, because it places the listener at an objectified distance from what is in fact immersive and so reinforces the artificial divide commonly erected between mind and matter. Ingold also questions the tendency to compare sound with vision or sight, rather than light. Studies of visual culture have virtually nothing to say about the phenomenon of light, he maintains, and studies of auditory perception also run risks of losing touch with sound. He gives the analogy of a landscape, seen on a fine day not as a 'lightscape', but as a landscape illuminated by sunlight. Similarly, by listening to our surroundings we hear within the medium of sound. 'Sound, in my view, is neither mental nor material,' he writes, 'but a phenomenon of experience — that is, of our immersion in, and commingling with, the world in which we find ourselves.'

Seeing may establish our place in what is verifiable in one part of the surrounding world, by revealing what is in front of us, but hearing allows us constant access to a less stable world, omni-directional, always in a state of becoming and receding, known and unknown. This is the world that surrounds us and flows through us, in all its uncertainty.

3   Dark senses

Bedlam: In *Rake's Progress*, produced between 1961 and 1963, David Hockney's etching of *Bedlam* shows five near-identical figures standing in a row, as if in a police line-up. All of them wear the same t-shirt; all are fitted (and they do look like medical devices) with headphones connected to some sort of small music player — in those days, a transistor radio. Whatever individuality they once possessed, they are now cool-looking robots. This was startlingly prophetic, since the Walkman era was far into the future at that time. Then in 2007, no doubt aggravated by the vertiginous rise of iPod listening, Hockney returned to his idea that portable music players are a symptom of hellish conformism. Whenever a public occasion presented itself — his opening of an exhibition of Turner watercolours at Tate Britain, or at a retrospective at the National Portrait Gallery — he complained that we no longer live in a visual age. 'In London,' he has said, 'everyone has something in their ears, so we're in an aural age.'

Setting aside Hockney's notoriety as serial complainer, there is the question of his deafness. The image of *Bedlam* also anticipated his own need to wear hearing aids. Since 1979 he has worn two of them and his hearing has deteriorated so completely that he no longer designs stage sets for opera. As his hearing has gone, so his interest in the minutia of looking seems to have increased, hence his controversial theories on the use of optical devices by painters from the fifteenth century onwards.

As Hockney told Bernard Weinraub in 2001:

I actually think the deafness makes you see clearer. If you can't hear, you somehow see. I read in John Richardson's book about Picasso that he didn't like music. It was rare then. He was the only artist who didn't go to concerts. I'm assuming he didn't hear the music. I'm assuming he was tone deaf. But he actually saw more tones than anybody. He was actually the great chiaroscurist of the twentieth century. Seeing and hearing — there is a connection.

It may also be true, as Oliver Sacks suggests in *Musicophilia*, that the 'filling in' effect of mental processing that enhances musical imagery through expectation and suggestion can be intensified by deafness. 'It is possible, indeed, that [Beethoven's] musical imagery was even intensified by deafness,' wrote Sacks, 'for with the removal of normal auditory input, the auditory cortex may become hypersensitive, with heightened powers of musical imagery.' In other words, it is possible to hear music in the mind that possesses the same, or even more, richness of detail and complexity as music heard in the air of the external world.

As a teenager I studied painting, graphic design and art history, but then abandoned my studies to be a musician instead. A passion for art galleries waned over the years, to the point where my ability to look, to really see visual art, began to atrophy. Part of the problem lies with the differing time bases of looking and hearing. Sound gives the impression of occupying time, even moving with time or determining time, so to hear we need to devote time to the activity. With music, speech and multi-sensory activities like meetings, television programmes, sports events and so on, this may be more or less identical to the duration of the event, but even to hear unfolding and unbounded audio events with accuracy, time needs to be given up to some part of their passing. Silence itself is conceived often as a version of time, a property of the world that may be shattered or obliterated but nevertheless runs continuously as a background condition that is always the same. Seeing also demands a commitment of time in order to understand and absorb what is there, but in the case of an object, what we see will be relatively inert, only changing through the play of light, and in the perception of the viewer. The whole can be comprehended in one glance, one sweep of the eyes or turn of the head, after which a period of deeper looking may begin to reveal more information.

Any form of disability can shift the balance. In 2007 I was invited to the White Cube gallery opening of Christian Marclay's *Crossfire*. To summarize, this is a four-screen video installation of film clips, all of them showing guns been fired directly at the camera. As it turned out, standing in the middle of the room, being shot up from four points of the compass, drowning in the noise of all these handguns and automatic weapons from westerns, war films, gangster films, John Woo two-fisted firearm orgies, you name it, was exhilarating.

Afterwards, Marclay introduced me to Louise Stern, an artist who was working as an assistant to Sam Taylor-Wood. 'You'll have to write,' he said. Louise is deaf, so we communicated by silently exchanging notes. These were written rapidly in her book, passed back and forth, and since I was examining and questioning the concept of silence at that time, that was one of the subjects we discussed. Now scribbling furiously, she expressed some anger at the writings of John Cage, who in her view overlooked the possibility that silence can differ dramatically according to each person's capacity to hear or not hear. As our conversation intensified, she mounted an attack on durational media that troubled me sufficiently to provoke a reconsideration of much of what I believed about sound. The narrative qualities of sound, music and other time based arts are coercive, she argued, whereas visual arts allow far more latitude for the perceiver. Later she emailed me an extended essay, in which the following paragraphs articulated this idea further:

> Objects stand still. They stare back. They are silent. They won't allow us to push them anywhere they don't want to go. They look back at us with understanding; but it is a demanding understanding, not a complacent obese one . . . Like a cat delivering a dead mouse, art shows it has a certain control over what it gives us. This control is simply the physical silence and stillness of the work. The silence allows us to approach the work and circle around its entirety again and again. We can view the work on our own time, stay with it for as long or as short as we wish, come back to it for a moment or two, choose whatever rituals for getting acquainted. Unlike a book or a movie, there is nothing pushing us into any particular, and ultimately false, direction. We can just be around the work in total intimacy, without having to keep pace with it. The silence of the work allows us that.

I am too attached to the unfolding, the commitment and delay of music, cinema or novels, or their deconstruction of time, to entirely share this view, yet a seductive alternative exists, crystallized by T. S. Eliot in 1935, in the first seven lines from part V of *Burnt Norton*, the air element of Eliot's *Four Quartets*:

> Words move, music moves
> Only in time; but that which is only living
> Can only die. Words, after speech, reach
> Into the silence. Only by the form, the pattern,
> Can words or music reach
> The stillness, as a Chinese jar still
> Moves perpetually in its stillness.

This theme was explored by Virginia Woolf in her final novel, written in wartime, *Between the Acts*:

> Empty, empty, empty; silent, silent, silent. The room was a shell, singing of what was before time was; a vase stood in the heart of the house, alabaster, smooth, cold, holding the still, distilled essence of emptiness, silence.

Both Eliot and Woolf were echoing the words of John Keats, in his poem from 1819, 'Ode On a Grecian Urn':

> Heard melodies are sweet, but those unheard
>
> Are sweeter; therefore, ye soft pipes, play on;
> Not to the sensual ear, but, more endear'd,
>
> Pipe to the spirit ditties of no tone

Those of us who are partisan have moments of believing that music is a superior art, simultaneously physical and evanescent, a transient presence in space that plays subtle games with time and atmosphere. Yet the limitations inherent within these qualities can diminish the attractions. Why can't music make an instantaneous impact, a sweep of time comprehended in its totality in a single moment? Why can't it stay still for examination, in the same way that we can ruminate over a passage in a book, or freeze-frame a film on DVD? A moment of music may be held in a computer programme in much the same way that a faulty CD stutters when it glitches on one fragment, but though a fragment may be identified, any intelligible link between the sound of that stutter and the greater whole is a tribute to the human brain rather than the music.

The lines from *Burnt Norton* are deeply ambiguous, but Eliot seems to be speaking about a sudden moment of illumination, a state of being in which feeling and consciousness is not short-circuited by words, worldly concerns and the ticking of time. The object, the catalyst, remains, in stillness; persists, also, in a state of flux, as a dynamic object. There are moments of illumination in music, of course (though less than we might wish for); busy with the volition and fragile energy of its own life, music rushes towards its own death.

Coinciding with the onset of adolescence, my eyesight declined dramatically. Shame and other painful emotions emerged with this loss, as if the weakening of one of my senses signalled a bigger crisis of identity. I had started at a new school and could no longer see anything at distance, so my work deteriorated to the level where I was, as they used to say, bottom of the class. This was the end of the 1950s, still a time of secrecy and acute repression in England. At all levels of public and family life, concealment was valued, emotional confession deplored. Sight, for me, will always be associated with this pivotal and difficult episode in my life. Teachers were unhelpful; my mother was insensitive. Nothing positive remains of the memory except for the sensation of walking home wearing my first pair of glasses, the glittering of an ordinary pavement revealing to me once again a world that had grown dulled and discoloured through myopia.

In the end, wearing spectacles is really not so difficult. Without them, life is a blur. My field of vision is restricted in all directions by the frames of my glasses; in low light levels I find it increasingly hard to read; swimming in the sea is a form of sensory deprivation. A rock might be a shark for all I know. This inability to see objects in focus unaided, or really understand subtle fluctuations of light, must accentuate the other senses and reconfigure an imbalance in the socially constructed hierarchy of the senses. In certain circumstances it can heighten feelings of interpersonal distance. Over time, I believe this has sharpened my sonic focus. As James Joyce wrote in *A Portrait of the Artist as a Young Man*:

> Did he then love the rhythmic rise and fall of words better than their associations of legend and colour? Or was it that, being as weak of sight as he was shy of mind, he drew less pleasure from the reflection of the glowing sensible world through the prison of a language manycoloured and richly storied than from the contemplation of an inner world of individual emotions mirrored perfectly in a lucid supple periodic prose?

David Hockney's more general complaint can be set against an equal number of complaints stating exactly the opposite: that we live in a society of ocular dominance in which all other senses are downgraded to varying levels of triviality. Then there is the utopian end of the scale, the technocratic optimism for a new age of digital sound and image (despite the magnetic pull that screens impose upon the eyes, to the detriment of listening). Can all these beliefs be reconciled? The quote from Hockney was inserted into a news item about a flash mob event set in motion by mobile-clubbing.com. A surprise venue and time was chosen, in that particular case London's Liverpool Street Station during evening rush hour. Mobile clubbers gathered in flash mob style, through the contemporary magic of online social networking and texting, and then danced to personal choices of music heard privately, without synchrony, and more or less silently, on their MP3 players. This music lacking sound, through which the communal physicality of social music is witnessed, without being heard, seems an ironic counterpoint to Hockney's lament for the demise of seeing.

At the same time, the critique is reinforced. Headphone listening is a form of voluntary deafness. This is temporary, admittedly, though listening for long periods at high volume will convert that into a permanent condition. External spatial characteristics of hearing are reduced by the construction of a predominantly imaginative space for sound to inhabit: this depends upon the type of headphones, playback volume and the environment. Lightweight earbuds allow ambient sound to mix with the listener's music, whereas the increasingly popular noise cancelling headphones create a relatively autonomous space that isolates the listener, not just from external sounds but from a sense of full presence within the environment. Ears enclosed by headphones, the body relinquishes the feedback function of its own sound. Contact between the body and its surroundings is so reduced as to be eerie and dreamlike. Instead, the body expands inwards by extending the perceived space of the mind. Music that can be recalled approximately through memory is suddenly reproduced in all its detail, apparently inside the head of the listener. I have tried to locate sound played back in this way, and its subjective placing within my head (since this is where it seems to sit). This depends on the stereo image of the recording and other illusions of receding distance, vertical height and depth, but mostly the music hovers in a narrow band between the ears, the greater part contained within the headphones themselves. Air and depth are no longer important; instead, the music builds a room of its own, of many dimensions and occupied by a single listener (or two, if earbuds are shared).

This is the attraction, and throughout the evolution of personal listening devices, many researchers into Walkman, Discman, MP3 player and mobile phone use have encountered similar evidence. People use headphones and portable audio playback to create distance, private space, and a personal soundtrack that counteracts all the unpleasant, inconvenient and tedious effects of the world through which they pass. In case this sounds judgemental, I can happily admit that I do the same myself, though only in certain circumstances, since most of the time I feel a need to locate myself through what I hear as much as what I perceive through other senses. 'We visit the land of our secret grandeur in fantasy or in books and movies,' writes Lewis Hyde in *Trickster Makes This World*, 'and on the road between these imaginings and the actual house where we must sleep and eat, to the degree that we are able, assemble a life from the usable fragments of each.' This is an eloquent expression of why an iPod can be a lifesaver during extended delays in airport departure lounges or on long-haul flights, though even in these non-places the inner soundtrack occasionally adds glamour to the outer reality, injecting once again a dreamy modernist beauty that was tarnished long ago. Through withdrawal, their presence as physical spaces is reinforced.

A SHIFTING SOUND FIELD

Seeing is believing; what you see is what you get; I can see what you're getting at; read my lips; you took the words out of my mouth; her name is on the tip of my tongue; I can't grasp what you're saying; I must be hearing things; can you see what I'm saying? Common in the English language, these are telling expressions, trans-sensory metaphors confirming a tendency toward what philosopher Casey O'Callaghan has called 'visuocentrism' in his book, *Sounds*. According to O'Callaghan, visuocentrism, 'the tyranny of the visual', dominates the belief system of this world, the world in which his book and mine are most likely to be read. For O'Callaghan, the only way to explain sounds is to regard them as events, rather than things, or objects. 'Since objects as we experience and conceive of them are intuitively wholly present at each moment at which they exist,' he writes, 'and since properties or qualities do not inhabit time in the way that sounds do,

I argue that events are poised as the best candidates for a theory of sounds '

There is a strong pressure in many societies to privilege materiality and substance — what we can see, touch, possess, or assess through physical relations, and what we can readily describe or represent. The reasons for this are easily appreciated: seeing tends to be more specific than other senses. People who suffer no vision impairment make the assumption that they locate themselves primarily with sight. Broadly speaking, this seems to be the case. The chaos, panic, societal collapse and degradation that ensues following the epidemic of blindness depicted in José Saramago's novel, *Blindness*, would be difficult to imagine if transposed to any other sense. What is seen can be easier to verify and share than what is heard. This is particularly true of sounds whose source is hidden or too far away to see. Can we trust them to be what context, previous experience and common sense tells us they are? '. . . the blind man had turned his head to the side where she was standing,' wrote Saramago, 'as if he had sensed something unusual, a sigh, a tremor in the air . . . What nonsense, how could anyone be there, at this hour everyone is asleep.' There is no certainty about such sounds; many are impossibly ambiguous or mysterious. In addition, sound is transient. Though some of it lasts far too long for comfort (even a few seconds of certain noises as they invade the body with great violence), we can sensibly believe that the energy of any noise will dissipate in time. If an event is known to be short-lived, then there seems to be less cause to note its brief existence and little desire to address any problems or distress it provokes.

'Seeing is believing, we say, but don't believe everything you hear,' writes O'Callaghan. 'Seeing Elvis in the flesh holds evidential weight we do not grant to merely hearing him in the next room.' Robert Pasnau is another philosopher who has wrestled with these problems. 'Our standard view about sound is incoherent,' he stated in a paper entitled 'What Is Sound?', published in 1999. Pasnau made a distinction between odour and sound, placing sight and hearing on the side of locational sensory modalities. 'This is not the case for taste and touch, or even for smell,' he claimed. 'Despite the fact that odours come to us from a distance, through a medium, we do not perceive odours to exist at the place where they were generated.' At best, this seems to simplify the issue. To give an example: I am sitting on a bus. A man reeking of urine sits next to me. Immediately, I perceive that the man is both the source and the location of the smell. If the smell becomes so bad that the bus became uninhabitable, then this smell would not be perceived to exist solely at the place where it was generated, yet it would still be traceable to its source, being at its most intense at that point. But Pasnau goes further with this distinction by arguing that sound exists at the place where it is generated. He gives the example of a disco, where the sound may be loud enough within its confined space to be immersive: 'But we should not conclude that the sound is anywhere other than in the speakers.'

From this, we have to assume his knowledge of clubs doesn't extend to places where the volume actually vibrates internal organs. The body passes through sound but sound also passes through the body. As a teacher at a Boston school for deaf children in the 1870s, Alexander Graham Bell encouraged his young pupils to hold balloons in their hands when walking in the streets. Horse-drawn wagons, driven very fast but silent to the children so a threat to their safety, could be heard as vibration, transmitted up from cobblestones through the balloon and into the child's hands. Like Bell's mother, his fiancée, Mabel Hubbard, was deaf, but they would experiment together using a communication based on the physical vibrations of vocal sounds. 'And time after time, as she tried different sounds, he had touched her throat,' writes David Bodanis in *Electric Universe*, 'and she had touched his, quite properly, with other students around, ostensibly just for the sake of identifying how different words produced different vibrations.' The image is at once tender and intimate, erotic and yet without passion, since we know that Bell would enfold these touching discoveries into his controversial role in the invention of the telephone.

The coherence of Pasnau's analysis flows from empirical evidence — a sound can be precisely located at a verifiable source — but the effect of hearing, once we begin to listen carefully, does not match this coherence. On the contrary, the self is doubled, or split, or dispersed: a sound is over there, very specifically, but around here and in here (also very specifically), within the physical and cerebral self, a fluctuation between these vectors and all around, all at the same time. The locational nature of sound is graphically illustrated in cinemas fitted with Dolby Digital Surround. Sounds clearly generated by events on screen may suddenly be heard from the back of the cinema, yet the illusion of experiential depth lies behind the image, or beyond its edges. In these situations, sound seems to have detached itself from the reality of the narrative (which keeps within its space at the front of the audience) to join the reality of the audience in their space. Nonetheless, as a rendition of experience, Pasnau's locational emphasis is misleading, since we live not within a fixed geography of sound objects but within a perpetually changing flow of intermixing sound events, some linked to discernable points, others emanating from hidden or unknown sources. Leonardo da Vinci realised that sound is simultaneously located at its point of emission and in a field that spreads all around the listener, as we learn from an entry on acoustics in his notebooks, in the section on the four elements: 'Although the voices which penetrate the air proceed from their sources in circular motion, nevertheless the circles which are propelled from their different centres meet without any hindrance and penetrate and pass across one another keeping to the centre from which they spring.'

Seeing is now-now-now-now-now-now-now-n-n-n . . ., whereas hearing is then-and-now-and-then, over there at the source of the sound and then here, within the body, already gone but still dispersing into ambience. To locate sounds only at their source is to fix them, like a display of pinned butterflies. But hearing is an improvisation: walking through King's Cross underground station during morning rush hour I can hear hundreds of footsteps. Yes, I can listen very closely and tell that each pairs of steps has a location, but the constant movement on all sides and in all directions of a multiplicity of steps would demand superpowers to locate each individual source in its place. Instead, I move through a shifting sound field of events that is closer to sea or heavy rainfall than signs of human activity. Even if I could be convinced by Pasnau, I would regret the loss of poetic links between ethereal phenomena such as perfume, smoke, mist and sound. This is where the philosophy of Duke Ellington, to take one example of a composer fascinated by intangibility, seems more valuable to human existence than this level of parsing.

Given its contradictory properties, the most sensible approach to sound is through incoherence. Coherence, after all, can be problematic in unforeseen ways, often leading to the opposite of what was intended. To give one example of sonic rationalism leading to an unwelcome outcome, the technology of public address systems has improved immeasurably in recent years. Announcements on railway stations were once notorious for being garbled, their spreading reverberation in tunnels and large public spaces blurring the specifics of whatever information the traveller was waiting to hear. Consequently they were rarely used. Now each word is perfectly clear, so use of the system has become a nervous tic, a justification of its existence that delivers an invasive stream of messages, some vital, some trivial or superfluous, some cautionary or threatening. How easily communication failure tips over into the efficiency of authoritarianism.

One of the most compelling aspects of hearing sound is the tension between its simultaneous attributes of specificity and generality. Listening to a symphony orchestra in a concert hall involves a rapid oscillation between these two modes. On the one hand, individual instruments can be picked out and located precisely in physical space; on the other hand, the overall sound is perceived to have a form and to inhabit the entirety of the space. At the same time as this spatial movement between local and global, there is an oscillation between what the psychologist and art educationalist Anton Ehrenzweig described as a conflict between two types of attention — differentiation (focussing) and dedifferentiation (dispersing). This unconscious scanning between the microscopic details of a work and its overall balance is achieved by an emptiness of attention. In Ehrenzweig's view, this is how the improvised variants that affect any musical performance are balanced with the organisation of the whole. As he wrote in *The Hidden Order of Art*:

> Spontaneously applied form elements are fragile and subject to unpredictable changes of mood. A performer may readily change the inarticulate micro-elements of his interpretation from performance to performance. But this instability does not make them arbitrary. Any change forces the performer to recast his interpretation of the whole work on the spur of the moment. This total integration can only be controlled by the empty stare of unconscious scanning which alone is capable of overcoming the fragmentation in art's surface structure. The relative smallness of micro-elements defies conscious articulation; so do the macro-elements of art owing to their excessive breadth.

SECRET PHENOMENA

As a musician who has trouble with spatial awareness, being short-sighted since childhood and prone to getting lost, I empathize with O'Callaghan's challenge to the idea of sound as a sub-set of visuocentrism. Another philosopher, Jonathan Rée, has explored the history of the senses, finding that the eighteenth-century aesthetic theorist, Gotthold Ephraim Lessing, privileged eyesight to the extent of describing smell, taste, touch and hearing as 'the dark senses.' Lessing believed that seeing allowed a uniquely instantaneous perception of many realities, and this was sufficient to prove the basis of eyesight's superiority as a medium for art. For Rée, this is an absurdly polarized conception of the senses, through which music, for example, can only be imagined as a succession of discrete events. An element of spatialisation, of pattern recognition, is what allows us to make sense of music and speech. 'If you heard a portion of language as a set of separate sounds passing through your consciousness one by one, like sheep jumping over a stile,' he writes, 'you would not even be able to recognize words in it, let alone grasp their meaning and syntactical relations, or appreciate their tunes and rhythmic patterns.'

This seems questionable, since events can be understood both in simultaneity and over varying temporal trajectories without being translated necessarily into visual patterns or intangible equivalents of solid forms. This is exactly what musicians do, particularly improvising musicians. But O'Callaghan, Rée and Ingold are in agreement on an important point: the senses do not operate in isolation; though language persistently fragments and disjoints the world, sense impressions cannot be separated and defined as self-contained properties. The environment is not 'sliced up along the lines of the sensory pathways by which we enter into it,' Tim Ingold says. 'The world we perceive is the same world, whatever path we take, and each of us perceives it as an undivided centre of activity and awareness.' Those novelists and poets who are particularly sensitive to sound can enhance our understanding of this complex flux; there are instructive parallels to be found between the idea of hearing as perpetual movement through sound, and the experiential drift of walking journals written by authors and flaneurs such as Robert Walser, Walter Benjamin, J. A. Baker, W. G. Sebald, Robert Macfarlane, Kathleen Jamie, Roger Deakin, Richard Mabey and Rebecca Solnit.

Such writers open themselves to a totality of experience, scrutinising the finest details of near-secret phenomena, vastness and intimacy, fluctuations of weather and mood, natural rhythms, fugitive traces of memory cached within place, space and dwelling. Their sensations may be transient, yet their register is profound. Sound is only a part of the drift, but in their accounts it rises to the surface as a crucial element of movement and refined awareness. The multi-sensory insights derived from moving through an environment differ from those deduced from a more static, detached viewpoint. 'Looking out into the landscape', inscribed on used stationery in 1927 by the Swiss writer Robert Walser in his tiny, near indecipherable pencil script, suggests from its title this detached, ocular relationship, yet Walser was alert to the subtle ecology of events. 'Looking out into the landscape,' he wrote, 'I'm able to observe that what moves can appear more graceful, more beautiful, more noble than what stands firm or is stable. For just now, simply and evidently because they are stable, the trees and saplings are being shaken by the wind. Now and then, insofar as they yield, they are shaken. If they weren't rooted, there'd be no rustling of their leaves, and consequently no listening. The listening depends on the rustling, the rustling on the shaking, the shaking on the fixity of the objects, which grow out of a definite place.'

In Kathleen Jamie's book, *Findings*, she writes with great feeling and elegance about listening for the crex-crex call of the corncrake. For her, this process of aural searching is a new discovery, and she notes the contrast between her own way of engaging with nature, and that of the two travel companions who accompanied her on a boat trip to the Monach Islands in the Outer Hebrides of Scotland. They were both sound recordists. 'In the five or six days we spent together,' she writes, 'I grew to appreciate the company of people who listen to the world. They don't feel the need to talk all the while. They were alert to bird cries, waves sucking on rocks, a rope frittering against a mast. Sometimes I'd notice them catch each other's eye, give a complicit smile, and I'd wonder what I'd missed.'

My earlier remarks about the difficulties of notating bird song are emphasized by the late Roger Deakin in *Wildwood: A Journey Through Trees*. Listening closely to the sounds of an Essex rookery, 'the roughest of folksong . . . the strongest of county burrs . . . rasping, leathery, parched, raucous, hoarse, strangled, deep-throated, brawling, plaintive, never reticent,' he hears not a universal and unchanging song, but the nuanced intimacies, conflicts and contentments of social life.

Such writing can be read as notations of discoveries made within the interstices of experience. How easy it is for human beings to lose their sentient capacity, to be dumbed not *by*, but *to* the charm, and what an adjustment it is to become attuned to nuances, wildness and unseen resonance, to confront this lack and the filling of its emptiness. In less-responsive circumstances, the presence or absence of sound may be a matter of indifference. Only when it clicks into focus — as an alarm or vital signal, as speech directed at the listener or overheard, intolerable noise, oppressive silence, affective music or some ambient sound that has curiosity

value or distracts — does it excite attention. This kind of selective, sophisticated audio analysis is now mimicked by digital listening machines that
can separate sounds such as gunshots, graffiti scratched into train windows,
or a car crash from background noise, but many species possess similar
skills. 'Should some alien being watch humanity during a thunderstorm
he might quite similarly decide that thunder was to us inaudible,' wrote
Lorenzo Langstroth in 1852, in *On the Hive and the Honey Bee*. 'Clap might
follow clap without securing any external sign of recognition; yet let a child
with tiny voice but shriek for help, and all would at once be awakened
to activity. So with the bee: sounds appealing to its instincts meet with
immediate response, while others evoke no wasted emotion.' But these
apparent deficiencies — vagueness, unconscious selectivity, invasiveness,
evidentially suspect, transient and insubstantial, ambiguous in its place in
space, painful yet pleasurable in its evocations of mood and memory — all
become qualities that distinguish sound and hearing as vital elements in
full knowing of the world and alert movement through it.

4 Writing sigla

What can we learn from sound? What is it giving or taking from our lives? These are the kind of questions we ask of sound, thinking of it as an active force, like thunderclaps, voices on the radio, a flock of geese, or a bass drum heard from a passing car. Already, things are upside down, but this is hardly surprising. Sound enforces itself in many contemporary environments, urban or rural, central or remote, with an iron fist: the brutal percussion of digging machines, the scream of an overhead fighter jet, the banshee wail of sirens, loud music and the dull undertow of motor traffic. The steady growth of these sounds has been barely noticed except by its most prominent victims. Along with all other side effects of relentless expansion and progress, they have been tolerated as signs of commerce, movement, and the infrastructure at work, but they obscure and eradicate the intimacies of the social, or those sounds that alert us to the peculiarities and flow of a community, its inhabitants, organic life, ceremonies, rhythms, disturbances, surfaces and spaces. If we expect sound merely to give, or to invade, just like the earth digger on the building site or the bass drum, then we miss the other side.

Better we should think of sound as an ear, a mirror, a resonant echo, a carrier, a shell. A word in your shell-like. Dylan Thomas has blind Captain Cat listening closely at the open window of Schooner House, hearing the finest details of the children's voices and their feet on the cobbles, Billy Swansea with the dog's voice, Jackie with the sniff, and the hitting of Maggie Richards by a boy he guesses to be Billy Swansea because you should never trust a boy who barks, and then the postman knocking at Bay View, identified by the soft sound of the knocker that

Mrs Ogmore-Pritchard has muted with a kid glove, and then by counting the postman's feet heavy on the distant cobbles his ears follow him to Mrs Rose-Cottage, due that day for her letter from her sister in Gorslas. In the introduction to the Penguin Classics edition of *Under Milk Wood*, a radio impression as Thomas once described it, Walford Davies writes of the marvellous scope of the work, 'narration, description, commentary, dialogue, monologue, song, poem, ballad, children's games, cockcrows and mere noises.' The slip is unfortunate: these are not mere noises, but one map of memory among many, a profoundly detailed combining of listening with local knowledge, drawn in consciousness by an old blind man who has lost so many connections with the world.

Sound is a composite, moving through an environment like a bird building a nest, rigging transient structures from the materials it collects. A lack of sound can say, quite simply, wait here, because a remarkable moment may happen. In the waiting, we discover how little we wait, expectations alerted to the finest of unknown sensations, all of them a part of the place in which we find ourselves.

Winter breaks and back to spring. Walking in Queens Wood, north London, in mid-March — a beautifully tranquil, bright morning. As usual, magpies strut across the path, their forty-fags-a-day rasp and hack returning a spirited response to traffic noise filtering through from Archway Road to this small but venerable woodland of oak and hornbeam, wild service tree, holly and hawthorn. Woodpeckers drum from all points today, a range of pitch and volume, rapid and deliberate, distance and direction. I stop, press the record button on my digital recorder. Missy, our miniature schnauzer, snuffles among the drying leaf layer near my feet, her investigations audible as a high-frequency whisper. In our line of sight, one woodpecker hammers out a richly sonorous, deep rattle; to the right, jays are squabbling. Imperceptibly, a low-pitched droning mixes with these spatially separated, distant signals. As the drone grows louder, piling on pressure, it spreads sonic glue, solidifying the audio scene to the consistency of dark treacle, a black balloon suffocating the sky. Suddenly the lower thickness of the drone falls away to uncover higher, more transparent frequencies. In the wake of its noise, a helicopter flies overhead. With its passing from sight and hearing, the tiny chirps, whistles and clicks of hidden birds are elevated in gentleness to the surface of listening, as if bubbles of pure air were released miraculously out of an impenetrable, noxious liquid. In normal circumstances the noise of helicopters poisons vast swathes of public air, but on this occasion, far from objecting, I felt excited by the effect, transitory but dramatic.

The woodpeckers may take the blame. *A Talking Fool*, a woodcut illustrating Alexander Barclay's sixteenth-century translation of humanist scholar Sebastian Brant's long moralistic poem, *The Ship of Fools*, shows a fool in full costume, tongue sticking out, striding past a tree on which a woodpecker is drumming. 'Of to moche spekynge or blabynge,' the poem warns, 'take example by the chatrynge pye. / Whiche doth hyr nest and byrdes also betray.' By its volubility, the pye (or woodpecker, as we know it now) attracts disaster to its own nest.

In Queen's Wood one month later, tiny caterpillars hang suspended from the trees, each dangling from a single near-invisible thread at about the height of a human being. Green, brown, grey, or mixed white and black, they writhe or bide still in the air, small and mysterious calligraphic sigla that invite the passing walker into a fruitless decipherment of an impossible text. Drops of rain are falling, so infrequent that the impression of their falling is too soft for the skin to know of their existence; as isolated drops they whisper the end of their fall as sound, a faint crackling within the dead-leaf forest floor. As I leave the woods I realize I am covered with caterpillars, their deception complete, since I am now the carrier (one crawls onto my ear as I write this) rather than the observer. Earlier I read an amusing story in an interview with saxophonist Evan Parker. Walking home I replay it in my mind. According to Parker, Numar Lubin, who ran Nimbus Records, lived in the same apartment block as Sydney Bechet in Paris in the 1930s. He could hear Bechet practice scales and arpeggios on his soprano saxophone, then finishing each session with strange animal noises. One day Lubin asked Bechet, why the strange sounds? Bechet replied: 'You know, I sometimes wonder if what they call music is the real music.'

In the high winds of January 2007, the window in my loft studio squeaked furiously, like warning signals sounded out by very tiny primates. I recorded a stretch of this monkey business, using two contact microphones and a stereo air microphone. The result was strange though far less eerie than the experience of being in the space itself, hearing one side of the room activated by this alien chatter. Days later, I was woken on a Saturday night by sounds that through the mist of sleep could have been a gang of cannibalistic human babies, crawling around our house, wet, cold, hungry and in search of an entry point. They were urban foxes, of course, but in the almost instantaneous lapse between a moment of waking and the moment of realization that they were indeed foxes, those predatory supernatural babies mewled at the threshold. Back in bed I listened to the wind, still high, and then the hysterical barking of a dog nearby, clearly spooked by those same foxes.

A week earlier, lying in darkness at 2.00 am after watching a gaunt James Brown play the last televised concert of his long career (and still puzzled though delighted by his frequent references to guitarist Wes Montgomery throughout the show) I listened to dogs begin a barking relay; one dog barks in the distance, another answers, then another, gradually developing a pattern in invisible space, close, far, north, east, close again. Why is it, I'm thinking (in the throes of insomnia and the Wes Montgomery question) that these long-range canine feedback sessions don't expand to cover huge distances, enveloping the planet, extending to infinity and lasting until the end of time? Typically for such labyrinthine explorations of the night, the two subjects converge, so that the diminishing echo of a jazz guitarist largely unknown to a James Brown audience of 2007 will bounce off some unexpected object (in this case, Brown, who on the brink of his own death was surely revisiting some of his own ghosts) and insert itself back into cultural discourse.

Lying down, I experience sound as physical sensations. Lying in wait for sleep, or in the hypnagogic zone of transition between waking consciousness and sleep, I feel sounds (loud or soft, familiar or uncanny) as a shock or surprise; shivers, a sudden prickling sensation, shudders, small waves of hearing that are haptic more than aural, as if a hand has brushed across my scalp, as if a quick jolt of electricity has been shot into my back. My body moves under the influence of these sounds; perhaps these nervous movements are related to hypnagogic myoclonic twitch, the falling sensation that sometimes happens just before sleep.

Then summer, the woods dark under leaf cover after persistent rain. I sit by Dog Pond in a clearing of trees. Robins are hidden high in the branches, five or six of them moving quickly. They are all sounding repeated, percussive, high-frequency calls that move randomly back and forth around the circle of trees: dip-di-di-dip, dip-dip-di-di-di-dip, di-di-dip, dddddip-didi-dip. If I close my eyes, I am in Renaissance Italy, sitting in the centre of a sizeable workshop, a sculpture studio in which artisans chip out fine details from white marble blocks, tapping quickly, hammers on tiny chisels.

In December 2006, staying with Lawrence English in Brisbane, I was woken frequently by bizarre, totally unfamiliar sounds from close by in the garden — perhaps the mass murder of cats or a large piece of polystyrene rubbed against the windows of a greenhouse. Bats, possums, and other creatures of the night, Lawrence told me. That, and the heating and cooling of the corrugated metal roofs. One evening he took me to the botanical gardens to feed possums. As growing numbers limped and rolled, such is the possum gait, towards our apple scraps from all directions, I found myself transfixed by a weird bird, moving slowly on stiff legs, radiating an air of nervous pedantry, of curiosity spiked with fear. A faint aerated noise seemed to escape from its beak at high points of caution. This was a bush thick-knee, Lawrence told me. The nocturnal duets of these peculiar birds have been described as 'a hysterical jumble of sound,' and 'eerie wailing calls.' We also visited the evening roost of flying foxes, hanging messily from the trees as if a cargo of broken black umbrellas had been dumped from a plane flying overhead. Squabbling and clambering, making ready to fly in one collective cloud for the hunt, their sound made me think of a large man wallowing in a bathtub filled with squeaky rubber ducks.

5   The jagged dog

Sound may say — these are the invisible traces of memories that have collected over centuries; this is the unique atmosphere of this precise spot, too humble to be noticed in the rush of ordinary life. The revelation comes through pausing, listening. 'In the deep woods they could hear no sound except the slow flowing of the water and the songbirds.' This was Carson McCullers, writing in her novel about a deaf-mute, *The Heart is a Lonely Hunter*. 'Harry held his stuffed egg and mashed the yellow with his thumb. What did that make her remember? She heard herself breathe.'

There is a conversation between place and person that is articulated through sound, in much the same way that the same or similar conversations are visible as buildings, hedgerows, landfill sites, illuminated signs, motorways unspooling into night or plastic bags floating in the ocean. The relationship of person to place is more straightforward, perhaps, in the reading of such material signs: evidence of their history is easier to track through written records, oral history, photographs, film, a shock of sudden disappearance or the lingering sight of decay. Then how can we listen to sounds never before noticed, sounds long vanished, or sounds that are not sounds, exactly, but more like the fluctuations of light, weather and the peculiar feeling that can arise when there is a strong awareness of place? Sounds can linger as vital presence, an intervention that existed for a time to reconfigure environment, and whose absence makes us pause for thought or deeper feeling, in our walking, working and waiting; our agitated, ceaseless inner thoughts; our shopping and drift; our anxieties, pains and pleasure.

What goes unnoticed in the general run of life still exists, in its colouration, its echoes, its affects, its atmospheres and definitions of place. An unnatural silence, a bell in the night, the dizzying flight of swallows, a sharp cry across the river whose audible flowing is a constant and would be missed if it ever froze or dried up, the murmur of a quiet pub, wind rippling through grass and at the far edges of hearing there is the scoot of a dry leaf caught in the breeze, the bringing of the milk and the emptying of the bins, a particular street in the hush of early morning, and maybe the name of that street, rolling around in the imagination with the patina of its age and the mystery of its sound.

A few years ago an email arrived, via my website, through which I learned about Steve, previously unknown to me, a man in Havre, Montana, walking through the drizzle and listening to a CD on his Discman (already the story is dated by this technological detail). The CD is *Live In Japan*, by the Viennese musician, Christian Fennesz, and as Steve walks, his CD skips and glitches of its own volition. The technical breakdown adds to the allure of the music, he says, apologising for sharing such a modest story. 'Plus,' he adds, 'who else am I gonna tell about it in Havre?'

Modest the story may be, but I like it for a variety of reasons. Steve is out there, in the rain, walking through landscape and the elements with his hearing transported to a live show in Japan. Fennesz performs on a laptop computer, but his starting point can be a guitar, building a song on his first instrument, then transforming it through a computer software program. He creates glitches, hitches, loops, distortions. Listening to his records seems to me not unlike eating Japanese natto, those pungent fermented soybeans that extend out into thin strings as you lift them to your mouth. Fennesz pulls his melancholy tunes in all directions without totally working them out of shape.

Then Steve's Discman has something more to say about this, adding another layer of glitch and skip to the mix. Steve enjoys the accidents, though his pleasure in technological imperfections may be a little esoteric for his friends in Montana. Never mind; he can contact a stranger on the other side of the world, elicit a response, and so feel that bit less isolated with this very personal, and perhaps slightly eccentric experience.

Penetrating to the smallest details of hearing, whether as a listening practice or methodology of sound-making, may seem to be an entrance-ment with silence, peace, meditation, all those religious and quasi-religious practices that fall under the rubric of spirituality, but really, it's an engage-ment with the noise that exists at all levels of the dynamic spectrum. In his book, *Microsound*, Curtis Roads has described transient audio phenomena and microsounds as ubiquitous in the natural world. Some of these may be what he calls subsonic intensities, those sounds too soft to be heard by the human ear such as a caterpillar moving across a leaf; others are audible but in their brevity as micro-events, their infinitely subtle fluctuations, or their placing at the threshold of audible frequencies, they lie outside the conventional notion of pitch, tone and timbre. They are difference; the differentiation of one voice from another, or the activation of one instrument from another. 'One could explore the microsonic resources of any musical instrument in its momentary bursts and infrasonic flutterings,' Roads writes, '(a study of traditional instruments from this perspective has yet to be undertaken).'

In the springtime, I sit outside in my garden sometimes at night, waiting quietly in the dark until I can hear the tiny chewing sounds of slugs and snails eating the leaves of my plants. I have to allow every part of myself to slow down, to forget what has happened earlier and what might happen later, to use the 'emptiness of attention' that I learned from Anton Ehrenzweig when I read *The Hidden Order of Art* in my late teens. To use a spatial analogy, it's like descending in a slow lift, moving down through the floors and stopping somewhere near the basement of hearing, where the tiniest of sounds seems amplified. Once down at this level, sounds that are normally considered quiet can shock the system. As snails move from leaf to leaf, snail's pace of course, the leaf they vacate snaps back into its unburdened position with a bang. This is more disturbing than peaceful.

On a still night in spring, in the darkness, there is little to see other than the static design of my garden, obscured by a shadow world. What I hear is a dynamic sonification of the animate life hidden within that shadow world, eating its ways through hosta, iris, and other succulent leaves, and so the experience of being within that particular place, also hearing the atmospherics of late night traffic noise, spiked by drunken shouts from distant streets and the occasional wailing police siren, contains endless variety at a level of perception so remote as to demand attention that is both focussed and relaxed. Detail is picked out from a low noise floor that can only be described as air sound — a sound that evades analysis or recording because it combines the sound of our internal functioning, the body sounds we would hear in the total silence of an anechoic chamber, with a blend of near-field and distant-field atmospherics. This undifferentiated background can be comforting, in the immediate present as an indication that life is perpetuated, the world still turns, and at the level of emotion and memory, a reminder of the sonic presence of loudspeakers, amplifier hum, recording noise, ear sound and human presence — the sound of a person sleeping, for example — but it acts also as a grainy context in which detail feels spatially settled.

This connects to Bart Kosko's analysis of information noise in his book, *Noise*. It looks at the way in which noise of all kinds — pixels, neural spike trains, air noise used by crickets to detect killer wasps, 'faint fields of electrical noise when [the long-snouted river paddlefish] feeds on tiny zoo-plankton in murky rivers and lakes' — can act as a field of interference out of which essential signals can be isolated. Noise is not a sudden incidence of disruption, but the constancy through which events of high value — a silence, for example, or breath heard against the slow flowing of water — are highlighted. 'So it is not just that we will never win the war on noise because noise is in the physical nature of things,' Kosko writes. 'Careful analysis shows that in many cases we should not even be fighting it.'

Exercises in microsonic listening — neither dramatic nor particularly impressive to anybody other than the recipient — can be discounted or forgotten so easily, or deflected in the need to move quickly, achieve, extract the maximum from being alive. In fact, they can ground us in the sense of being in the moment, open us to a form of concentrated attention, are essential for developing skills in the habit of listening to peripheral and subliminal sounds, all of which is a lesson in becoming aware of how strong feelings emerge in relation to barely noticeable elements within an environment.

This is a productive area of investigation, particularly since sound, like scent, seems to be such a potent carrier of memory, as well as being a powerful influence on the formation of a sense of identity. A friend of mine — radio DJ Steve Barker — emailed me to say that memories had surfaced from his teenage years, the sound of hundreds of looms clattering in the cotton mills of Lancashire. Despite his open, inclusive attitude to music, he felt that this enveloping sound, and its associations with factory work, had shaped one aspect of his sonic aesthetic. 'Now I understand why I am so averse to total noise musicians,' he wrote.

Seeing in normal circumstances has a kind of frame for me, determined, to some extent, by a pair of spectacles. I can range across the visual field, but the external limits are always there. Sound, on the other hand, is all around, and existing in ambiguous locations, articulating time at the same time that it describes space. Hearing and sounding happen simultaneously: she shouts and hears her shout, so there is movement out, in and through the body. This shout reaches back to the first shout that tested an alien space, when a baby cries out for the first time as his or her response to the unpleasant shocks of light, air, temperature and other people.

As I am writing this I read a news story about a young man named Tomohiro Kato, who ran amok in Tokyo's Akihabara district, ramming a rented truck into pedestrians, then stabbing others in the vicinity. Witnesses heard him grunting incomprehensibly, screaming and roaring as he slashed at shoppers with a 13-inch survival knife. Seven people died. In the lead-up to the attack, Kato sent 30 messages from his mobile phone to an online noticeboard. Although the messages were ostensibly public, their solipsism rebukes the rhetorical question he asked himself at 6.03 that morning: 'Am I incapable of having friends?' What little he has to say, what unknown depths there are to express — all mediated remotely through staccato words, texting, mobile phone, internet — but his true feelings are hurled out into the streets by those incomprehensible noises. From the gut. From the child. Howl.

Sound is not easy to describe, not always easy to comprehend. Though the metaphors of a visuocentric world cause confusion and relegate hearing to the role of a lesser sense, they can also connect the senses in ways that reflect our experience of being. 'The speaking animal is also a visual animal and does not wholly grasp what he projects into space,' wrote Vladimir Jankélévitch in his subtle and profound examination of music's *charme*, its enchantment, *Music and the Ineffable*. 'More than any other, the dubious, vague, controversial truth of musical Becoming solicits metaphors: it is vision layered upon hearing, and projects the diffluent, temporal order of music into the discussion of space, onto spatial coordinates.'

Touch and sound lie together: the sending out of a sound that touches objects and surfaces at distance; sounds that can vibrate water; sound waves caressing tiny hairs in the cochlea. Walking downstairs, I hear my feet as a composite of their sound — their contact with each wooden stair, the sensation of touch, and the impact that shoots up my body. If I walk down the same stairs with my fingers in my ears, the external aural effect is almost cancelled out, yet I still feel the sensation of sound. The emotional register of the voice is affected profoundly by this sense of texture and resonance in constant flux. Roland Barthes wrote of the grain of the voice: 'The "grain" of the voice is not — or is not merely — its timbre; the significance it opens cannot better be defined, indeed, than by the very friction between the music and something else, which something else is the particular language (and nowise the message).' In the realm of metaphor, voices are soft, hard, smooth, smoky, broken, rough, cracked, warm, cold, like silk, felt, wood, honey, fibres, earth, ice, bubbles, leather, tobacco or oleaginous liquids. Felt as a subtle contact, almost physical, this grain distinguishes the original voice of an Al Green, Chaka Khan or Nat 'King' Cole from the performance of an *X Factor* copyist.

Silence can occupy space with the stealth of fine white sand in subtle movement, an unoccupied chair in an empty room, an abandoned car, sifted flour falling on a chopping board, the cooling of boiled water. During an experiment in which Walter Benjamin took 0.4 of a gram of hashish, the following observations were recorded: 'A dog barks. Test subject speaks of a jagged dog and explains barking as an acoustic serration. The jagged dog is contrasted with the polished dog — that is, the quiet dog.' The dog sounds out to scour the hearer.

Sounding out is the expression used in Cork, in southern Ireland. The phrase gives a sense of outer movement counterbalanced by cautious ingress, which is to listen and investigate with openness, not knowing quite where the listening will take you. To sound out a person is to probe their opinions; to sound out a word is a tentative discovery of a sound, and these implications of edging forward in quizzical silence derive from the maritime origins of the expression, which comes from an equally tentative sounding out of depth in water, using a lead or line and calling the depth, feeding out the lead into what may be unfathomable, mysterious depths, or may be dangerously shallow, listening acutely within the surrounding silence to gauge clear passage or disaster as the vessel progresses. 'I leaned on the rail and turned my ear to the shadows of the night,' wrote Joseph Conrad in *The Shadow-Line*. 'Not a sound. My command might have been a planet flying vertiginously on its appointed path in a space of infinite silence.' But sounding has another, less cautious meaning. To sound is to dive into the black abyss. On the third day of the chase of Moby Dick, brief pause, breath held and muted sound before a final reckoning, the white whale is invisible yet present somewhere beneath the boats. 'Ahab knew that the whale had sounded,' wrote Melville, 'but intending to be near him at the next rising, he held on his way a little sideways from the vessel; the becharmed crew maintained the profoundest silence, as the head-beat waves hammered and hammered against the opposing bow.'

PART II

Vessels and Volumes

6   Act of silence

'Hush! Don't tell Courbet.'

– JAMES MCNEILL WHISTLER

In January 1911, Marcel Duchamp began work on one of the most intriguing paintings of his early life. His personal re-evaluation of the making and meaning of art, so influential in so many ways from the early twentieth century until the present day, had its beginnings in this period. *Sonata* shows a group of three elegant young women grouped in front of an older woman. The younger women are Duchamp's sisters: Yvonne, Magdeleine and Suzanne. Yvonne plays the keyboard of an otherwise invisible piano, Magdeleine plays violin and Suzanne is depicted in profile at the front, sitting in the centre of the image, and she listens intently to the music. The woman standing behind this trio of performers occupies an alternative centre, a formidable counterweight to this aerial, angular gathering of the foreground. She is heavier, more solid than the willowy insubstantial forms of the sisters, and her expression is emotionally remote, darkened by the heavily outlined eyes and a solid line that accentuates the shape of her nose, lips and chin. She looks straight out but avoids the direct gaze of the person who is looking at the painting, as if her wide eyes are wandering in the silence within which she dwells. Her mouth is pursed tight, her demeanour mute. This is their mother.

The picture shares some characteristics of the conversation piece, that peculiarly English genre of art that transplanted the vitality of seventeenth-century Dutch painters such as Metsu, de Hoogh and Mieris to rather more staid depictions of the wealthy landed families of England. Sacheverell

Sitwell wrote of the '. . . sufficiency of the Conversation Piece, which must have an existence to itself as the unfolding of some anecdote or situation.' In other words, they show scenes of two or more people posed in some activity or languid idleness within a stately home or garden, and from that scene we might imagine movement, air, sounds, smell, temperature and other impressions, not least conversation itself. Yet these paintings give little room for imaginings beyond the central subject, which is the wealth and position of the subjects; with a few exceptions the genre is inert. There is an interesting comparison to be made, however, between Duchamp's *Sonata* and J. M. W. Turner's unfinished sketch in oils, *A Musical Party at Petworth*, painted in about 1830. Both show women making music, the unfolding of some mystifying anecdote or situation, yet unlike most conversation pieces, in which those who are portrayed stare down the viewer or seek to dominate the viewer's gaze, as if to say, we are the important ones here, Turner and Duchamp avert the gazes of their subjects. In both cases all details are blurred and diffuse, which leads us to ask deeper questions about what exactly is going on. Sitwell describes the Turner as a 'transcendental experiment . . . no other painter of that day could dissolve his vision into this abstract informality.' The activity of making music is depicted simply enough, yet both artists seek to approximate with visual means the imprecise volumes and movements of sound that suffuse their spaces.

In 'Notes for a Lecture', written in 1964, Duchamp spoke of *Sonata* with affection, almost as if it were painted by a dear friend: 'The pale and tender tonalities of this picture, in which the angular contours are bathed in an evanescent atmosphere, make it a definite turning point in my evolution.' These qualities of paleness and evanescence typify almost all parts of the painting, except for the central upper wedge, taken up by the mother. There, tones darken, gathering clouds. The three sisters float in translucency, the three graces, anticipating Duchamp's later interest in the properties of glass, which shows only those images that are painted upon it. Like sounds, their bodies lack defined edges. But the mother, Lucie Nicholle, seems pulled back into the materiality of the room. Her presence is stolid. Her absence is a difference — not absorption into the aerial flux of sound, but emotional disjunction. A photograph of the Duchamp family, taken in 1895, when Marcel was seven or eight, reveals a similar situation — nine people focussed towards the central action, a game of cards, with Lucie Nicholle distant and leaning back from the group. Evident in images and in Duchamp's infrequent references to his mother, this distance grew for a specific reason. 'Lucie Nicholle suffered from a progressive hearing disorder that had made her almost completely deaf by the time Marcel was born,' wrote Calvin Tomkins in *Duchamp: A Biography*, 'and she dealt with this by withdrawing more and more into a private world of her own.' Duchamp's description of her as 'placid and indifferent' was the unwitting reaction to her deafness — a child alienated by alienation.

Sonata is a representation of an event more than a place. Any representation of spatial depth has begun to vanish as if erased and replaced by simultaneous unfoldings of time, and within that oscillation of time and space are three modes of auditory act: sounding, hearing, and not hearing. 'Sonata' is the feminine past participle of the Italian word 'sonare', to sound, and sonata form in music is typically a composition in three or four movements, written for a solo instrument or small ensemble. As the eyes scan across this painting and settle on the gloomy, isolated figure of Duchamp's mother, the mood of the movement might be indicated on a score as *très grave*. The painting is a reflection of the difficult family dynamic, no doubt, but its core is heartless, since the mother's stern silent world is untouched by this pleasure of sound flowing by. A lesser artist might have sentimentalized the scene; Duchamp could only reveal a truth.

Duchamp's sensitivity to sound, air, gases, visual illusions, weight, tobacco smoke, shadows and similar evanescent or intangible properties was typically refined and arcane. There was, for example, his idea that a full box of wooden matches is lighter than an opened box because it doesn't make any noise, or the recommendation of an article of lazy hardware — the tap which stops dripping when nobody is listening to it. In notes that he collected and 'published' in an edition of three, called *The 1914 Box*, he wrote the following fragment:

[see]
One can look at seeing;
one can't hear hearing.

Later he modified this a little, though to lesser effect: 'One can look at seeing. Can one hear hearing, feel breathing, etc. . . .?' Also in *The 1914 Box* was a note apparently addressed to himself, 'Make a painting of frequency' and a curious observation, headed '*Electricity Breadthwise*': 'The only possible utilisation of electricity "in the arts."' Along with his use of glass, a material in which signs of materiality are almost absent, this deliberate confusion of apperception could be interpreted as part of his resistance to the com-mon sense idea of art, the purely visual, or retinal representation of reality epitomized, in his opinion, by the paintings of Gustave Courbet.

Duchamp was in search of another dimension, and in that search was a refusal of the partition of arts into sensory categories. 'Each second, each breath is a work which is inscribed nowhere, which is neither visual nor cerebral', he told Pierre Cabanne in an interview two years before his death. Another of his *texticles*, published in 1945, proposed the 'infra-slim' ('infra-mince') as a category to be studied. 'The sound or the music which corduroy trousers, like these, make when one moves, is pertinent to infra-slim', he wrote. 'The hollow in the paper between the front and back of a thin sheet of paper. . . . To be studied! . . . it is a category which has occupied me a great deal over the last ten years. I believe that by means of the infra-slim one can pass from the second to the third dimension.' This quasi-scientific focus on what is so precisely fugitive as to be absent yet measurable by finely attuned human sensibilities, seems to rest at the other end of the spectrum to his 'Musical Sculpture', published in the *Green Box*, which in its vague inclusiveness could be a prototypical definition of audio arts: 'Sounds lasting and leaving from different places and forming a sounding sculpture which lasts.'

A WOMAN DESCENDS THE STAIR

Though silent in actuality, the inference of Duchamp's *Nude Descending a Staircase, No. 2*, painted in 1912, is of a sounding sculpture lasting and leaving. Duchamp insisted that the nude was female, though truthfully she looks more like a humanoid built from plywood. In her descent, she clatters, freezing a sequence of moments both sonic and kinaesthetic. Duchamp was not alone in his pursuit of movement and duration through fixed media. Giacomo Balla's *The Hand of the Violinist*, also known as *Rhythms of a Bow*, was painted in the same year, though Balla and Duchamp were unaware of each other's experiments. Whereas Duchamp rejected what he called 'cinema effects', the blurred hand of Balla's violinist is stretched and shuttered like stop-motion photographs. Balla was influenced by Futurist Photodynamism, a movement started by photographer Anton Giulio Bragaglia, who used slow shutter speeds to capture the sweep of a cello bow, a slap, or ghostly hands hammering at a typewriter. The laborious hatchings of small parallel brushstrokes in *The Hand of the Violinist* used Divisonist techniques to create an approximate illusion of the frenetic body in action. They shiver with intensity, yet even so, the picture is too literal to be particularly surprising. The philosophy of Henri Bergson was highly influential during this period, but Bergson spoke of transitions, not one visible state followed by the next, the next, and so on.

Balla's aim, outlined in a joint manifesto with Fortunato Depero, was to find 'abstract equivalents for every form and element in the universe, then combine these at the whim of our inspiration into plastic complexes, which we set in motion . . . Plastic complexes that simultaneously disintegrate, speak, make noise, ring out . . .' As for Bragaglia, his beliefs touched on spiritualism, paranormal phenomena, and the ideas of Bergson. 'The truth is that we change without ceasing,' Bergson wrote in *Creative Evolution*, 'and that the state itself is nothing but change.' Bragaglia's attraction to the spectral is not surprising, given the grey traces of presence that his photographs of kinetic transitions revealed. 'When a person gets up,' he believed, 'the chair is still full of his soul.'

Along with Balla and Bragaglia, two other important Futurists — Luigi Russolo and Umberto Boccioni — addressed this challenge of representing the intangibility of sound though a static visual medium. Russolo's *La Musica* is a theatrical work of rather overbearing symbolism, but Boccioni's *The Street Enters the House* (*La Strada Entra Nella Casa*) of 1911 vibrates with sufficient sound and colour to question Duchamp's conundrum. Maybe we can't hear hearing, but we can certainly observe the act of hearing. The window of the painting has been flung open. A woman leans over her balcony rail and looks down into the street. We see her left ear, as if she is tilting her right ear in the direction of noise. Buildings encircle her. Like her, they lean forward, startled and curious; their windows are eyes, nostrils and ears to the chaos of construction work that buzzes below. Two neighbours lean over their balconies. In the revolutionary mood of the time, a racket of progress and creation has penetrated the tranquillity of domestic space. Like all Futurist manifestos, Carlo Carrá's manifesto of 1913, *The Painting of Sounds, Noises and Smells*, proposed a formula, a dogmatic enshrinement of these aims. 'In order to achieve this total painting, which requires the active cooperation of all the senses, a painting which is a plastic state of mind of the universal, you must paint,' he commanded, 'as drunkards sing and vomit, sounds, noises and smells!'

Duchamp was dismissive of the Futurists. He told Pierre Cabanne they were 'urban Impressionists' who had simply switched from countryside to city. *The Sound of the Stream*, painted by the Italian Divisionist artist Emilio Longoni in 1903, adds support to Duchamp's diagnosis. Longoni shows a woman playing her violin by an isolated waterfall. Despite the sickly colours and insipid symbolism, his representation of the musicality of complex noise is not so far from Luigi Russolo's celebration of waterfalls and other sounds of nature in his essay of 1916, 'The Noises of Nature and Life (Timbres and Rhythms)'. Russolo's explosively dramatic painting of 1909–10, *Lightning*, attempted to breach the limits of visual representation. Its demonic clouds clearly unleash a crack of thunder along with the visible rendering of lighting and rain, yet the painting is of course silent. Logically, the next step was to devise a technology that could mimic such sonic dramas. This was precisely the decision made by Russolo.

Ultimately the Italian Futurists were realists, just like the retinal Courbet, banal for the literalness of their representations of noise and movement in industrial society. Drunk on Futurist belligerence and self-aggrandisement, Carrá was deaf to sound in any painting prior to the Impressionists. 'Before the nineteenth century,' he wrote, 'painting was the art of silence. Painters of antiquity, of the Renaissance, of the seventeenth and eighteenth centuries, never envisaged the possibility of rendering sounds, noises and smells in painting, even when they chose flowers, stormy seas or wild skies as their subjects.' If Carrá had taken the trouble to look more closely at the work of his predecessors, he would have realized the arrogance of his error. It's all the more regrettable then that such pronouncements have been cited uncritically as the origins of twentieth-century experimental music. Though modernism is synonymous with various forms of clamour, whether Dadaism, Futurism, James Joyce, Virginia Woolf, William Faulkner or Duke Ellington's Jungle Band, and though painting is (as Poussin and Delacroix made clear) a silent practice, the representation of listening and sound through visual arts is an ancient history.

7   Art of silence

'Stay, illusion
If thou hast any sound or use of voice,
Speak to me.'

HORATIO TO THE GHOST
(WILLIAM SHAKESPEARE, *HAMLET*)

A WOMAN DESCENDS THE STAIRS

In the Wallace Collection's gallery of seventeenth-century Dutch painting, a woman descends the stairs. Her knee is bent under a voluminous red dress and white apron, one foot poised, as if she knows that to lower her weight onto the stair would risk a creaking of the wood. The composition of the picture is built around a familiar device in Dutch painting — the doorsien, a 'looking through', a hole, opening or threshold that leads through to a secondary scene. Behind her is an open doorway through which we can see an airy, high-ceilinged room in which two well-dressed people are sitting at the table, drinking wine. Their expressions, from what we can see of them, are almost comical. The conversation seems to have hit an awkward silence; their faces are positively dyspeptic. To the left of the woman, in the centre of the painting, are familiar objects that add symbolic depth to Dutch art of this period: a mirror, a globe, a map, all three showing reflections or representations of spaces that lie outside the frame of the work. Thrown with insouciant haste over a chair, a scarlet cloak invites the painter to demonstrate his skill in rendering the folding and falling of fabric, his love of blazing colour within the sober, shadowed hues of a bourgeois Dutch interior. A sword propped up next to the cloak tells us that a soldier has entered the house.

To her right of the woman and downstairs we can see into another room, lit by a roaring fire. The contrast between the light of this cellar space and the surrounding darkness is extreme. To modern eyes, this makes the square of light look like a television or computer screen. What can be seen in this isolated square is the man who owns the cloak and sword, and he is seated next to the maid of the house, clearly in the process of seducing her. He is leaning in close to her face, whispering; his hand is on her breast. Head angled away from him, her hand is on his hand, either in affection or pushing it away. By her feet, a cat is eating food, and this is another familiar motif, of a pet taking advantage when somebody neglects their duty.

The woman in the centre of the picture carries a wine jug in one hand, so from this we can deduce the situation: the wine has run dry, the maid has disappeared, and so the woman of the house has gone to fetch it herself; in the course of doing this she has heard some part of the seduction scene below stairs. She is smiling, collusive, claiming silence, but her gaze seems myopic. There is a clue to this. On the side of her head, behind the left eye, is a black dot, and this shows she is undergoing a cure for an ophthalmic problem. She seems to be leaning on the banister rail with her right elbow to steady herself in mid-step and her finger is raised to her lips, as if to whisper 'shhh.'

The painting is called *The Listening Housewife*, or *The Eavesdropper*. The name of the artist and the date of the work are both very clear because they are inscribed on the stair just below the eavesdropper's foot: N. Maes, 1656. Nicolaes Maes was a pupil of Rembrandt. Born in Dordrecht in January 1634, he entered Rembrandt's studio in Amsterdam as a teenager in about 1648, returned to Dordrecht to marry in 1654 and then settled again in Amsterdam in 1678 until his death in 1693. From the age of 26 he restricted himself largely to fashionable portraits influenced by the work of Rubens and Van Dyck, though there is one exception, an interesting picture — psychological or supernatural in its implications — of a woman suffering from a grave illness. No doubt his prolific output as a portraitist was a reward for his facility in capturing the placid, self-satisfied vanity of his wealthy Dutch and English sitters and their unfailingly grotesque children. The paintings of children are noteworthy for being surreal to the point of nightmare, fat young cherubs with painted faces dressed in ostentatious headgear and adult clothes, naked in drapery, or even winged. Infant Ganymedes ascending Mt Olympus, they ride eagles through lowering clouds. Others cuddle deer or dogs, or sit like pink pygmy despots in miniature chariots pulled by goats. Maes's humour was sharp, even cruel — we know that from his genre paintings. Is it possible that in the course of making a decent living churning out portraits of burghers and aristocrats he made sly fun of them through his pictures of their children?

Many of the genre scenes of his early twenties, however, embraced the spatial, social and psychological implications of sound and silence, largely within domestic interiors. He is almost unique in meditating so explicitly on the contradiction of using a visual medium to represent the ineffability of one moment of hearing, though his fascination with sound as an implicit means of articulating complex spaces is a trope familiar from other works of the early modern period painted in the Netherlands.

Maes was so captivated with the theme of the eavesdropper, or so responsive to its popularity with clients, that between 1655 and 1657 he painted six versions. Four hang in London, one in Boston, and one in his hometown of Dordrecht. All of them are different in quite subtle aspects but all depict this errant, suspect, uncontrollable, betraying, dislocating and uncanny quality of sound. Moreover, they assume a listener, listening to nothing.

He shows a captured moment of listening to what is, or should be, secret. The sound in the silent painting is sustained over centuries, but the silence in the sounding room, the gallery in which the painting is experienced, is transient. There are many paintings of noise and silence from this early modern period of Dutch art, many representations of music both drunken and refined, of people reading, sleeping, peeling apples, scraping parsnips, pouring milk. With scientific detachment, they experiment with the possibility and impossibility of bringing sound into life through a mute medium; with humanistic engagement they locate the significance of sound and silence within human events, specific places and the world of objects. But they also locate us in a haunting, participating in events from more than 350 years ago, placing us in liminal space, colluding with the woman with her finger to her lips, her foot poised over the wooden stair, the stair that threatens to creak and so reveal the guilty pleasures of her intensive listening.

We have stumbled onto a scene as it unfolds. Perhaps the stumble is actual, a transition of movement and time, as well as metaphorical, since we have disturbed a person interrupted, engaged, absorbed, in an act that could be construed as shameful. Through being enjoined to silence by the eavesdropper, we become a second eavesdropper. The space in which we stand is shared, yet the assumption is that the viewer of the work is hidden from all but one of the characters inhabiting the painting. If we were visible, as we are in actuality in relation to the extended space of the picture, then we would be visible simultaneously to all parties in the house, so exposed as a voyeur. That finger on the lips would be too late. Silence would be irrelevant. Yet the hearing of this stilled moment is, in reality, non-existent, and the viewer's point in this extended space is also non-existent. The viewer oscillates between being and not-being: a noisy silence.

LOVERS, OVERHEARD

Apsley House, London: 5 July 2007. Another Maes *Eavesdropper* of 1656, this one subtitled *Lovers with a woman listening*. Again, the listening woman is poised above the lowest step. A forefinger to her lips gives her a quizzical, simpering look; simultaneously it enjoins silence and points to her left, where an open door into another room reveals two lovers, framed against an open window with a windmill visible in the distance. One of the lovers is a maid; her abandoned broom is propped against the door frame. The man is leaning in to her, pawing her breasts. She slumps into him, heavy and tired, somewhat reluctant. A baby basket is by her feet on the floor, and the maid holds a string in her left hand, presumably to rock the cradle.

As for the woman who listens, she has left her work at a book that lies open, probably the household accounts, to eavesdrop. Duties have been neglected by all parties; the invitation to stop work and become a voyeur implicates the viewer in this scheme, part moralistic, part prurient. Keys hang from the listener's dress; perhaps they clink faintly. In the decipherment of these paintings, which is one way to approach them, as a riddle to be decoded and understood, keys play a significant role. Here, they are virtue and responsibility, and elsewhere in Maes, they stand for the forsaking of these qualities, but in this context, attached to the clothing of this woman who is trying to keep still, they are percussion that must be kept quiet. The stairs will creak once her foot descends. Through the open door we hear the rocking of the cradle, though if the sound stopped in the preceding moments, then its silence will have alerted the listener to mischief.

The painting hangs in the Piccadilly Drawing Room of Apsley House, and in this ornate room, gold and white, I hear the constant roar of traffic behind me as it circles Marble Arch, and the strange quavering of a window frame vibrated by the unseasonable high winds that blow outside.

Why so many versions of the eavesdropper? They are like performances of the same play, a short season during which slight variations of a theatrical scene are presented to an audience that becomes curious, this curiosity growing into a compulsion to return over and over again. They are also operatic mysteries, even the seeds of tragicomedies, the weight of blame hefted with each new viewing. Who is the victim? Who's cheating who? The dynamic shifts from player to player, drawing the beholder of the painting into this web of seduction, reproach, dereliction, snooping and collusion.

Speech is marginalized and repressed; action is stilled. After all, each eavesdropper has the choice of interrupting the tryst, berating the maid, ejecting the suitor, but spying is too delicious. The denouement can wait. The story of the space is neither visual nor aural, nor even a flickering fusion of the two, since the eavesdropper cannot see, only look out into an unknown future, and the viewer who she shushes cannot respond by speaking back into the image. How is it possible to bridge this gulf? Speaking of England rather than Holland, Bruce R. Smith makes this suggestion in *The Acoustic World of Early Modern England*: 'The multiple cultures of early modern England may have shared with us the biological materiality of hearing, but their protocols of listening could be remarkably different from ours. We need a cultural poetics of listening.'

The fulcrum of these paintings (the punctum, Barthes might have said) is the silent 'shhh'. Sounded or implicit, this point, sibilant and cautionary as the serpent, falls into the category of stop, sneeze, aerosol spray, all close relations to sudden pain, orgasm, heart attack, broken stick underfoot, camera click, the sudden closing of a book, a slammed door, a thrown glass, a car crash, an explosion. There is a punctuation, a pointing (though the finger points upwards to the heavens as it bars the way to speech) a crossing out. The purpose of its whisper is to still sound, to cut through unwanted noise like a blade, but in so doing it must evade silence. Hence, a finger on the lips, the silent 'shhh', the hush. Making noise to stop rogue noise, the 'shhh' identifies itself with errant sound yet signs for nothingness: my sound is the sound that obliterates, and because there is no such thing as a sound, only sounds mixing together in the course of becoming and fading, the 'shhh' is a stoppage of flow. We hear the contraflow in Björk's song from her 1995 album *Post*, 'It's Oh So Quiet': 'Ssh, ssh, it's nice and quiet, ssh, ssh, but soon again, ssh, ssh, starts another big RIOT.'

Extending from this stoppage of sound is a blockage of secrets. The finger to the lips can also be a sign cautioning the wisdom of silence on subjects that should not be broached, secrets that should not be divulged, things better left unsaid. A Henry James story, 'The Ghostly Rental', uses the 'shhh' in this sense. During his country rambles, the narrator comes across an isolated house that strikes him as 'spiritually blighted'. Passing a young woman at her gate nearby, he enquires about the house; her response is evasive, provoking his curiosity:

> But I laid a hand on her arm, respectfully. 'You mean,' I said, 'that the house is haunted?'
>
> She drew herself away, coloured, raised her finger to her lips, and hurried into the house, where, in a moment, the curtains were dropped over the windows.

Any verbal exchange on the subject of this uncanny place is stoppered, sent back as if by a spell, shut out by a blinding of the canny house's eyes. Returning to Freud and *The Uncanny*, the unhomely feeling emanating from the haunted house (not haunted at all, as it turns out) is warded off, plugged, banished by a retreat into the security of the home. That is the intention, but as with any form of censorship, the desire to know becomes stronger.

Most art historians prefer not to speak of sound in Maes's paintings, or indeed any others, though Richard Leppert's writing on the representation of music in paintings is a notable exception. Sound is not their speciality, so this is understandable, but there is another factor. The hearing of sound in a painting can only be speculative and uncanny. Take, for example, the anonymous Flemish painting, *Boy at a Window*, c. 1550–60, which is in the Royal Collection at Buckingham Palace: a boy looking through a window pane. The frame of the window is also the frame of the painting, so the intended illusion of the work is that this sinister smiling boy who looks out at me is tapping at the leaded glass with his fingertip to attract my attention. In reality, the soft tap-tap-tap is silent, though its imaginary, uncanny presence resonates very effectively. Despite the visual evidence of its effects, there is no material evidence of sound, no proof, no trace, no clear historical context within which a theory can be constructed, no documented history of the significance of sound and silence, no scholarly tradition of discourse, and what little is known of Maes gives nothing further with which to work. In an otherwise stimulating paper that considers Maes's eavesdropper series, Georgina Cole downplays the importance of hearing in these paintings. She writes of the eavesdropper's power to 'see' the structure of the painting (though the woman at the centre of the painting 'sees' only the imaginary viewer in front of her — the structure of the painting is hidden from her eyes so she must use her ears to understand the entirety of the scene), and even interprets the raised finger in visual terms, as a pointer rather than a silencer. 'Capturing our attention with both look and gesture, the housewife makes contact with the viewer,' she writes, in ''Wavering Between Two Worlds': The Doorway in Seventeenth-Century Dutch Genre Painting'. 'With raised finger, she demonstrates how we should "look" at the painting, gesturing to the maidservant's seduction, and guiding the viewer to perceive its clandestine quality in relation to the civil group upstairs.'

Similarly, in *The Self-Aware Image: An Insight into Early Modern Meta-Painting*, Victor I. Stoichita concerns himself with seeing, rather than hearing. 'A powerful dialogue is established between painting and spectator,' he writes, 'because it is actually interrupted. From her gestures, attitude, and expression, the person in the foreground — "the eavesdropper" — intimates, beckons.' In her detailed study of Maes's eavesdropper paintings, Martha Hollander concedes some significance to sound: '[The raised finger] recalls the emblematic figure of Silentium, shown with her finger to her lips, who encourages silence to avoid jealousy and strife.'

Yet sound is indisputable within these spaces, palpable absence, uncanny in its visibility. It is true, adding to my difficulties here, that the gesture varies from painting to painting, angled or slightly curved, never unequivocal, never a clear indication of anything other than a stoppage. The gesture itself, finger on lips, has no secure place in the history of signs, since it arose from a misunderstanding. In ancient Egypt, a naked young Horus, god of the sky, was sometimes depicted sitting on a lotus blossom, with one finger to his lips, signifying the hieroglyph for 'child.' After the conquest of Egypt by Alexander the Great, the young Horus was transformed into a Hellenistic god named Harpocrates, personification of the new sun. Later Greek and Roman poets interpreted this finger to the lips as a gesture for silence and secrecy, even though silence in Egypt was signified by the whole hand placed over the mouth. In *Metamorphoses*, Ovid wrote of Isis and her attendants:

> The barking bug Anubis and the saint of Bubast and
> The pied-coat Apis and the god that gives to understand
> By finger holden to his lips that men should silence keep

More grounded in immediate realities of sexual deceit, Catullus wrote:

> If any secret's whispered by a friend,
> To one who's known for silent loyalty,
> Cornelius, I'm steadfast to this end:
> You'll find a mute Harpocrates in me.

Despite the error, the gesture was accepted and has persisted as a commonly understood visual symbol denoting or demanding silence. Examples include Michelangelo's statue of Lorenzo de' Medici, Gerrit van Honthorst's *Samson and Delilah* from around 1619, in which a maid looks out and gestures for silence at soldiers only she can see, as Delilah cuts Samson's hair, Werner van Valckert's etching of 1612, *Sleeping Venus Surprised by Satyrs*, which shows a satyr with a finger to his lips, ogling the naked Venus, and Quentin Massys's *Allegory of Folly*, painted around 1519, which shows a stupid looking man wearing the bells, ass ears and cock's head costume of a fool. His finger is on his lips and an inscription on the painting reads '*Mondeken toe*': 'Keep your mouth shut.' We are back again in Sebastian Brant's *Ship of Fools* and its moralising — the noisy woodpecker drawing predators to its own nest, and the chattering fool who is equally a hazard to human society. More whimsical as time passed, it could be found on garden ornaments of cherubs and drawings of satyrs, yet centuries later, the sign was still powerful enough to be used in propaganda posters issued by the American Office of War in World War II — Uncle Sam with a finger on his lips, with a message that read: 'I'm counting on you! Don't discuss: troop movements, ship sailings, war equipment.' More recently, the patriotic hush was subverted for political satires aimed at American media compliance with the Bush administration. Uncle Sam was now saying 'Don't discuss: election fraud, corruption, civil rights, impeachment.'

INDISCRETION, OVERHEARD

The Harold Samuel Collection at Mansion House, London: 23 January 2008. *An Eavesdropper with a Woman Scolding* (1655) shows a variation on the drama inherent in what can be heard but not seen. In this case, silence is not the issue. No foot is poised above a stair. The maid has neglected work, leaving crockery in disarray, in order to enjoy the sound of her mistress giving a tongue lashing to some hapless victim. Her finger is not quite raised to her lips, so the scene seems frozen at an earlier moment than other versions of this theme. A painted green curtain hung from a trompe-l'œil pole obscures the right-hand view of the interior and conceals the victim. The detail is tantalising: was the curtain drawn open at the beginning of the ruckus, but only partially drawn because it threatened to ruin the pleasure of witnessing this loss of control? Was it open already, so we have the misfortune of missing half the scene through an accident of placement? Or is Maes thinking that a total visual scoping of an incident such as this is unnecessary, because hearing tells us most of what we wish to know?

The inherent theatricality of the eavesdropper series is further heightened by this curtain. Nine years earlier, *The Holy Family with Painted Frame and Curtain* by Rembrandt provided Maes with a template, though the curtain device relates back to Greek myth: in a contest to decide the best artist, Zeuxis painted grapes that were so realistic that birds tried to eat them; he then asked Parrhasius of Ephesus to pull back the curtain to reveal his work but the curtain itself was Parrhasius's painting.

Rembrandt's humanisation of the Christian theme of the holy family shows a woman and child huddled by an open fire, while in the background gloom, a carpenter is working. In every sense — frame, lighting, depth and atmosphere — their room is portrayed as a miniature stage set, an illusion completed by a painted curtain drawn aside to reveal two-thirds of the scene. Another reality, belonging neither to the subjects of the painting nor to the beholder, is introduced. As in theatre and opera, many genre scenes of Dutch painting in this period suggest a fourth wall, with painters like Maes and his celebrated contemporary, Gerrit Dou, delighting in 'breaking' the wall by using experimental pictorial devices to address or approach an audience directly.

Dou, another member of Rembrandt's studio, specialized in meticulously rendered illusions. His *Violin Player* of 1653, for example, shows the musician leaning out from an open window, the music book from which he plays propped casually on the ledge as if in danger of falling off with a thud into the viewing space. A birdcage is attached to the edge of the window frame, its food container protruding into the non-space between observer and observed. In the darkness behind the musician we can see a painting on an easel and two figures — a young man grinding pigment and a man smoking a pipe — but the musician's eyes are fixed on the bird cage, rather than on these men or the pages of his music. Music is represented as an inspirational force within the artist's studio, but perhaps birdsong is even more inspirational to the musician. Dou plays not only with these ideas but also with the illusion of paintings within paintings: the bird song, the violinist and his music projecting into our world and leaving behind the paintings at his back. The presence of a caged songbird adds a reminder that sound can escape confinements in which solid bodies are trapped. Ultimately, the violin player will never escape from the painting of which he is the subject, no matter how far he leans into our world.

Dou repeatedly used the same device of a character leaning out through an open window in combination with an opened curtain, as in *Painter with Pipe and Book* (1645), *The Doctor* (1653), *Girl at a Window* (1657), *The Trumpeter* (1660) and *Self-Portrait* (1665). Life is short, many of his paintings seem to say, and perhaps an illusion anyway. Certainly one of his less flamboyant works, the Dulwich Picture Gallery's *Woman at the Clavichord*, presents a poignant moment of theatre. A heavy curtain has been lifted up to the right of the picture; wide-eyed, the young woman seems startled, interrupted in her playing by this intrusion. As the world penetrates her solitude, both her physical presence and the sensuality of her music flood out of this claustrophobic yet secure place in which she plays. But perhaps it is not so secure: gathered around and on a table behind her, a viola da gamba, glass of wine, flute and music book all suggest an absent lover who has somehow dematerialized in the sudden shock of light. The message is clear: that the male viewer should step onto the stage (or into the frame), pick up an instrument, or the wine, and perform the role of stand-in for the evaporated actor.

Martha Hollander traces the subject of eavesdropping back to medieval Dutch love poetry, with its focus on secrecy and shame, and to sixteenth- and seventeenth-century farces for the stage, such as the anonymous *Esbatement van den luijstervinck* (*Eavesdropper's farce*), in which lovers constantly try to evade the snooping of a gossip. 'In soliloquies addressed to the audience, or to another character,' she writes, 'a lady might complain about a lazy or lustful maid, or a maid might comment on her angry mistress — the portrayal in *An Eavesdropper with a Woman Scolding*. In Bredero's 1617 farce *Moortje*, for example, the choric character of the "careless maid" (*Morssebelletje*) appears in only one scene during which she soliloquizes about her mistress's amorous difficulties.'

To be part of an audience is to experience audentia, a hearing and a listening, and every audience, whether for theatre, opera, cinema, television, video, webcams, and even media that may be 'inaudible', such as written texts, painting, sculpture and site-specific installations, is a listener or eavesdropper. Either we experience scenes at a distance, in which we have no overt part, or we are directly addressed, as is the case in interactive arts and media, and many television formats such as news and weather, game shows, party political broadcasts and so on vacillate between the two modes. Often, the relationship fluctuates, or is maintained at two levels simultaneously, or in the case of so-called reality TV, is a contract of unknowing in which all parties wittingly suspend reality.

Firmly lodged in collective memory, even as the original becomes an increasingly inaccessible source, is the film noir voiceover, which works hard to give the impression of speaking to an audience in an intimate, confessional mode. Person-to-person, a voice speaks with confessional intimacy into a collective ear, yet the film unfolds remotely in another space and time, as in a dream. Convention encourages the peculiarity whereby the audience is expected to be more or less silent and invisible as helpless witnesses to unfolding drama. The extent and power of cinematic conventions can be surprising. In his essay 'The Silence of the Silents', Rick Altman gives the example of a *Philadelphia Inquirer* review reporting the 1904 showing of a landmark silent film, Edwin Porter's *The Great Train Robbery*: 'There is a great amount of shooting. The smoke of the pistols is plainly seen, and men drop dead right and left, but no sound is heard. Nevertheless, while witnessing the exhibition women put their fingers in their ears to shut out the noise of the firing.' Altman's research leads him to the conclusion that the film was not accompanied by music or sound effects. There was no noise of firing: 'Silent films were in fact sometimes silent, it seemed, and what's more, it did not appear to bother audiences a bit.' And why shouldn't silent film be silent? Why should it be supplemented or 'assisted' by the addition of live music and effects? In its early days, film was closer to the tradition of painting than it was to theatre. Painting stilled the past, froze sounds and movements; film was its spectral equivalent, a reanimation of the past.

'Look with thine ears,' says King Lear. In *Hamlet*, Polonius eavesdrops behind an arras, a tapestry concealing an alcove. 'I'll silence me even here,' he says, but in moments he has broken his silence. Hamlet draws his sword, thrusts it through the arras, then through the 'wretched, rash, intruding fool', to kill him. Earlier, in Hamlet's playlet within a play, 'The Mousetrap', and the dumb show that precedes it, the King is poisoned by a 'mixture rank, of midnight weeds collected', poured into his ears while he sleeps. In Shakespeare's plays, characters soliloquise as soon as they are alone on the stage, speaking to themselves, speaking silent thoughts aloud, or speaking directly to the audience; others hide and eavesdrop on conversations, or on the revelations of such solitary speeches. *Othello*, for example, is a tragedy that unfolds through asides, soliloquies, the unsaid, and through information that the audience has overheard yet despite its growing discomfort cannot replay back into the narrative. 'It is engendered,' Iago says, as he reveals his evil intent to an unseen audience. 'Hell and night must bring this monstrous birth to the world's light.' His asides — 'O, you are well tuned now!' — are words and observations that only the audience can share, while they hear him 'pour this pestilence into [Othello's] ear.' Deception is audible but the truth is silent. Secrets tumble into earshot, anxieties gather around the protection and invasion of privacy. Cumulative punishments lurk, both for characters within the plays and for the audience as they hear what should not be heard, fail to hear what they need to hear, hear what they might not wish to hear, yet cannot resist hearing.

ILLUMINATED LOVERS, OVERHEARD

Buckingham Palace, London: 19 February 2008. *The Listening Housewife* was painted in 1655. This is the most compact of the series, richly dark, warm and mysterious. The woman, wearing a white apron, keys hanging from her belt, descends a complex winding stair. 'We don't think enough about staircases,' Georges Perec wrote, in *Species of Spaces*. 'We should learn to live more on staircases. But how?' Here is a life on staircases. Again, Maes shows her caught, movement arrested in a moment of listening, foot poised above the stair (a shadow runs under her foot) and finger to lips. Again, the myopic gaze, the quizzical look, as if to say that sexual life is still new and puzzling. Below stairs is a familiar scenario — a man is kissing a servant woman — but this time there is the disturbing addition of an old man standing behind them, a Christ-like shepherd illuminating two errant members of his flock with a lantern. He looms over the couple, an unseen paternalistic voyeur. A cat sleeps on a chair; another broom lies abandoned on the floor. Other paintings in the series murmur and whisper, sound rising and creeping, entering and leaving, animating spaces that recede, rise and descend, disgorge and enfold, but this space is profoundly enclosed, a claustrophobia intensified by tightly wound stair and deep shadows. I feel I hear the cat breathing. Standing in the Picture Gallery of Buckingham Palace with only a curator of the Queen's collection for company, I am conscious of the wonders that surround me: Steen, Metsu, Cuyp, the strange stillness of Vermeer's *A Lady at the Virginals with a Gentleman*, the dynamism of Rembrandt's *The Shipbuilder and his Wife*, and his solemn *Agatha Bas*. Like a sonic mirror of the class divisions articulated by Maes's hidden and hierarchical spaces, maids whisper in adjacent rooms within this hushed atmosphere.

DISTANT AND PRIVATE, OVERHEARD

Dordrecht Museum store, Netherlands: 25 April 2008. Painted in 1657, this version of *The Eavesdropper* is the most complex of the series. A woman stands at the foot of a flight of stairs leading down from the main dining room of the house. She is older than the other listeners, and her amusement is more generously given. As usual her foot is poised above the lowest step, one finger to her lips, and in her left hand she holds an empty glass. Yet again, the wine has run out; yet again a suitor paws at the maid's breasts. She stands at the bottom of another short flight of stairs, in a high-ceilinged hallway. There is very little sense of pleasure here; she appears to be tolerating attentions that are both intimate and proprietorial with a gaze into the distance that is either steely or resigned. Also in view, through an aperture, is the ubiquitous cat, eating what may be a chicken. While the maid falls into damnation, the cat gets fat.

A large door opens behind them, showing a distant view of another house. Two characters, a woman and a man, can be seen in the garden of this house, mirroring the couple. They are deep in conversation. Despite their remote position, far out of earshot, the viewer is implicated a second time. Inaudible, and clearly private (their placement in the garden could be innocent, though they may be removing themselves from the risk of being overheard), their talking invites another eavesdropper. The view is innocuous, yet it harbours a mystery, as if anticipating a Peter Greenaway film yet to be made (some might argue that the film has been made, or one version of it, with Greenaway's *Nightwatching*, his investigation of a crime hidden in the clamorous darkness of Rembrandt's *The Militia Company of Captain Frans Banning*, better known as *The Night Watch* — the published screenplay begins with an exegesis of the sounds circulating within the painting).

Behind the eavesdropper, in the room at the top of the stairs, a moustachioed man is proposing a toast, or alternatively, he could be holding up his empty glass as if to say, 'Where's the maid with the wine?' Somebody else is standing (only one of their hands is in the frame) and three people sit at the table. Two of them conspiratorially lean their heads together, ignoring what is happening around them and looking through the opening. Maes is ambiguous here: they could be looking to see what the eavesdropper is doing, or they may have spotted the viewer. This group is lit by a high window, behind which lies a murky, unclear world.

Lying on the floor, at the nearest point to the viewer, is a stick and what looks like two stones. Is this some kind of toy? If so, it could have been discarded by the children of the house, who are sitting at the table and looking down the stairway. Nobody has cleared the object away; Maes is as thorough as ever in his penchant for scattering blame. The colours are typical of Maes in this early phase of his career: vivid vermilion and scarlet bursts outwards from a homely enclosing darkness of greens and browns. This is one of his most complex depictions of spaces, interiors and exteriors, and the most intricate articulation of acoustic spaces: high ceilings, an enclosed stairway, and openings into other spaces in all directions. The silvery pale greys of the map hanging on the wall, the wall on which the map is hung, and the eavesdropper's apron, emphasize the mirroring that is such a strong feature of the work (a triangulation of reds, from the eavesdropper, to the woman in the garden, to the maid and the man's cloak).

The eavesdropper emerges from shadow, only the implicit sound of a creaking stair signalling her stillness. Can the children have heard this creaking board, and the maid also, since her right eye has turned to her left, even in the middle of an embrace? As for the eavesdropper, she seems so absorbed and amused that there is a danger of her dropping the glass she holds — its tipping to the left is another line pointing to the subject of her audio gaze, a transparent cone that seems aimed to capture transgressive sound. At the same time its phallic angle in her hand is a clear allusion to sex. References to sexuality abound in Dutch paintings of this time. As Simon Schama wrote in 'Wives and Wantons: Versions of Womanhood in 17th Century Dutch Art', '[sex] is represented by the visual equivalent of a wink, a leer or a nudge: the proffering of a single coin, or a glass of wine held at the stem, or a strategically placed foot. The point of this symbolism was not to expose sexual behaviour but to shroud it behind a gauze of allusions and metaphors.'

THE GRAIN OF AN INEXPLICABLE NOISE

Maes painted other works dealing specifically with sound as a betrayer of the illicit and forbidden. In the style of the *Eavesdropper* series, *The Jealous Husband*, painted in 1655 or 1656, shows a man at the foot of a staircase, smiling but looking slightly sorry for himself. His finger is close to his mouth but it points in the vague direction of the clandestine scene. What he hears in a room only visible to the viewer is the maid in conversation with another man. The title suggests that he is having an affair with his own maid, which makes him look both pathetic and salacious: his voyeurism embraces his own humiliation, as he hears himself usurped from a position which he should never have held. A related painting from 1655, *Sleeping Man*, shows a man asleep at a table, his pipe and wine jug emptied. A woman stands behind him, leaning over to dip into his pocket. Her finger is raised to her smiling lips; this is the clearest case of the raised finger signifying silence, since it points away from the victim. To look at the painting is to become complicit as the silent witness to a crime.

The Naughty Drummer, or *The Drum*, from 1656, is lighter and less judgemental. A small boy has been banging his drum in the same room where a baby is sleeping in a cot. Exasperated, the mother seems to have struck him. The painting freezes this moment, the quelling of noise, since the striking implement in the mother's hand seems to quiver in mid-air, the stick in the boy's right hand is still lifted above the drum, the other stick lies on the floor and his left hand moves up to his eyes as his face crumples. Percussive reflections echo between walls, fading, then tears begin; the tattoo on a drum head is replaced by the noise of wailing. On the wall behind the scene is a mirror, reflecting the painter's face — another presence which, like sound, is there but not there.

Sound offered Maes many possibilities through which he could distinguish his work from other artists in a crowded field. First, there was eavesdropping, which delineates species of spaces: physical, social, gendered, sexual, moral, acoustic. Then there was time. In slicing through the frontage of a house to reveal the physical relations of a scene as it unfolds, Maes layers each stoppage of time, each 'shhh', upon the next, so that time stutters in the way that digital media such as DVDs and CDs glitch at a standstill. Eavesdropping is a mode of hearing that requires delineated spaces. Ear pressed to the wall of a house, the secret listener stands under the eaves, the overhang constructed to protect the walls of a house from rainwater. The word is probably derived from the Old Norse *upsardropi*, which correlates with the Old English *yfæsdrypæ*. Originally, it may have referred to both the person who listened under the eaves and the drops of rain as they fell from the eaves.

To the person inside the house, the sound of rain outside is a background, just as words can hum and blur as background, but to the person outside, their intensity of listening gathers into itself all the detail of a separate interior in order to hear what is secret, private, and contained within its own space. There may be culpability on both sides: the private information may be malicious or duplicitous, but the eavesdropper deceives by creeping around, sneaking up, invading auditory space not through transmission, but through reception. Like other writers, I eavesdrop on conversations not intended for my ears. Sometimes this is a relatively casual form of overhearing, often involuntary, in which a public conversation becomes intrusive or mildly interesting. A person's voice, their tone or turn of phrase, their topic of conversation, may be interesting or amusing in some way. Sometimes the eavesdropping is involuntary, an unwanted hearing of noises created by actions that can't be seen. These are known as 'vicinal' noises, the sound of activities that transmit through partitions, the intimacies of private domestic life that soak through architecture to invade the lives of others. Research into this phenomenon is quoted by Erving Goffman in his study of social encounter as performance, *The Presentation of Self in Everyday Life*. Through party walls, every private noise penetrates and the awareness of this produces a corresponding self-consciousness. 'It does make you feel a bit restrained,' one informant told the researchers, 'as if you ought to walk on tiptoe into our bedroom at night.'

Freud believed that all human beings store within themselves an unconscious fantasy of watching their parents have sex, based on childhood instances of overhearing the sound. An example was given in his case study of a young woman named Dora, which was documented in 'Fragment of an Analysis of a Case of Hysteria':

Dora's symptomatic acts and certain other signs gave me good reasons for supposing that the child, whose bedroom had been next door to her parents', had overheard her father in his wife's room at night and had heard him (for he was always short of breath) breathing hard during their coitus. Children, in such circumstances, divine something sexual in the uncanny sounds that reach their ears.

In *A Voice and Nothing More*, Mladen Dolar quotes the passage in which Freud spoke of an accidental sound triggering a primal fantasy, describing such noises as 'an indispensable part of the phantasy of listening [Belauschungsphantasien], and they reproduce either the sounds which betray parental intercourse or those by which the listening child fears to betray itself.' In this scenario, even the smallest sound can reverberate far beyond its initial space of resonance. In Dolar's interpretation.

The situation of the patient would thus be a displaced reenactment of a paradigmatic fantasy which is constructed entirely around the kernel of the voice, the grain of an inexplicable noise, a mysterious sound, which can appear even with the tiniest click. At the origin of fantasy there is a traumatic kernel materialized by the voice, the noise — we should allow full latitude here to a sonority not pertaining to language.

Though I have no memory of overhearing sexual sounds as a child, so have to take Freud's theory on trust, I have retained an extremely strong memory of eavesdropping on my parents arguing in their bedroom at night. Perhaps eight years old and woken by their voices, I listened, petrified and absolutely still, as they argued with unfamiliar venom. The usual threats were traded — 'I only stayed with you for the sake of the children,' and so on — their seriousness falling like depth charges into my life. Though they never repeated the argument in my earshot, the shock and guilt of that moment is burned into my memory. Like Jim Hawkins of Robert Louis Stevenson's *Treasure Island*, concealed in the apple barrel and overhearing Long John Silver's treacherous intent, I realized that adult life is fraught with disillusionment and the unknown.

With the ubiquity of mobile phones, many so-called private conversations are shared by all those who occupy a public space such as a bus, a train, a waiting room or a cafe. This may be fascinating, irritating or deeply uncomfortable, but the experience is coloured by its unavoidability. The ears cannot hide themselves or save themselves from shame.

The more serious form of eavesdropping, in which intimate information previously withheld is discovered by stealth and close listening, compromises the listener with a confusing mixture of self-righteousness, ambivalence and shame. What I want to know, I may not wish to hear. During eavesdropping incidents of this kind I have experienced a heightened, almost hallucinatory sensation of being enfolded in two discrete spaces, each of them connected only by the auditory space flowing between them. Each vibrates with a peculiar intensity, since the speaker concentrates on secrecy — intelligible yet quiet — and the listener concentrates on stealth — intent yet silent and invisible. Both parties may feel guilt, and within the heightened emotions of this scenario, revelations of betrayal come as a physical shock, yet what they reveal is accompanied by absence. In discussing the important role of sound and eavesdropping in the novels of Proust, Ann Gaylin argues that for Proust, sexual knowledge is intimately associated with 'epistephomilia', the primal desire to know. 'No matter how much we know, we almost always want to know more,' she writes, in *Eavesdropping in the Novel from Austen to Proust*. 'Eavesdropping usually provides us with partial information and whets our appetite to possess the complete story. It not only dramatizes the exchange of information that forms the crux of storytelling, but in its incomplete acquisition of information, encourages us to create additional stories to account for what we may have heard.'

This entwinement of sexuality and epistomophilia lies at the core of Maes's *Eavesdropper* series. Each incident is a moment of theatre, an interruption of a narrative in which each interpretation is frustrated by its opposite. Moral admonitions concerning laziness, dereliction of duty, and immorality are undermined by the amusement of the eavesdropper, while the delineation of social and economic territories is ruptured by the flow of erotically charged sound that titillates the employer, implicating her (and him, in one case, and the viewer of the picture whenever it is seen) in these lapses into sin.

Some painters seem to work with a consciousness of sound, incorporating suggestions of its presence within their otherwise silent work; others show no interest in audibility? Maes's ingenious representation of the moment of listening is a curiosity. In a sense, he might be described as a pioneer of sound art, since so much of his youthful work dwells in this auditory hinterland of the incomplete story. Hearing is so transient. The idea of recording sounds for posterity must have been imagined long before it could be achieved — the desire in grief to hear the voice of a loved one who has died. One can't hear hearing, said Duchamp, but through Maes there is the inference, even though his medium is soundless. He experiments with the depiction of complex spaces, relationships between people, the character of individuals, and with the atmosphere of a single space. This is achieved both with impressive technical facility in the use of perspective, and with the implicit hearing of hearing. We know so little of Maes, how he lived or what he believed, but for the modern viewer his early paintings hover on the brink of replaying audio events from the distant past. In one sense they are theatre, yet they go beyond the conventions of our time, in which the audience for many productions is either expected (or forced by the technology) to be passive, looking ahead to the twenty-first-century world of digital interactivity.

BE SILENT

His *Eavesdropper* series was not the first to go beyond visual representations of sound by depicting a hypothetical zone of audible communication, shared by the inhabitants of both pictorial space and viewing space. Martha Hollander finds a model for the eavesdroppers in F. Laquy's eighteenth-century watercolour copy of a lost painting by the Leiden painter Isaack Koedijck, dated by the clothing to the late 1640s. The composition clearly anticipates Maes's *Eavesdropper* series, though Koedijck pushed sexual content a little further towards pornography by showing the visitor lifting the maid's skirt. The Flemish painter, David Teniers the Younger, also scrutinized the complex dynamics of domestic affairs. As with Maes, sound is a leading actor in his mini-dramas. *Interior of a Kitchen with an Old Woman Peeling Turnips*, from the early 1640s, shows a large kitchen, gloomy and dusty. In the right foreground an old woman sits peeling turnips, and in a chimney nook behind her, two men converse conspiratorially, while another slumps against the wall. At the rear, a man looks in through the open door, looking and listening at this group; above them, another man's head pokes through a hatch, gazing down with a curious expression as he eavesdrops on their private machinations. Just to complicate the audio scene further, a seated dog in the far left foreground is staring away from the scene, as if it has heard something through the open window set into the wall above. A later Teniers painting, *Interior of a Farmhouse with Figures, 'The Stolen Kiss'* (c. 1660), reworks this potent confluence of sex and the raised index finger (yes, that smutty implication might be a consideration, just like the wine glass held by the stem). In another room of earthy, rural gloom, this one shared with chickens, cows and a dead hare, an old woman milks cows in the background; to the centre of the picture a servant steals a kiss from a young woman. She is holding the hand of a little girl who seems oblivious to this moment of sexual opportunism. The dog, however, is not, and registers disapproval by barking at the servant's leg. Perhaps this racket has raised the farmer, who comes unsteadily down the stairs, knife in one hand, index finger of the other hand raised to his lips. He seems to have seen them, though the open door may obstruct his view. If he has seen them, and this young woman is surely the old couple's daughter, then his raised finger is puzzling. Is he, like Maes, instructing the beholder to keep silent and spy on the amorous young couple? If so, the implications might suggest a number of salacious stories.

Equally intriguing is the theme of the reclining, or sleeping water nymph. Lucas Cranach's *Reclining Water Nymph*, 1515–20, is a sublime example, the naked nymph lying in the open air by a fountain, her expression serious rather than erotic. A later version of 1533 is more playful in its sexual implications. In this version, the fountain has been replaced by a rustic grotto. The nymph is naked but she is using her clothes as a pillow and a transparent veil is entwined around her right foot. A partridge, a bird associated with promiscuity, stands by her, beak open as if speaking and one foot raised to indicate an inscription written along the bottom edge of the painting: 'Fontis nymphae sacri somnum ne rumpe quiesco.' The same inscription can be read on Cranach's *Sleeping Nymph* of 1518, its message a distillation of a longer text:

> Huius nymphae loci, sacri custodia fontis,
> Dormio, dum blandae sentio murmur aquae.
> Parce meum, quisquis tangis cava Marmora, somnum
> Rumpere. Sive bibas sive lavere tace.

Leonard Barkan, author of *The Beholder's Tale: Ancient Sculpture, Renaissance*

Narratives, translates the poem as follows: 'Nymph of this place, custodian of the sacred fountain, I sleep while I hear the murmuring of the smooth-sounding water. Spare me, whoever touches upon this marble cave, do not interrupt my sleep. Whether you drink or wash, be silent.'

Both sound and silence are vital in this image: the somniferous properties of running water, the 'silence' implicit in depictions of sleep, and the request (or is it a command?) addressed to beholders, that they should drink or wash in silence. 'It is a speech that cancels speech, thereby introducing a maze of linguistic paradoxes,' writes Barkan. 'An object which is inanimate but for a representational illusion "speaks," only to establish that it is in a condition (i.e., sleep) which forbids speech.' His interpretation of the inscription is that the interruption of the viewer is sexual; a sleeping naked woman (or boy) is a voyeur's dream. 'From at least the perspective of those who are, or identify with, heterosexual males (and one of the powers of Western high culture has characteristically been to universalize this identification),' he writes 'the beautiful woman asleep with a notable promise of nudity is in herself a perfect object for the voyeur — an object that may be watched with impunity.'

This underlying meaning was made explicit in a series of woodcuts published in Venice in 1499, the *Hypnerotomachia Poliphili* of Francesco Colonna. One of these images showed a satyr with two fauns looming over a naked sleeping woman. As he pulls up the curtain that shields her from prying eyes, the satyr's erect penis makes his intentions unequivocal. Rembrandt's 1659 etching of *Jupiter and Antiope* visits similar territory. This story was depicted by many painters, including Correggio, Titian, Watteau, Ingres and Poussin, though none of them are so scrupulous in their examination of the ruthlessness of male desire. Rembrandt shows the naked Antiope sprawled asleep, mouth open and arms thrown behind her head. Savouring this still contemplation even though he knows that what will follow is the violence of rape, Jupiter quietly lifts the covering over her legs to expose her fully to his studious, surreptitious lechery. In *Rembrandt's Nose*, Michael Taylor compares this image with Rembrandt's *Anatomy Lesson of Dr. Tulp*. 'The cadaver and the sleeping girl,' he writes. 'They are both objects of lust, after all — the lust for knowledge and the lust for knowledge in the biblical sense. The lust to understand and the lust to possess — or, in both cases, simply the lust to see, to draw, to paint. Like Picasso in his countless variations on the theme of the old satyr and the beautiful young woman, Rembrandt has given us a mythological equivalent of an historic relationship between male artist and female model or, to put it in more general terms, between the artist and the world.' Though Maes was never so frank in reflecting back to the beholder this rapacious aspect of the gaze (or so sexually graphic as either Rembrandt or Koedijk), his paintings collude in the erotic frisson of unimpeded voyeurism.

MURMURISM

Confusion surrounds the sleeping nymph and the origins of the inscription. Was it from Giorgione's *Sleeping Venus*, a Roman fountain relief from antiquity, or a fountain constructed by the Hungarian King Matthias Corvinus, based on an antique water nymph shrine on the banks of the Danube? A version by Alexander Pope can be found in the classical setting of Stourhead landscape garden in Wiltshire. Created between 1741 and 1780 by Henry Hoare II, the owner of the Stourhead estate, with buildings by architect Henry Flitcroft, the garden is an artistic, poetic and mythical journey, leading the visitor through Neo-classical landscape and buildings inspired by the paintings of Claude, Poussin and Gaspar Dughet, and the allegory of Aeneas's voyage after the fall of Troy, as recounted in Virgil's *Aeneid*. By the lake, fed by the river Stour, the path leads down into a grotto of two chambers. Within the main chamber, sheltered within an arch, is a white statue said to represent Ariadne, sleeping on a marble plinth (after being abandoned on Naxos by Theseus, slayer of the Minotaur). Water runs constantly from either side of her plinth into a shallow pool, a continuous trickle that lulls, a sleeping draught, a draught of sound that creeps through the chamber almost unnoticed.

Down into gloom in the wake of Aeneas, the underworld descent, to the cryptoporticus, the shades, Naiades, oracles and diviners, where words are liquid murmurs and sibilant whispers. For a moment, we should be still and quiet in the darkness. Listening closely to the constant burble of water we hear a murmuring of phantom voices — imagined choirs, conversations in a language that eludes meaning, tantalisingly incomprehensible monologues and inner voices that seem to live within both the imagination and air. Phantom voices are buried just below the surface of water flux. In his study of Greek oracles, Robert Flaceliere unearths many examples of sonic divination and oracular listening used in ancient Greece: the sounds of sneezing, bird song, the murmuring of oak trees in the wind, the crackling of laurel wood in a fire, even singing in the ears. 'Since the physical act could not be voluntarily controlled,' he wrote, 'it was considered reasonable to attribute it to divine influence.'

The nymph sleeps; subduing the eroticism implicit within the scene, the poet requests silence of movement, washing, drinking: 'Nymph of the grot these sacred springs I keep, and to the murmur of these waters sleep. Ah, spare my slumbers, gently tread the cave, and drink in silence or in silence lave.'

LIVING STILLNESS

To watch a conversation in progress is unremarkable. To see a conversation in which the words are completely silent is uncanny. Even Maes's conversing couple in the far distant garden, in the Dordrecht *Eavesdropper*, piques my curiosity.

By the time that Maes turned his attention exclusively to portraits, sound was no longer relevant to his subjects or style, but from the earliest stage of his career, he had experimented with sound, silence, listening and auditory space. From 1653, *Abraham Dismissing Hagar and Ishmael*, in the Metropolitan Museum of Art in New York, is his earliest known dated work. Abraham speaks to his concubine, Hagar, who listens with her eyes down, head turned away, while their son, Ishmael, walks away down the steps, his head and eyes turned back, as if listening to a private conversation. *Vertumnus and Pomona*, painted in the same year, shows an intense conversation between two women. The old woman of the myth (Vertumnus in disguise) is leaning in, gesturing to emphasize a word as he praises his own virtues as a lover. Unaware of his deception, Pomona gazes into the middle distance, chin resting on her hand, her face serious as she listens intently. Again, the innovations of Rembrandt preceded him.

Drawing on the research of Julius Held, Svetlana Alpers argues in *The Art of Describing* that Rembrandt went against the common practice of his time — depictions of two people speaking at once, or actions taking place as words were spoken — by painting one person speaking as another listens to what they say. The example given is Rembrandt's etching of 1645, *Abraham and Isaac*, in which the two of them have stopped on their way to the mountain. Abraham is gesturing to his son in the course of speaking, and Isaac listens quietly. 'Held is surely right that Rembrandt is trying to represent an actual conversation,' Alpers writes. 'What is at stake for him is his deep respect for the power of words and the privilege that he gives to the sense of hearing. Rembrandt shows the spoken word to be a prime way of bringing or binding people together.'

But Maes was not all conversation and comedy. Another of his specialities during this early period was the quiet or silent scene, in which a woman, almost always a woman, is engaged in domestic work, sleeping, writing, praying, or reading. Men are conspicuously absent from this aspect of the bourgeois interior. 'The visual lack of adult men is essential to these paintings,' writes Nanette Salomon in her book, *Shifting Priorities*, '. . . these images partake of the Netherlandish visual convention that figures the domestic interior as the pure, virginal space of the woman's body.' Such scenes of domestic quietude were common in Dutch genre painting, raised to extraordinary levels of beauty and sadness by Rembrandt and Vermeer, but when he is not chastising yet another maid for her dereliction of duty, the deep atmosphere of tranquillity and concentration of Maes's work in this sub-genre is conveyed with great sensitivity.

There is the strangeness, comforting and uncomfortable, of watching a person sleep, listening to their breathing; another kind of voyeurism; another kind of eavesdropping, either devotional or sinister. In a state of bliss and relief, parents watch their children sleep; in a state of anxiety, children watch an ageing parent sleep. Young children and old people often appear to have died in their sleep: still lives. We vanish in our sleep (to quote Bootsy Collins from his song of that title); living stillness. Haruki Murakami describes this watching of sleep in *After Dark*, watching on a screen, then passing through the screen to be close to the woman who sleeps in a silence so deep it hurts the ears. The Man with No Face also watches her and so the narrator and the reader watch the watcher: 'We seem to be looking at a picture that has been paused, which is not the case.' John Giorno, briefly Andy Warhol's lover and the subject of his first film, awoke one night after a party to see Warhol watching him sleep. In 1964, Warhol went on to film him sleeping naked, looping and repeating parts of the footage, then projecting the film at sixteen frames per second, for a final length of eight hours. The film ran silently. Jonas Mekas recounted the contents of a letter he had received from Mike Getz, manager of the Cinema Theatre in Los Angeles, where *Sleep* was screened. At one point, when the shot changed to show a close-up of Giorno's head, a man rushed up to the screen and shouted 'Wake up!' into his ear.

To be near to a person you love, watching them as they sleep, is one thing; to watch an interminable film of a sleeper as if through the unyielding eyes of a remote stranger is quite another. Deriving anything from the experience depends upon a radical shift of temporal consciousness, a slowing of tempo, a conscious restriction and intensification of perception that zooms in on minute detail. From 1971, this was filmmaker and theorist Peter Gidal's analysis of what can happen in the viewing of Warhol films like *Sleep*: 'Concentration on nuances of movement (in time) not only makes the slightest change of position (even breathing) important but also is involved with silence in visual terms. It is not stasis, but a silence filled.'

Paintings are different again. They allow choices: how to see, and the duration of seeing. Between 1654 and 1657, Maes invited his audience into these pictures. Animate life seems to have been paused: a young woman sleeps, her arm resting on a baby's crib; a woman nurses her baby; a woman embroiders, lit as if in church; a young woman leans out of a window, pensive, lost in thought; a child eats from a spoon, distracted, dreamy, her bowl of food leaning on the crib of the baby she is minding while a cat waits, sphinx-like, for its opportunity; an old woman snoozes over her open book, pen in hand; an old woman prays, surrounded by symbols of mortality: a skull, an hourglass, time running out. In New York's Metropolitan Museum, *The Lacemaker* by Maes: a fat baby sits imprisoned in what looks like a junior pulpit; a cup lies on its side, the woman's horsey face is slightly twisted by her concentration. In this room at the Met, the parquet floor creaks in fine gradations of high tones shading into lower frequencies. The floorboards in the painting would have creaked. The window is open. The baby looks directly at me, as if to say, 'Can you see what is going on here? Can you hear this quietude?'

Young Girl Peeling Apples, also in the Metropolitan Museum collection, is all soft light. There are no sharp edges. The corners of the walls are rounded, buttery, so the only sharpness, emerging from the girl's hand but black and only glinting in one spot, is a blade. Her concentration seems not absolute — a flicker of amusement passes over her young, slightly plump features, as if she is thinking of an amusing incident. In London's National Gallery, *A Woman scraping Parsnips, with a Child standing by her*, shares a similar soft-focus quality and muted tones, almost photographic or cinematic. The humble parsnip holds the centre of the picture, the woman and the child looking down. The vegetable occupies their gaze, but both seem lost in their own thoughts. The child looks rather sulky, as if held in this quiet, diligent space against her will. Deep shadow envelops most of the scene, emphasising the private, contemplative mood, only disturbed by the sounds of scraping. Simon Schama finds a link between education and nourishment in such paintings, the peeling of vegetables depicted as an instruction in household virtue. '*Opvoeding*, the word for education, was, after all, etymologically rooted in the verb *voeden*, to nourish or feed,' he writes in *The Embarrassment of Riches*, 'and if learning was supposed to nourish virtue, nourishment was supposed to be a form of learning itself.'

As representations of piety and virtuous duty the moral messages of these paintings may be too strictly judgemental for modern tastes in art. They remind us that silence can signify docility; women fixed within the domestic grid training younger women to a future occupancy of the same spot within the same grid. Mona Hatoum's 1999 work, *Home*, views a similar scene, but from the perspective of a world radically transformed: the knife that scrapes the parsnips has been industrialized but the woman who operates the machinery is not longer prepared to be subjugated by the task. A table is covered with gleaming steel devices designed to bring efficiency to kitchen work: grater, colander, whisk, pastry cutter, sieve, scissors, pasta maker. These metal instruments are interconnected by electrical cables. Electricity passes through them, lighting small lamps as it does so and humming malevolently. Just as the silence of Maes is a beguiling affirmation of the home and its continuity through acquiescent acceptance of transferred knowledge and gender roles, so Hatoum's dangerous humming is unheimilich, an invader that envelops the enforced silence of domesticity, the tyranny of the home.

Nevertheless, as more universal images of quietude, Dutch genre scenes of domesticity and concentration can be profoundly affecting: Rembrandt's *Mother as the Biblical Prophetess Hannah*, Gerrit Dou's *Old Woman Reading*, Gerard ter Borch's *Woman Writing a Letter* and *Mother fine-combing the hair of her child*, Caspar Netscher's *The Lace Maker*, Pieter de Hooch's *A Woman Peeling Apples*, Johannes Vermeer's *A Maid Asleep* and *Woman Reading a Letter*, and originally thought to be by Rembrandt but now known to have been painted by one of his followers, *A Man seated reading at a Table in a Lofty Room*. This latter work, in the National Gallery, London, is unusual within the genre, since the more familiar custom was to place either a solitary individual, or a mother and child, in the foreground of the composition. Instead, the man reading in a far corner, barely visible, is absorbed and engulfed almost by the dark shadows, looming refractions and cavernous dimensions of his room. Light floods in through a high window, yet there is little diffusion; only the projection of the window glass and its frames on one wall. Most of the room remains completely dark.

Inevitably, many academic studies of art privilege sight and text. When Garrett Stewart looks at this painting, for his book *The Look of Reading*, he sees space as a metaphor for text, the window acting as a '. . . refracting lens for a vast figurative projection, at an appropriately oblique angle, of the tome's glowing diptych: a case of Bachelard's 'intimate immensity' writ large in the roominess, indeed potential loftiness, of reading's inferred textual space.' All this feels right, but additionally I hear the resonant silence of concentration and study, the sound of air and thought. As the light fades, the room will grow darker and darker, the painting moving towards the condition of Ad Reinhardt's so-called black paintings.

Perhaps even more than in paintings in which dynamic actions unfold, the feeling of being a voyeur and eavesdropper is particularly strong when the subject is so still the room is so quiet. As with the sleeping nymph, the beholder hovers on a threshold that delineates a barrier between exclusion and entry. Svetlana Alpers discusses this in relation to Gabriel Metsu's *The Letter Writer Surprised* and Vermeer's *Woman Reading a Letter*. The Metsu shows a man in the act of spying, peering over the shoulder of the woman who is writing a letter. Using the device of a painted curtain, drawn back to reveal the scene, Vermeer shows a woman utterly still, absorbed in the moment, her hands at the bottom of the page suggesting that she has read the letter and is contemplating its contents. 'Vermeer in effect turns the relationship between the Metsu couple ninety degrees and puts himself in the position of the man,' writers Alpers. 'Vermeer discovers that the artist is a voyeur with a woman as his object in view.'

In his study of Vermeer, Lawrence Gowing proposed a similar idea: 'It was in his camera cabinet perhaps, behind the thick curtains, that he entered the world of ideal, undemanding relationships. There he could spend the hours watching the silent women move to and from.' Speculative but powerful, Gowing's image is hypnotic, entrancing, yet also slightly creepy. Of course, it is reminiscent of T. S. Eliot:

> In the room the women come and go
> Talking of Michelangelo.

WRITING TO VERMEER

I read somewhere that a judge at the Hague tribunal seeks brief respite from the evils wreaked by war criminals by visiting the Mauritshuis. He goes to this most sublime museum to spend some moments with Vermeer's *Girl with a Pearl Earring*, I assume for silence, solace and tranquillity, and for lasting physical evidence of a human propensity for simple beauty in the face of horror and all its specious justifications. This is one of the themes of an opera named *Writing To Vermeer*, composed by Louis Andriessen with a libretto by Peter Greenaway. Women write letters to Vermeer in his absence, while outside the house, during the Dutch Year of Disasters in 1672, there are street fights, Spanish brigands, the Orange mob. Drawn to the transparency, the colour, the music, the women, of Vermeer, Andriessen had this to say about his 'concrete' reasons for agreeing to Greenaway's proposal: 'I feel very close to the attitude of the painter who fixes on his canvas brief 'stolen' moments that are eternally beautiful.'

A crude reading might find in this a retreat from politics into the sublime, but Vermeer is not so simple (nor, come to that, are Andriessen or Greenaway). Moments are indeed stolen. We are back with John Berger in *Ways of Seeing*, the silence and stillness that permeates the material trail of brush strokes, and that connection made between the concentrated physical moment of the painting and the moment of the beholder, absorbed in the painter's gestures, the painter's silence. 'Only the silent, brooding interaction of presences is allowed to burden the stillness of the air,' wrote Lawrence Gowing.

As Timothy Brook demonstrates in *Vermeer's Hat*, reflections of the outer world of conflict and commerce, emanations of disquiet and fragility, constrained eroticism, shadow places of the uncanny, are deeply embedded within Vermeer's paintings, only accessible to subtle divination: in *Young Woman Reading a Letter*, the Turkish carpet laid over the table that separates us from her, and on that carpet a Chinese dish from Jingdezhen. More impressively, these intimations crackle and stir at the threshold of a silence so deep as to be a well of still volumes. 'Often it is not matter that occupies the eye,' Gowing wrote, 'so much as the reciprocal play of nearness and distance. Overlapping contours, each accessory to the next, confine the space, an envelope of quiet air.'

ABRUPTLY, AS A SUDDEN SOUND

Paintings are static; this distinguishes them from the experience of hearing. 'One might be tempted to say that paintings preserve a moment,' wrote John Berger in *And Our Faces, My Heart, Brief as Photos*. 'Yet on reflection this is obviously untrue. For the moment of a painting, unlike a moment photographed, never existed as such. And so a painting cannot be said to preserve it.' The contradiction of the still life has been examined thoroughly by art historians, but in this context it demands to be revisited. If silence (which is a form of sound) can legitimately be described as an element of painting, then time is out of joint.

In the Hague, at the Mauritshuis, I saw a small exhibition of tiny, exquisite still life paintings by Adriaen Coorte. Overlooked until 1958, Coorte was active between c. 1683 to 1707. Very little is known about his life — perhaps he lived near Middleburg, in the province of Zeeland. The appeal of his painting is not easy to describe — an acquired taste, perhaps, and yet immediate. From 1684, he devoted himself to still lives, diminutive works of consummate skill, usually delicate fruit or vegetables arranged on a stone table against a background of profound darkness. Glowing asparagus, redcurrants, strawberries in a Chinese Wan-li bowl, translucent gooseberries, intricately marked shells, hazelnuts still enfolded in their green, squid like outer cases. In some of the paintings, a butterfly hovers in the air above food that is inert yet we know that it moves towards decomposition, and in this tension between the vastly differing speeds of life and death, a silence gathers. There is a secret music in these 'still lives' that I would like to hear, not a formal music of regulated construction, but an organic music which can register the infinitely slow decay of strawberries, the inconceivably condensed life cycle of a butterfly, the audible atmosphere of a Chinese interior overlaid by its palimpsest of a Dutch interior, and the quiet hum of darkness.

NOISE AND SHIT

Why was it that these northern painters were so fascinated with the effects of sounding and hearing, quiet air and silent women? Many Flemish and Dutch artists painted allegories of the Five Senses; there are examples by Jan Brueghel the Elder, Rembrandt, Adriaen van Ostade, Jan Steen, Dirck

Hals, Jan Miense Molenaer, and David Teniers the Younger. Jan Brueghel the Elder's allegories of hearing are analysed by Richard Leppert in *The Sight of Sound*; he finds Brueghel's choice of objects used to represent hearing, ranging from instruments of art music to hunting horns, birdcalls, clocks, guns and infantry guns (and not a peasant bagpipe in sight), revealing in its bias towards wealth and power: 'In the end, Brueghel's allegory of hearing fails to map this human sense as something universal, hence natural, or simply biological. Instead, hearing is rendered culturally, and radically historical, whatever the painter's intentions. For only certain sounds are available to be heard, and they are the sounds of a world organized and valorized for the benefit and honour of the few.'

Inevitably the challenge of finding a static image that could illustrate senses such as sound, smell and taste, without resorting to the obvious — musical instruments or flowers — threw up a challenge to these ingenious artists. Consequently, the odoriferous and cacophonous are never far away. Noise, babies (both bawling and arse-wiped) and dog shit were typical responses to the problem: Adriaen Brouwer's *Tavern Scene* shows seven dishevelled and riotous men at a late stage of a serious drinking session, one in the foreground laid out cold and probably snoring, the three at the back bellowing out a song, and Jan Miense Molenaer's *Two Boys and a Girl Making Music* groups together a trio — violin, rommelpot (a friction drum) and spoons on a soldier's helmet — so sonically intriguing that the absence of an audio version is deeply frustrating.

Equally enticing as a visual notation of rough music is the deep brown cavern of horrors painted by the seventeenth-century Flemish artist David Teniers the Younger. One of his versions of *The Temptation of Saint Anthony*, in the Musées Royaux des Beaux-Arts de Belgique in Brussels, draws up from hell a menagerie of bawling winged monsters, a skull man playing the oboe, another skull man and a dwarf harmonizing together, a huge toad howling up to the ceiling. Saint Anthony tries to read his bible in the centre of this bedlam, distracted by the noise, by the horned woman who shouts in his ear, the toad pulling at his cloak, the woman who approaches him with a glass of wine, the monstrous creatures flying overhead. Though this gloomy painting is not as inventively profuse as Hieronymus Bosch's triptych of the same theme, nor as authentically nightmarish as Matthias Grunewald's version, nor as intense with the humming, screeching and wing clatter of diabolical flying monsters that lift Saint Anthony into the air in Cranach's woodcut of 1506, Teniers is hearing a dark underworld sound of his own.

In *Hubbub: Filth, Noise and Stench in England*, Emily Cockayne notes a change of mood in the seventeenth century, a growing intolerance of the noise that came with expanding populations, burgeoning commerce and the infrastructural developments that struggled to keep pace with all this activity. 'The types of noise that attracted most complaint among the literate and vociferous citizens were those sounds made by the poorest citizens,' she writes, 'especially the sounds made by popular entertainers and low-profit traders.' She gives the example of a caricature by Marcellus Laroon, a drawing from 1770 entitled *The Execrable Concert*. As above, what glorious racket might we hear from this quintet? The ragged fiddler, the man who saws away at a one-string viol, the percussionists — one banging on a box, the other crashing fireirons together — and the 'keyboard' player whose instrument is a wooden frame in which three cats are imprisoned. The cats are arranged according to the pitch of their squawk when he pulls their tails, and so from the pain of the animal world comes the most extreme of unregulated discord.

I imagine these paintings not only as notation, but as records (in all senses of that word), ethnomusicological recordings that will play back, if only the phantom frequency can be tuned, if only Virginia Woolf's 'plug' to switch on the past can be invented. 'Feel at once on terms with the picture,' Samuel Beckett wrote in his notebook, after seeing Emil Nolde's *Christus und die Kinder* in Hamburg, 'and that I want to spend a long time before it, and play it over and over again like the record of a quartet.'

SOUNDING SPACES

In *The Eyes of the Skin*, Finnish architect Juhani Pallasmaa fashions a telling critique of ocularcentrism in contemporary architecture. Unless architecture acknowledges the interpenetration and distinct qualities of all the senses, he argues, it celebrates impressive visual spectacles that increasingly detach themselves from the body and time. City streets and the interiors of buildings lose their echo. 'Our ears,' he claims, 'have been blinded.' On the importance of sound in domestic interiors, he writes this:

'One can also recall the acoustic harshness of an uninhabited and unfurnished house as compared to the affability of a lived home, in which sound is refracted and softened by the numerous surfaces of objects of personal life. Every building or space has its characteristic sound of intimacy or monumentality, invitation or rejection, hospitality or hostility. A space is understood and appreciated through its echo as much as through its visual shape, but the acoustic percept usually remains as an unconscious background experience.'

Emanuel de Witte's *Interior with a Woman Playing the Virginals*, painted some time after 1660, is an intriguing work for a number of reasons, not least the emphasis on abstract shapes which makes us think ahead some two and a half centuries to the geometric abstractions of Piet Mondrian. Here is a woman playing the virginal, sitting off-centre in the frame and with her back to the viewer, the top of her head reflected in a large mirror which looms like a cavernous hole into nowhere. The virginal is placed very close, unnecessarily close perhaps, to an open doorway, and the view through that doorway opens onto other open doorways, a succession of high-ceilinged, hard-floored rooms.

Close inspection reveals that the woman is playing for a man who lies in the curtained bed to her left, or perhaps she is playing despite him, unconcerned that he is sleeping. All sorts of ideas are at work in this painting: not least eroticism; conflicts of morality; chaos and order; social identity; phenomena of light and colour; experiments in the representation of spatial depth through perspective, and a powerful metaphor of the domestic interior as a body that may be biological, psychological, social, gendered, sexualised, political. But what fascinates me also is the unknown unspeakable — the way of hearing through which we can listen and hear a rather complex auditory environment transmitted over a lengthy historical delay, even though in actuality we hear nothing at all. As a person who has developed the faculty of listening, perhaps to the detriment of other sense acuity, I can hear this quiet keyboard music reverberating in silent chambers, reflecting from glass and stone, losing the sparkle of its upper frequencies in the plush darkness of the bed, then hear it again, more faintly now, through the ears of the maid, the model of dutiful virtue, sweeping two rooms away at the centre of the image. Like the mirror that reflects the face of the woman who plays the virginal, the recessing rooms imply their own double, a reversal that projects outward into the world of the beholder. The maid's ear, one might say, is one ear of the painting; my ear, as I absorb the painting, is the other.

There are many interconnecting and conflicting interpretations of Dutch painting from the seventeenth century. Given an explosion of demand, these artists were so prolific, and so inventive and experimental in their approach to entirely new ways of seeing, being and representation, that they left a rich legacy for continuing study and exegesis. Through their virtuosity in exploring and articulating illusions of architectural space, particularly the intricacies of interior space, they deployed sound, silence and hearing alongside other expressive devices. Martha Hollander describes Nicolaes Maes's conception of the Dutch interior as a cluster of spaces recreated for visual gratification. 'Maes displays the house like a dollhouse,' she writes, 'a showpiece designed to present his artistic ingenuity and the furnishings of the house at the same time. Exploiting the multilevel, compartmental quality of the Dutch house for its social implications, he relates the physical structure of the household to the social relationships of its dwellers. Just as cabinets and dollhouses vouchsafe a privileged look at their secret miniature contents, Maes's "eavesdropper" series reveal the anatomy of the household. The resulting tension between secrecy and disclosure, between hermetic doorway and invading eyes, also reflects the contingent relation between public and private spaces.'

But implicit within visual gratification was an acknowledgement of all the senses and their interpenetration. This included those that are not easily conveyed by visual media, such as hearing, smell, taste, and even proprioception, the body's internal sense of itself, a mix of conscious and unconscious awareness that locates the body, inside and outside, and registers the state of all those elements. In *The Object Stares Back*, James Elkins has described proprioception as: '. . . the inaudible muttering of a body in good health as well as the high pain of illness.' From all points on the spectrum, from the inaudible muttering of Vermeer to the acute listening of Maes and the rowdy noise of Adriaen Brouwer or Jan Steen, a full engagement with the sensorium is celebrated. The materiality of sound also flows through these supposedly secure and enclosing interiors, an elusive event entering and leaving through open windows, inside to outside, passing from public to private and private to public, from open space into hidden and secluded spaces, through economic, class and gender boundaries, through solid walls, around corners. What seems safely bounded inside is dislocated by the act of hearing.

Mariët Westermann's *Art and Home: Dutch Interiors in the Age of Rembrandt*, argues the similarities and differences between Dutch seventeenth-century interiors as represented in paintings and contemporary interiors represented in catalogue photographs. The soothing perfection and tranquillity of these interiors is disrupted by those elements in life that we find difficult to control: sex, animals, sound, sleep. There is a fixation with the moral universe in which wayward forces are constrained as a defence against their seductiveness, their irrepressible powers. Conceived and executed at an extraordinary level of intensity and virtuosity, these depictions of home exist to be subverted and disrupted. To paraphrase Delacroix: 'Sound is tactless, it interrupts one's peace, demands attention and provokes discussion.'

8 A conversation piece

On the flat page, a drawing, within an irregular, rectangular frame of cross-hatched diagonal pen lines, of an ear. The ear lacks a head. Lines slash across the ear, not violently, but like static, or sleet. The outer edge of the ear looks perforated, and the ear canal is dark, abnormally large, a well, a cave. The title of the drawing is *Untitled*.

Now we are in physical space, a volume of open air, a room, a vessel in which other people move and step, murmur and clatter, pushed and pulled from here to there by their wretched whispering audio guides, as if the problems of seeing can be solved by words insinuated directly into the ear. A small, sightless man leans his right ear against a wall, listening. *Listening Figure* has no legs; his eyes are webbed, mole-like decayed fossil genes. His lower half is a giant ball, a toy that always returns to an upright position no matter how many times a child pushes it over. His arms and hands are stretched back flat against his sides. He is built for eavesdropping, built to listen in to the dull murmurs of conversations belonging to others, to whispers and secrets.

This is the work of Spanish sculptor Juan Muñoz, who died in 2001. These figures in spaces might be mistaken for what we call the real world, with their verisimilitude, the way they share space with their audience, yet they are presences more than figures, and these presences are an occupation of potential spaces, volumes and durations of silences, and the implicit sounds that resonate within and beyond these spaces. Take the *Conversation Piece* of 1996. One figure, the isolated one to the left of the group of five figures, is inclining its head, straining, intent on the conversation itself, though that looks as much a business of touch, presence and listening as voice. Really, it seems an examination rather than a conversation, like a blind person feeling out thoughts from a map of facial structure and musculature. The two other figures are connected by wires. Either one is pulling the other forward, or the one in the rear is holding the leader back. Actually, who is in the front? Listener or speaker, sound or silence; who leads, who follows? As I intrude into their space, I think of Mukai Kyorai's seventeenth-century haiku:

> Which is tail? Which head?
> Unsafe to guess
> Given a sea-slug.

Like Nicolaes Maes's *Naughty Drummer* (which, incidentally, hangs in the Museo Thyssen-Bornemisza in Madrid, the city where Muñoz was born), he silences drums, cutting out noise, breaking the skin. *Wax Drum* is spiked with scissors; the weapon has been left in the wound, a stoppage for sound. As if another evolutionary selection through which humans have been reduced to a single sense, seeing has superseded hearing. We are all deaf. In conversation (with James Lingwood) Muñoz once said: 'The conviction has to originate in the gaze, because now we don't believe in anything but our eyes — and very soon we're going to disbelieve them too.'

Wax makes us think of light in darkness, the illumination of candles, but also deafness in the midst of sound, when an ear becomes blocked from a build-up of wax. Many years ago, suffering from temporary deafness after swimming, I went to the cinema. Through most of the film I could hear only muffled sound but occasionally the blockage would clear for a few seconds. The impact of these unpredictable bursts of noise, particularly from the higher frequencies, was overwhelming. In Homer's *Odyssey*, Ulysses used kneaded, sun-softened wax to block the ears of his crew, as a protection against the song of the Sirens, then had himself tied to the mast so that he could hear the song without succumbing. The effect of their bewitching music is described by Circe as a threat to the integrity of the home: 'There is no homecoming for the man who draws near them unawares and hears the Sirens' voices; no welcome from his wife, no little children brightening at their father's return.' In his short story, 'The Silence of the Sirens', Franz Kafka derides this childish defence. The Sirens could use two methods of seduction: first there was song, then silence. For Kafka, silence was a deadlier weapon by far. 'And when Ulysses approached them,' he wrote, 'the potent songstresses actually did not sing, whether because they thought that this enemy could be vanquished only by their silence, or because the look of bliss on the face of Ulysses, who was thinking of nothing but his wax and chains, made them forget their singing.' Kafka, incidentally, was a dedicated user of Ohropax (or 'ear peace') earplugs, the invention in 1908 of Maximilian Negwer, a German pharmacist who was initially inspired by the same episode in the Odyssey. Ohropax was designed to give the wearer 'ear peace' in response to the industrial century's growing noise problem. As an unconscious riposte to the Italian Futurists, who glorified the noises of war and industry, one of its first applications was to protect the hearing of German troops and medical staff during the First World War. 'Without Ohropax day and night,' Kafka wrote to his distant fiancée, Felice, sounding like an advertising copywriter, 'I really couldn't cope.'

As symbols and sound, drums are dense, foetid, reeking of tyranny, fear, entrancement and the mastery of time. In every drum there is politics, particularly for an artist who grew up under Franco's dictatorship. Drums speak a secret language, both in repression and rebellion. In *Percussion Instruments and Their History*, James Blades quotes from English military tactics drawn up at the time of Mary Tudor:

All captains must have drums and fifes and men to use the same, who shall be faithful, secret and ingenious, of able personage to use their instruments and office of sundry languages; for often-times they are sent to parlay with their enemies, to summon their forts or towns, to redeem and conduct prisoners, and divers other messages, which of necessity requireth language. If such drums and fifes should fortune to fall into the hands of the enemies, no gift or force should cause them to disclose any secrets that they know.

A drum is both noise and silence then, but also ear, cavity, chamber, cave. Again, James Blades, though this time speaking scientific language mixed with some romantic speculations cloaked in faux ethnography of a vanished era: 'The uncanny power of the drum is almost certainly an extension of that mystery — the phenomenon of sympathetic resonance. To the untutored savage, the roaring sound experienced when he placed his ear to the slit of the drum (as one places the ear to a suitably shaped sea shell) was a message from the supernatural; the voice of the gods.'

The snares, thin strings or wires stretched across the bottom head of a side drum, will rattle when another sound — a singing voice, a wind instrument — converges with its sympathetic resonant frequency to produce a phenomenon known as forced resonance. At the point of the sound, at the drum, this needs no human agency (drummers who forget to turn off their snares will often be cursed by other bands as certain pitches in their music set off metallic buzzing). Like the sound of wind in trees, a seal, a bee, or water, the snare drum's rattlesnake drone exudes out of nowhere: a ghost (and let's not forget that a version of the military side drum with its snares, became part of what was once called the trap set, that collection of bass drum, snare, cymbals and percussion now known as the drum kit).

The first line and repeated refrain of one of the first songs I learned as a child at primary school in the 1950s lingers in my memory: 'Oh, soldier, soldier, won't you marry me, with your musket, fife and drum?' The death rattle of the snare drum expels humour from the absurdity of ceremonial marching and the parade ground (those Monty Python silly walks). Of all faces in Rembrandt's *The Night Watch*, the most serious and composed (the composer of action) is that of the drummer, playing at the right-hand edge of the painting: a dog cowers beneath him and barks, startled by the sound; shots have been fired, all of these sounds a shock to the night. Ensnared within the sound of a drum are gunshots, cannon fire, marching feet, clocks striking, a knock on the door at dawn (listen to the military drum and piccolo that punctuate Scott Walker's 'Patriot (a Single)' from *Tilt*, or on *Drift*, the chilling BAM BAM BAM BAM of 'Cue' beaten out on a huge box constructed in the studio). Drums measure out strict time through rituals, rallies and battles, parades and marches, imposed order, regulation and oppression; in resistance to this Martian urge, they possess as much potential to release bodies into pleasure through subtle, propulsive games of time. In the darkness of a theatre, in Ingmar Bergman's *Silence*, a troupe of Spanish dwarfs, costumed out of Velásquez, tumble to the circus tattoo of a snare drum; at the edge of the stage, a woman and a soldier fucking, heads thrown back. Drums are loudness, a sudden impact, yet the eardrum, the tympanic membrane, is a delicate amplifier of sound. This is the contradiction of all drums: both shamanic and military, their violence is their vulnerability — the perforated eardrum.

We step into another Muñoz room, join another group, living among the dead: *Seated Figures with Five Drums*, five white figures sitting on strangely asymmetrical armchairs in a conversational group, each in possession of a snare drum. Solid, soft, creamy companions, dusted in flour or volcanic ash (the instant death of Pompeii's citizens after Vesuvius erupted; its residue), the composition's spectral atmosphere is suggestive of Pieter Brueghel the Elder's mid-sixteenth-century grisaille paintings, *Christ and the Woman Taken in Adultery*, and in the Frick Collection, New York, *The Three Soldiers*. In the latter, a tiny, exquisite work, three soldiers stand in uneasy relationship to each other. Half-hidden in the background and shadowed, the colour of verdigris, a flag bearer looks up at the banner he is waving. The foreground musicians, a lighter sepia, play fife and drum, the flute player looks forward, out of one corner of the painting, the drummer balances a huge bass drum on his hip, peering into the dark corner at the rear, his drum a yellowing block of grey wax, out of Joseph Beuys. They could be playing after the end of time, the dead celebrating war's final victory, or before the mother of all battles, sounding their own death song, one foot in the grave.

As if experimenting with a mysterious object experienced for the first time, each of Muñoz's seated figures engages with their drum in a different way, studying it closely, for example, or using it as a footstool. One of them seems to speak into his drum. The drum becomes a resonator, an amplifier, a mirliton (again the buzzing), a voice disguiser. In her essay on Muñoz, 'A Mirror of Consciousness', Sheena Wagstaff draws a connection between *Listening Figure* and another representation of a voice projector and disguiser:

> Its relationship to the group has been likened to Seurat's painting *Bathers at Asnières* by writers quoting Muñoz's stated admiration for the way in which each figure in the painting is placed within its own space of silence. The exception is the boy in the river, hands cupped in mid-shout — the drawing for which Seurat titled *The Echo*. The dramatic potential for sound, not just to infuse the scene evocatively but through its subsequent return as an echo, gives the painting a unique sense of a-temporality in relation to its space.

Georges Seurat's *Bathers at Asnières*, exhibited in the National Gallery collection in London, was painted in 1884. The scene is drowsy, though not idyllic: as a backdrop to the river and its boats, factories pour smoke into the summer sky. Five young men, perhaps factory workers, are grouped separately, yet together. Three of them relax on the river bank, one lying, two sitting. Two stand in the river, one looking away from the group, the one wearing a hat looking beyond the edges of the painting and calling through hands cupped into a trumpet. The two figures on dry land seem to look in the direction of his shout. Except for the reaction of a small dog, nestling into the back of the man who is lying down, the feeling is not urgent; perhaps the boy in the hat has seen a friend on the other side of the river. The directionality of the painting moves in an arrow from left to right, its point culminating in the shout, a moment of sound, from which we can imagine the sound waves fanning out, opening into a mirror triangle that moves beyond the frame, into the unknown, then returns as an echo to the apperceptive dog. Strangely, the atmosphere is heavy with silence, as if the shout transcends human hearing, only disturbing the more aurally sensitive animals.

Though anticipated by the hazy, Japonistic *Nocturne* series of paintings begun by James McNeill Whistler in 1866, which in turn were closely associated with the 'impressionism' of Debussy's compositional innovations, it was scientific influences that enabled Seurat to develop a pictorial method to net those regions of the sensory spectrum that, despite their materiality, elude solidity of form: light, sound, atmosphere, fleeting sensation. The shimmering points of light and colour of his pointillist technique, visible in a formative stage in *Bathers at Asnières*, dissolved the certainties of visible reality, moving the act of seeing closer to a more immersive world of vibrations and waves. His 1890 *Beach at Gravelines*, in the Courtauld Gallery, is empty light almost without boundaries, a complex, enharmonic flood of high-frequency silence. Seurat was famous among his contemporaries for taciturnity. 'In looking at Seurat's drawings, such muteness and reserve is far more than an idiosyncrasy of personality,' wrote Jodi Hauptman in her introduction to the 2007 MoMA catalogue, *Georges Seurat: The Drawings*. 'Seurat's silence is, in fact, an aesthetic . . . Not simply quiet, these drawings are aggressively silent. To make use of an anachronism, it is as if a mute button has been pushed on, evacuating all sound. No matter how hard we look, no matter how evocative of person or place, we cannot hear the turning of a cart's wheel's, rain on the trees or sidewalk, the snap of an umbrella, the call of a merchant, the swish of a broom, the turning of a novel's pages.'

Like Muñoz, Seurat was drawn to aspects of theatricality, yet his tableaux are eerily soundless. *La Parade de Cirque*, for example, captures the ritualistic aura of circus; time is suspended. A trombonist stands in the centre of the picture. On close inspection he seems to be playing, but Seurat gives the impression that all sound, all movement, has been absorbed into a gauzy fug. Similarly, his sublime conté crayon study for *Bathers at Asnières*,

The Echo, is unequivocal in showing a moment of sharp sound, a close-up of the boy who shouts, yet the drawing itself is the softest diffused silence, like cellophane screwed up into a tight ball, then released to faintly crackle a return to its original form. The silence is not an omission, a gap in sensory awareness, but a deliberate, provocative absence.

The spaces of Muñoz expand into a similarly febrifugal air of anticipation, then like a bellows, magnetically pull inwards, toward the cool presence of the work. As with the work of Maes, theatre is an unreliable analogy. For Muñoz, his pieces were not theatre, but the stage sets of theatre. 'I would like the spectator to walk into the artwork very much as an actor within his own tableau,' he told Adrian Searle, in their BBC radio broadcast, *Third Ear*. Does that mean, Searle asked, the spectator could join in with the drama? 'No, no,' Muñoz replied, 'he's just a spectator in silence. The drama happens away from him.'

And yet, there are precedents in theatre. An illuminating passage from James Knowlson's biography of Samuel Beckett suggested to me the profound influence of Beckett on these works by Muñoz, particularly his mechanical mouths and the isolation of figures that are connected in some indefinable relationship. During a holiday in Malta in 1971, Beckett visited the Oratory of St John's Cathedral in Valletta to view Caravaggio's painting, *The Beheading of St. John the Baptist*. Early the following year, Beckett and his wife Suzanne took another holiday, this time in Morocco, where they travelled to El Jadida. Beckett watched a solitary woman, waiting for her child to finish school. Covered by a djellaba, she leaned against a wall in what seemed to Beckett to be a position of intense listening. According to Knowlson, drawing on Enoch Brater's analysis and Beckett's own testimony, these two images merged to form the inspiration for one of his most radical plays. *Not I*, begun in March 1972, began from a simple scenario: 'Mouth and Auditor'. The mouth, lit to reveal nothing else of the female actor, speaks a rapid monologue, while a silent listener, 'sex undeterminable, enveloped from head to foot in loose black djellaba, with hood' stands dead still throughout, except for four brief movements, 'simple sideways raising of arms from sides and their falling back, in a gesture of helpless compassion.'

Knowslon observed:

The source of this link between the Auditor and his Moroccan experience was Beckett himself. What probably happened is that the djellaba-clad figure coalesced with his sharp memories of the Caravaggio painting. For perhaps even more striking than the partially disembodied head of John the Baptist in the Caravaggio are the watching figures. Most powerful of all is an old woman standing to Salome's left. She observes the decapitation with horror, covering her ears rather than her eyes. This old woman emerges as the figure in Caravaggio's masterpiece whose role comes closest to the Auditor in Beckett's play, reacting compassionately to what he/she hears.

This is not entirely consonant with Catherine Puglisi's interpretation in her study of Caravaggio. 'The old lady alone reacts emotionally,' Puglisi writes, 'her whole body appears to shudder as she hunches her shoulders and presses her raised hands to her cheeks.' By looking closely at the painting, it is evident that both interpretations are possible. As in the case of the raised finger in Maes's *Eavesdropper* series, what the observer finds will be determined to some degree by personal sensory priorities and preoccupations. But what is indisputable, clearly felt by Beckett and articulated by Puglisi, is the poignant physicality of this emotional reaction, a sheltering or blocking out. 'Her horror in this instance disrupts the eerie stillness of the scene in which violence is matter-of-fact,' Puglisi writes, 'and no one but she protests when a man is butchered in cold blood.'

ROOM TONE

A series of large monochrome drawings by Muñoz, each titled *Raincoat Drawing*, depicts empty rooms, all of them leading to concealed spaces and corners, open closets, open doors, stairs leading down, or up, into darkness. One of them shows a short stairway of four steps ending in a wooden floor. To the right of the steps is black nothingness. I am waiting for Maes's eavesdropper to descend this stair. Others in the series are reminiscent of the empty rooms painted by Samuel van Hoogstraten in the seventeenth century, particularly the beautiful, enigmatic *View of an Interior (The Slippers)* of 1658, or his *Peepshow with Views of the Interior of a Dutch House*, a three-dimensional anamorphically painted miniature theatre in which a cryptic narrative — a woman in a bed, a seated maid, a shadow behind a window and a dog — is played out in silence. There is also the feeling of David Lynch's sound design for his 2007 film, *Inland Empire*, or the pioneering sonic sculpting of Alan R. Splet on earlier Lynch films, particularly *Eraserhead*. Lynch loves the sound of rooms, just as he loves rooms themselves and their emotional power.

Asked by interviewer Chris Rodley about the soundtrack to *Eraserhead*, its 'thickness', its 'continuous, almost subliminal "presence",' David Lynch responded enthusiastically: 'I'm real fascinated by presences — what you call "room tone". It's the sound that you hear when there's silence, in between words and sentences. It's a tricky thing, because in this seemingly kind of quiet sound, some feelings can be brought in, and a certain kind of picture of a bigger world can be made. And all those things are important to make that world.'

A very low frequency tone is recurrent in Lynch films as an indicator that the room is more horrible than we think, or even more horrible than we have already assumed. This tone comes and goes at will. Then there is a high frequency frizzing noise, electricity on the blink or perhaps the neural activity of the players. Subliminally, we can hear other sustained composites of sound, which act as a barely noted threnody. Rushing wind is another device to suggest the malevolent nature of empty interiors and implicit presences, but rushing wind is not quite it, since the sound could be amplified air conditioning. So many rooms in his films, all of them more ghastly than the last, and all of them sounding like the resonating chambers of multiple nightmares.

Seated on a narrow plywood box directly in front of two of Muñoz's *Raincoat Drawings* is a tiny man. The plinth on which he sits emits a random series of low frequency buzzing tones like a muffled organ. His mouth moves (the title of the piece tells us he is a ventriloquist), so I presume that the sound is a by-product of the mechanism that drives the movement. The images into which he gazes are almost mirror images of each other — a room, an armchair only partially seen, an open door into a clothes closet, light from the closet creeping into the darkness of the room — the whole scenario a vertiginous *mise en abîme* that could cause dizziness if considered too seriously. We are told that he is a ventriloquist, but he seems more dummy than operator. So there is the intriguing prospect of a tiny ventriloquist operating an even tinier dummy (Steven Connor has used the phrase, 'the motif of the boxed-up child', which is festeringly suggestive of all the dark places, material and psychic, that may be accessed through ventriloquism). Alone, sitting on a wall, gazing into flat drawings of seemingly empty rooms, he is either sinister or unbearably poignant, but which?

Has he been abandoned, is he waiting, or has he done away with his other half? His mouth opens but nothing comes out, which is doubly the reverse of what should happen: the closed mouth ensuing in the thrown voice. Confusions of identity are the stock in trade of ventriloquism; in this case, the roles have merged, though speech has been lost in the process. Only the grinding mechanism is left sounding, and this may be simply the noise of empty rooms. Held on the edge of a conundrum in which all the elements are familiar yet wrong, the 'spectator', as Muñoz called her or him, can only negotiate (with) the uncanny.

Absences are so ubiquitous as to cast suspicion on these figures: the *Dos Bailarinas (Cocina)* of 1989, two female torsos mounted on half spheres, one holding bells, the other holding scissors. Signs of music exist to reinforce the absence of music. *Shadow and Mouth* reveals the movement of the figure's mouth through its ventriloquial shadow — threatened by his own looming shadow, the figure with moving mouth sits close to the wall, as if whispering to *The Listener* on the other side. I am reminded of the title of Orlando Figes's book — *The Whisperers: Private Life in Stalin's Russia*. This speaking into a wall, and the uncontrollable outgrowth of the shadow double (the way that sound — the sound of the body and its technological selves — extends and grows outwards, moves through spaces, exists outside the body as a doubled self, ultimately has the potential to betray us) infers a crisis of privacy.

Another figure sits at a table, separate, sitting back to the wall at right angles to the shadowed figure, distanced but close enough to impose a presence, to eavesdrop on the soundlessness. He faces the same way as the shadow, could almost be the shadow of the other. In *A Short History of the Shadow*, Victor I. Stoichita discusses, among other images, the grotesque, enlarged shadows cast on walls in films such as Friedrich Murnau's *Nosferatu*, and Robert Wiene and Willy Hameister's *The Cabinet of Dr Caligari*, and the paintings of Giorgio de Chirico. Stoichita contextualizes their impact within Freud's writings on the uncanny, and in particular his observations on the impressions made by 'waxwork figures, ingeniously constructed dolls and automata' and the uncanniness ('a thing of terror', Freud wrote) of the double that acquires a life of its own. 'It is undeniable,' says Stoichita, 'that the most complex and mysterious narrative characteristics to be conferred on the shadow are to be found in the metaphysical paintings of Giorgio de Chirico.' He quotes De Chirico's notes on the enigma of the neo-classical buildings that inspired him: 'The Roman arcade is a fatality. Its voice speaks in enigmas filled with a strangely Roman poetry; shadows on old blue walls and a curious music, profoundly blue . . .'

The anticipatory air of silent stage set, of prelude, so powerful in De Chirico, generates the curious music (thinner than blue, one suspects) of many Muñoz works. *The Prompter* is a room in which a stage has been constructed. At the front of the stage, his head and shoulders concealed from behind within a small box but his back view visible to us, is a male dwarf. He looks straight ahead, impassive as a man resigned to his entrapment, his mouth closed. The surface of the stage is patterned with a characteristically bold Muñoz design of squares within squares, divided into light and dark. At the very back of the stage lies a side drum, the pattern on its skin a variant of the stage pattern. Either the drumhead is a miniature stage, or the stage is an expanded drumhead. Drumheads depend on tension for their full resonance; tension between the drum and the prompter (who has no actors to prompt, as yet, so no vocal function) vibrates in their mutual silence.

'Silence, you know, is something that can't be censored. And there are circumstances in which silence becomes subversive. That's why they fill it with noise all the time.' This was John Berger, writing for *Will It Be a Likeness?*, developed with Juan Muñoz in 1996 as an art/radio/theatre project. In the same piece, he wrote: 'Try turning the volume of the silence up — higher — higher. Higher still . . . [Total silence] Is this the silence of a likeness, of the mountains at night in south-east Mexico, or of us listening together?' And then in the first paragraph of the piece, ruminating on the barking of dogs, Goya's dog, language and history: 'And we decided it was better to look at paintings on the radio than on the television. On the TV screen nothing is ever still, and this movement stops painting being painting. Whereas on the radio we see nothing, but we can listen to silence. And every painting has its own silence.'

LISTENING AT DOORS

In the Courtauld Gallery in London, *A Conversation*, painted between 1913 and 1916 by Vanessa Bell, sister of Virginia Woolf. Three women huddle together by open curtains, one leaning forward, gesturing, her two companions leaning together, as if the convergence of their ears will shape this whispered gossip into something more substantial, more secret, more dangerous. The picture is almost a mirror image of Quirijn Brekelenkam's

Confidential Conversation of 1661, justifiably praised by Simon Schama for 'the candor and scrupulousness with which feminine gesture has been recorded in three variations: placid attentiveness (in profile), the maid's less polite hand on hip, and the emphasizing gesture of the matron — all three bound together by a triangle of gossip.'

The difference between the two works exposes just how much these configurations matter: Brekelenkam's three women face the viewer; listening would seem rude, and they are set at a respectful distance, whereas the closely observed back views of *A Conversation* act as a magnet, drawing the viewer in closer. To stare into Bell's painting, eavesdropping at its periphery, is to risk discovery and all the affronted humiliations that ensue from exposure as an outsider who longs to be inside. There is something deep about this discomfort that reawakens the outsider pangs of childhood and teenage years, the ache of being excluded from cliques, gangs, the most glamorous friends, the best parties (the elusive centre of the in-crowd) that grows into more deadly adult manoeuvres of power, paranoia and elitism among the cabals and inner circles of workplace, politics, arts, exclusive clubs, secret societies, even neighbourhood and friendship. At the heart of such exclusivity is the whisper, a quiet sibilance at the edge of silence through which the richness of the spoken voice is reduced to its highest frequencies.

An element of the hostile reactions provoked by music that declines to address or embrace an audience directly, particularly forms of improvisation that may seem more like inwardly focussed private conversations than outward communication, springs from these rooted fears of exclusion. Similarly, novelists who construct fictions of seemingly unmediated conversation also risk alienating those readers who come to feel more like eavesdroppers than intimates. Books constructed almost entirely from dialogue such as *Carpenter's Gothic* by William Gaddis, *A City on a Hill* by George V. Higgins, the novels of Ivy Compton-Burnett, or (a different case) the internal soliloquies of Virginia Woolf's *The Waves* demand high levels of concentration both from author and reader. They are conversation stripped of all description, but their naturalism is highly artificial. An instructive comparison can be made with Andy Warhol's *a: A Novel*, which was transcribed from rambling conversations between factory habitués such as Ondine, Edie Sedgwick, Paul Morrissey and Warhol himself, then published in 1968 as a novel. In the cases of Gaddis, Higgins and Compton-Burnett, their intensive focus on verbal exchange, thinned of the depth and colour of contextualisation, description or authorial distance, lays a tremendous weight of responsibility on the characters. Their nature and motivations, the trajectory of narrative, the dynamics of relationships and psychological undertones must all be carried by the formalities of conversation. For this reason, the method lends itself to claustrophobic atmospheres of brittle tension, suspicion, misunderstanding, spare savage wit and an acute attention to listening.

So, from *The Last and the First*, Ivy Compton-Burnett's last, unfinished novel:

'Does Mrs. Duff listen at doors?' said Angus. 'Or has she powers of her own?'

'Most of them listen,' said Eliza. 'They see no harm in it.'

And from her *Parents and Children*, published in 1941:

'The iron has entered the boy's soul,' said Daniel.

'Graham and Lester both have a squeak in their voices,' said Susan

'Lester must unconsciously try to catch a note from a different and more spacious world,' said her sister.

A

The first lines of *a: A Novel* (which I read, cover to cover, during my first year as an art student in 1968, at first naively believing the book to be a novel, then miraculously persevering even after it became apparent that I was eavesdropping on the poorly transcribed conversations of drug-addled airheads) are these:

Rattle, gurgle, clink, tinkle.
Click, pause, click, ring.
Dial, dial.

INTERSPECIES CONVERSATION

The Frick Collection, New York, *Lady with a Bird-Organ*, painted by Jean-Baptiste-Siméon Chardin, c. 1751: a woman sits on a chair, turning the handle of a bird organ with her right hand, looking toward the caged songbird at the left of the picture. Her lips are sealed, but a conversation is in progress, machine and bird in dialogue, human as intermediary. Something about Chardin, his engagement with stillness, convinces me that he was conscious, like Piero della Francesca and the chorale of angels and ass in *The Nativity*, of the curious sound of this otherworldly ensemble. His *House of Cards*, in the National Gallery in London, makes me think of Juan Muñoz, performing the card tricks of *A Man in a Room, Gambling*. And *L'Enfant au Toton* in the Louvre in Paris: the boy's face patient, placid, hands still, as he waits for his spinning top to complete its circumnavigation of the table top, erratic insistent buzzing in the stasis. Hélène Prigent and Pierre Rosenberg write of air circulating in the space around the figures in Chardin's paintings, and the familiarity in this eighteenth-century world of women with household objects and children with toys. 'These things are more than attributes,' they write, in *Chardin: An Intimate Art*, 'they are true companions, silent witnesses of a domestic world of which they also form an integral part.'

A forerunner of the phonograph, the French bird organ, or serinette, was an eighteenth-century French invention, a small hand-cranked barrel organ used by women to teach melodies to their singing birds, their serins or finches. In 2003, sculptor Martin Riches constructed his own version of the bird organ. In Aleksander Kolkowski's stage performance, *Mechanical Landscape with Bird*, the device is combined with the singing of live canaries, the songs of the canaries recorded by phonograph onto wax cylinders and played back by Kolkowski through one of his collection of magnificent phonographs, while a string quartet of horned Stroh violins plays music based on the sounds produced by the Belgian breed of Wasterslager song canary. Like the soundtrack to a steampunk novel, the music wheezes and crackles in some indeterminate space where ghosts and automata share a common history.

THE BACK OF SILENCE

Jodi Hauptman writes of absorption in Seurat, his drawings of subjects absorbed in reading or embroidery, their self-involvement in reverie, or working, or sleeping, the isolation, backs turned to the beholder, the obscuring of faces, the absence of expression, gesture or speech. 'It is hard to imagine another oeuvre filled so completely with human backs,' she writes. At the Royal Academy of Arts in London, I am immersing myself in the silences of the Danish painter, Vilhelm Hammershoi. The exhibition has been named 'The Poetry of Silence'. In fact, there are many backs in Hammershoi's oeuvre: women turned away, gazing out of the window, playing the piano, standing beside a piano, engaged in an activity, possibly the preparation of food, that is concealed, reading before the light of a window, yet seen from the side and behind, so that her face is obscured. Nobody speaks in these paintings. At a level below conscious sound, these spaces hum and whistle quietly in the spectrum of white and greys used by the painter. Like all silences, it is felt as a powerful presence. Hammershoi was said to be a silent man. The poet and art critic Rainer Maria Rilke felt conversation was difficult because of these silences; his friend Emil Nolde noted that Hammershoi's reticence imposed itself on any conversation, reducing its volume. 'We all spoke quietly,' he wrote in his memoirs.

There is something of Maes in these interiors, the doors that open into mysterious spaces, the indistinct view of life beyond the world of domesticity, a brooding aura of silence that speaks for the painter himself. Given the solemn reverence that certain kinds of silence induce, a subtle, dry humour revealed in certain paintings shows that Hammershoi liked to manipulate the idea of what his work might signify. *Strandgade 30*, painted in 1901, shows a piano against a wall. A woman is leaning on the window sill, her knee resting on a chair, looking down into the street below. A table, laid with a white tablecloth, has been placed in front of the piano, making it difficult for anybody to squeeze between the table edge and the keyboard. Moreover, the piano has only two legs, and the woman whose right leg rests on a chair has no left leg on the ground to support her. If she wishes to break the stillness and silence of this room with music then she must surmount the obstacles laid for her by the passive-aggressive wit of Hammershoi. These objects of silence, silent witnesses, whisper among themselves, their conversation piece.

Part III

Spectral

9   Chair creaks, but no one sits there

When the lights go out, hearing stays awake. *The Chimes: A Goblin Story*, was one of a series of Christmas books written by Charles Dickens in the 1840s. His tale opens with a hypothesis calculated to seduce, to lure in through its cold haunted design the reader who is settled in an opposite condition of warm secure comfort. Few people care to sleep in a church at night, alone, Dickens claims; the cause of this is not supernatural, nor even general discomfort, but the spooky noise of the night-wind as it encircles and penetrates the church. His anthropomorphic description of this night-wind is exhaustive. He gives it form and purpose, devious ingenuity and volatility of mood:

> For the night-wind has a dismal trick of wandering round and round a building of that sort, and moaning as it goes; and of trying, with its unseen hand, the windows and the doors; and seeking out some crevices by which to enter . . . Anon, it comes up stealthily, and creeps along the walls: seeming to read, in whispers, the Inscriptions sacred to the Dead. At some of these, it breaks out shrilly, as with laughter; and at others, moans and cries as if it were lamenting. It has a ghostly sound too, lingering within the altar; where it seems to chaunt, in its wild way, of Wrong and Murder done, and false Gods worshipped . . . Ugh! Heaven preserve us, sitting snugly round the fire! It has an awful voice, that wind at Midnight, singing in a church!

Charles Dickens returned to this theme of spectral noise in *The Haunted House*, written in collaboration with five other authors in 1862. In the haunted house, the dog howls when the narrator strikes an accidental discord on the piano, again when the servant's bell rings incessantly, even though no living person is there to pull the cord, and no servant in attendance to hear it. 'Noises?' he wrote. 'With that contagion downstairs, I myself have sat in the dismal parlour, listening, until I have heard so many and such strange noises that they would have chilled my blood if I had not warmed it by dashing out to make discoveries. Try this in bed, in the dead of the night; try this at your own comfortable fireside, in the life of the night. You can fill any house with noises if you will, until you have a noise for every nerve in your nervous system.'

Dickens suggests that noises, real and unreal, reveal themselves through conscious, intent acts of listening. The nervous body fills the vacuum of silence with phantom sounds generated by its own hyperacuity. If we believe that what we cannot see, we cannot know, then the possibility exists that inert and lifeless objects may have a secret life that only reveals itself when we look away or fall asleep. In Hans Anderson's story, 'The Sandman', the purpose of the Sandman is to create sufficient quiet for the imagination to be unleashed; unless they are quiet, or better still silently sleeping, children are unable to hear his stories. A little boy named Hialmar is the listener. One night when he is in bed, the Sandman touches all the pieces of furniture in his room with a magic wand: 'Thereupon they all began to chatter, and each piece talked only about itself, excepting the spittoon, who stood quite still, and was much vexed at their being so vain, all chattering about themselves, without ever thinking of him, who stood so modestly in the corner and suffered himself to be spat upon.' Images are brought to life by the Sandman's wand. As he touches pictures that hang on the walls, the birds within them begin to sing; with this enlivening of silence, the Sandman (as if inventing the animated film) lifts Hialmar into the frame of the picture so that he can cross over into the world of images.

The propensity for sound to summon or accompany uncanny sensations and atmospheres has been noted only fitfully in the extensive literature devoted to Freud's essay, *The Uncanny*; invariably its significance is set aside for more ocular concerns. In his own version of *The Uncanny*, a book-length study of this subject, Nicholas Royle takes the trouble to locate and analyse the obscure story from the *Strand Magazine*, which Freud described only in précis: a young couple move into a flat and among the existing furnishings is a table carved with crocodiles. As darkness falls the flat is filled with an obnoxious stench, the tenants trip over things and see some inexplicable creature gliding over the stairs. As Royle discovers, this story, entitled 'Inexplicable', was written by a now forgotten author, Lucy Gertrude Moberly. Royle's reading uncovers material that Freud chose not to consider. The opening paragraph, for example, revisits a familiar trope: the fateful crossing of a threshold, just prior to entering an unfamiliar house. The gate's rusty hinges creak dismally, and when the latch clicks into its socket, 'with a sharp clang', the narrator is startled into thoughts of prison doors and turnkeys. Once again, sound serves as a presentiment of events to come.

'This sense of eeriness in the ear, the "eariness" of the uncanny, recurs throughout the story', writes Royle. Incidents of 'eary' phenomena include a 'far-away bellowing . . . pregnant with evil' and the 'sliding and pattering' of crocodiles in the darkness. 'Once again, that is to say, this story provides striking examples of an auditory dimension that is crucial to a critical appreciation of "the uncanny".' Crucial it may be, but Royle's exploration of the auditory dimension takes us no further than this provocative remark.

In his *The Uncanny*, Freud described E. T. A. Hoffmann as 'the unrivalled master of the uncanny in literature.' Born in Königsburg in 1776, Hoffmann juggled a number of careers by using alcohol to obscure any incompatibilities that existed between them. He composed operas, stood as a member of the Commission for the Investigation of Treasonable Organizations and other Dangerous Activities, and in Berlin wrote the short stories and novels that made him famous. Freud's essay concentrates on 'The Sandman', a complex short story initially narrated by a young student, Nathaniel. He begins with a letter written to his foster brother, Lothario, but mistakenly addressed to his foster sister and fiancée, Clara. The letter relates a recent incident in which a seller of barometers has revived memories of a traumatic childhood experience. The narrative returns to this childhood, to memories of their father, and the evenings when their mother would hurry them to bed, telling them the sandman was coming. 'On these occasions,' wrote Hoffmann, 'I really did hear something come clumping up the stairs with slow, heavy tread, and knew it must be the sandman. Once these muffled footsteps seemed to me especially frightening, and I asked my mother as she led us out: "Mama, who is this sandman who always drives us away from Papa? What does he look like?"' The mother reassures him with a white lie, telling him that there is no sandman, only the feeling of being sleepy, as if somebody had sprinkled sand in his eyes. Others have a more sinister explanation. The old woman who looks after his sister tells him that the sandman comes for children who won't go to bed, throws sand in their eyes so that they jump out of their heads, then tosses them into a sack and carries them to the crescent moon as food for his children. The children have crooked beaks, like owls (or harpies), and peck out the eyes of these naughty children.

From this point, Nathaniel is terrorised by sounds or their absence — his father's silence on the nights when the visitor is due, the invader's feet as he clumps up the stairs, the noise of him wrenching open the door of his father's study, then entering for some unknown purpose. Years pass, the sounds continue, the intensity of Nathaniel's terror persists. Finally, he is moved to a bedroom closer to his father's study. As usual, he hears the stranger open his father's door, but with the closer proximity, he senses something new, 'a subtle, strange-smelling vapour' spreading through the house. Finally reaching a point at which these combinatory signs of an invisible intruder impel him to see their perpetrator, he hides himself in a cupboard behind a curtain in his father's room. Again the sounds reach him in the darkness of his eavesdropper's cubbyhole: 'The footsteps thudded nearer and nearer, and there was a strange coughing, rasping and growling outside. My heart quaked with fear and anticipation. Close, close behind the door — a quick footstep, a violent blow on the latch and the door sprang open with a clatter!' With the crescendo of this noise symphony, the rupture of heimlich by unheimlich, Nathaniel looks out and sees a familiar but repugnant figure: the aged advocate, Coppelius. Whatever horrors were imagined through the agency of the nursery tale, the silence of his father, the noises, or the strange odour, had been replaced by unpalatable visible reality, 'a repellent spectral monster bringing misery, distress and earthly and eternal ruination wherever he went.'

From these 'lifelike' beginnings, sympathetic to universal memories of childhood anxiety, Hoffmann's story grows stranger, more convoluted, as if preparing for all that follows. Nathaniel watches in horror as his father and Coppelius perform a ghastly alchemical experiment in which eyeless faces float in an atmosphere of smoke and confusion. Screaming when Coppelius demands eyes, 'in a dull hollow voice', he is discovered, narrowly avoids losing his own eyes, and is subjected to bizarre manipulations of his hands and feet. In the escalating tension of those intervening years in which Nathaniel has eavesdropped upon the auditory double of the unseen intruder clumping up the stairs of the family home, we can imagine the multifarious bodies and faces he has fitted to the disembodied sounds, banal in themselves but terrifying for their implicit threat. The climactic impact of this first phase of Hoffmann's story — eyeless faces in the smoke, the scream, the unscrewing of Nathaniel's hands and feet, a huge explosion that kills his father, more screams, wailing and lamentation — is a necessary trauma to justify the suspense of this auditory prolongation. After the explosion — 'a fearful detonation, like the firing of a cannon' — Nathaniel hears 'a clattering and rushing' past the door of his room, then the front door of the house slamming with a crash. By this point, Nathaniel is intimately familiar with Coppelius and his auditory signs. As sound, he enters the home, materializes, wrenches open a door, destroys both the father and the space of the father, then as sound again, closes the door to the home and exits.

The psychoanalytic conclusions of Freud's analysis of 'The Sandman', particularly his assertion that the fear of being robbed of ones eyes is a substitute for castration anxiety, have been exhaustively picked apart, notably by Hélène Cixous in 'Fiction and Its Phantoms: A Reading of Freud's *Das Unheimliche* (The "uncanny")'. All of these examinations of Freud and Hoffmann glide over the unsettling relationship between Nathaniel's initial 'blindness', in which the noises of the unseen sandman are an unreliable (and disbelieved) witness to events that later prove to be unimaginable, and the theme of enucleation that persists until Nathaniel's demise. In her sceptical reply to Nathaniel's letter, Clara tells him that almost everything in his story took place within his misdirected imagination. 'Perhaps there does exist a dark power which fastens on to us and leads us off along a dangerous and ruinous path which we would otherwise not have trodden,' she writes, 'but if so, this power must have assumed within us the form of ourself, indeed have become ourself, for otherwise we would not listen to it, otherwise there would be no space within us in which it could perform its secret work.' At the end of the story, when all seems settled, Nathaniel succumbs to the enucleating device planted by his nemesis. He roars, laughs hideously, screams and chants in a 'piercing cry', ending his own life by jumping from a high tower. The last paragraph of 'The Sandman' portrays Clara seated in a bliss of 'quiet domestic happiness', her space of repressed hearing a heimlich middle ground that Nathaniel, inhabiting a place of uncanny extremes, of forensic listening and unrestrained vocalisation, could never have supplied.

As a footnote to this complacent withdrawal from the sounding world, Metallica's 'Enter Sandman' draws out a further subtext of the story.

Though the lyrics are a litany of all the familiar defences against darkness — quiet obedience (children should be seen but not heard), lullabies, prayer and vigilance — the domain of night and nightmare gains ascendance over these fragile consolations as the song reaches its conclusion. With Metallica's retrospective approval, the song proved extremely popular with US psyops troops as an instrument of so-called 'torture-lite', played repeatedly at overwhelming volume to prisoners in Guantanamo Bay and in a prison facility known only as 'the disco', located somewhere on the Iraqi-Syrian border. Searching for a theoretical base for this practice, retired US Air Force Lt-Col Dan Kuehl, an instructor in psychological operations at the time, drew upon the Biblical story of Joshua, whose army used ram's horns and voices as sonic weapons in their conquest of Jericho.

THE HAUNTING

This interpretation of sound as an unstable or provisional event, ambiguously situated somewhere between psychological delusion, verifiable scientific phenomenon, and a visitation of spectral forces, is a frequent trope of supernatural fiction. In Bram Stoker's *Dracula*, after all the whisperings and susurrations, howling wolves, bats flapping at windows, the 'low piteous howling of dogs', the 'churning sound of her tongue' when Jonathan Harker is seduced by three voluptuous vampires, and their silvery musical laughter, 'like the intolerable, tingling sweetness of water-glasses when played on by a cunning hand', one of the first signs of Count Dracula's imminent arrival in Whitby is auditory:

> Shortly before ten o' clock the stillness of the air grew quite oppressive, and the silence was so marked that the bleating of a sheep inland or the barking of a dog in the town was distinctly heard, and the band on the pier, with its lively French air, was like a discord in the great harmony of nature's silence. A little after midnight came a strange sound over the sea, and high over head the air began to carry a strange, faint, hollow booming.

Whereas other omens are described as shared visual experiences — the erratic progress of the *Demeter*, the ship in which Dracula lies in his earth-filled box, and an unusually vivid sunset followed by a storm of spectacular violence — these notations of sound are given as a private occurrence. The hearing of anomalous sounds implies a degree of interiority that may border on hallucination or madness, yet through this ambiguity, the place of sound in the natural order is interrogated. A fictional archetype is established, in which the sudden and unnatural absence of sound opens up space in nature for supernatural sound, a sound that shares the characteristics of sound yet lacks its materiality.

Long John Silver, of all characters in fiction, challenges the false logic of supernatural sound in *Treasure Island*. As the last remnants of his pirate band search for treasure, they are taunted by the hidden voice of a marooned sailor. The more susceptible of the men assume it to be the ghost of the dreaded Flint, but Silver is unconvinced: '"Sperrit? Well, maybe," he said. "But there's one thing not clear to me. There was an echo. Now, no man ever seen a sperrit with a shadow; well, then, what's he doing with an echo to him, I should like to know? That ain't in natur', surely?"' If the form of an apparition has no physical substance, then its voice must also be insubstantial, otherwise contradicting nineteenth-century science's explanations of sound as a wave or pulse that moves through air to make a physical impact on the tympanic membrane. As physicist John Tyndall pointed out in his pioneering study, *Sound*, first published in 1867, sailors must understand something of acoustics. The use of lights as fog signals often proved useless when visibility dropped to zero. 'No wonder, then,' he wrote, 'that earnest efforts should have been made to find a substitute for light in sound-signals, powerful enough to give warning and guidance to mariners while still at a safe distance from the shore.' Victorian-era writers like Stevenson, Bram Stoker and Sir Arthur Conan Doyle shared a deep interest in the scientific discoveries of their time. Informed by this, Silver enacts a conflict between the sailor's pragmatic knowledge of natural phenomena and his tenacious superstition, engendered by the spectre of death haunting those whose occupation depends upon the sea.

This uncertain relationship between real and imagined shadows the fate of Eleanor, the central subject of Shirley Jackson's novel, *The Haunting of Hill House*. First published in 1959, the book was filmed as *The Haunting*, directed to unsettling, edgy effect by Robert Wise in 1963, then remade by Jan de Bont in 1999. The latter misses the point in its dependence on CGI effects, 'materializing' the haunting as a firework display of whizzing spooks, whereas Wise preserves the ambiguity and restraint of Jackson's story.

Eleanor has cared for her invalid, tyrannical mother all her life. One night her mother knocks on the wall, calling repeatedly for her medicine. For once, Eleanor sleeps through the noise. Subsequently, her mother dies, leaving thirty-two-year-old Eleanor with an ultimately fatal dose of guilt. A researcher in supernatural manifestations, Dr John Montague, is given the opportunity of investigating Hill House, notorious for its malign atmosphere. Searching through records of psychic phenomena for assistants who might be sensitive to presences in the house, he finds Eleanor. Shortly after her father died, Eleanor and her family were driven from their home by showers of stones falling from the sky for three days, 'rolling loudly down the walls, breaking windows and pattering maddeningly on the roof.' In her vulnerable state, liberated from her mother's needs, she joins the ill-matched group who assemble at Hill House under the paternalistic direction of Dr Montague.

What transpires in the house is inconclusive yet mysteriously power- ful. The horror, such as it is, might be described as 'mild threat' by those picturesque summaries now printed as warnings of what to expect in a film. More accurately, it is sonic menace. On arrival, Eleanor finds herself drawn into a silence, trying to put her suitcase down without making a sound, walking in stocking feet, conscious that the housekeeper had moved soundlessly: 'When she stood still in the middle of the room the pressing silence of Hill House came back all around her. I am like a small creature swallowed whole by a monster, she thought, and the monster feels my tiny little movements inside.' There are intimations of this swallowing, as the house resists all attempts to understand its spatial logic, yet noth- ing happens until the feeling of nothing happening is firmly established. Significantly, though the reader is waiting for ghosts, the first manifestation is a loud knocking on the door of the bedrooms shared by Eleanor and Dr Montague's other female assistant, Theodora. Shocked awake by this noise, Eleanor thinks she is back at home, her mother knocking on the wall. She and Theodora attempt to rationalize the noise and its physiological effects. 'Just a noise,' says Theodora; 'It sounded, Eleanor thought, like a hollow noise, a hollow bang, as though something were hitting the doors with an iron kettle, or an iron bar, or an iron glove.' The sound moves with a similar anthropomorphized purpose (though a more specific intimation of domes- tic violence) to the wind that probes Charles Dickens's church, searching methodically, diminishing, thundering to a climax and falling ominously silent, then, with silence, a spreading of cold air: 'Little pattings came from around the doorframe, small seeking sounds, feeling the edges of the door, trying to sneak a way in. . . . The little sticky sounds moved on around the doorframe and then, as though a fury caught whatever was outside, the crashing came again, and Eleanor and Theodora saw the wood of the door tremble and shake, and the door move against its hinges.'

Though Hill House has little to recommend it as a home, Eleanor imagines herself within a family. Her delusion is fragile, yet it serves to enclose the isolated space of repressed memories, misanthropy and loneliness that has grown within like a cancer born of too much harsh reality, and so the invasive sound that manifests with every significant death in her life is an uncanny response to her brief moment of security. Predictably, the sound offers unreliable evidence to scientific rationalist, sceptic, medium or Eleanor herself, who doubts her own fear. Not everybody hears the sounds, so Eleanor begins to question their material reality, their 'outside' existence: 'Now we are going to have a new noise, Eleanor thought, listening to the inside of her head; it is changing. . . . Am I doing it? she wondered quickly, is that me? And heard the tiny laughter beyond the door, mocking her.' Jackson's subtle mockery of the clichés of supernatural and gothic fiction echoes this laughter, yet she refuses to supply a rational explanation, or confirm the psychological undercurrent. In its scenario of flawed and incompatible individuals forced to share enclosed space, *The Haunting of Hill House* resembles Jean Paul Sartre's play, *No Exit*, whose message was that hell is ourselves. Hill House is, after all, one vowel away from Hell House.

Myth enters the story as they move into the grounds of the house, when Theodora describes the third assistant, Luke, as Pan. Soon after this invocation by naming, Eleanor's senses sharpen, turn to paranoia. She hears distant murmurs of conversation, a brush of footsteps, a voice: '"Eleanor, Eleanor," and she heard it inside and outside her head; this was a call she had been listening for all her life. The footsteps stopped and she was caught in a movement of air so solid that she staggered and was held. "Eleanor, Eleanor," she heard through the rushing of air past her ears.' Soon after this revelation, Eleanor sits and listens to the sounds of the house, her hearing capabilities expanded to animalistic sensitivity: a door swinging shut, a bird touching the tower and flying off, the stove settling and cooling, an animal moving through bushes by the summerhouse outside: 'She could even hear, with her new awareness of the house, the dust drifting gently in the attic, the wood aging.' At this point of fusion between the extended space of Eleanor's hearing and the projected soundings of the house, there is little reason to expect a happy outcome. In the final line of the book, all noise is stilled: '. . . doors were sensibly shut; silence lay steadily against the wood and stone of Hill House, and whatever walked there, walked alone.'

DARKNESS GATHERS

Seamus Heaney's poem, 'Personal Helicon', opens into boyish memories of wells — their smells and drop and sunken mirrors. As the undignified freedoms of childhood are lost to maturity — the digging in slime; the gazing, like Narcissus, at his own image in water — so Heaney calls upon the auditory reflections of wells to speak for poetry, and why poetry should be written: 'I rhyme / To see myself, to set the darkness echoing.'

A hole is dug into the ground, a journey to the centre of the earth in search of music, and as with all holes in the ground, the digging disturbs artefacts of the human trace. A cavity, hollow, vessel or pit deepens, unearthing memories of burying, hiding, storing, amplifying, echoing, tunnelling, sheltering, trapping, containing, planting, suffocating, sinking, secrecy, sacrifice.

In 'Musical Instruments Through the Ages', Klaus P. Wachsmann noted an Abyssinian (Ethiopian) instrument known as the Lion's Roar, a narrow tapered hole dug in the ground to fashion a resonating, transformative vessel for the voice. Is it possible to imagine a more economical diagram of pre-scientific cosmology than this prototypical loudspeaker? Sound is earthed or grounded within place and human society, yet it extends in all directions: outwards to intersect with the communications of non-human organisms; upwards to air, sky, the heavens; downwards into the dark underworld. With a shout — raaagh — the connection is made.

Documentation of terrene instruments is rare, perhaps because of their ephemeral nature, or because they had been largely superseded by more portable and sophisticated technologies by the time ethnomusicology was sufficiently advanced as a scholarly discipline to pay attention to such devices. More important than this, they were safe from collectors and explorers. Shipping home a hole in the ground for future collection in museums such as the Horniman in London or the Pitt Rivers in Oxford was hardly a practical option. In *Musical Instruments of the South American Indians*, Karl Gustav Izikowitz described an elaborate signal drum made by the Brazilian Catuquinarú Indians. First reported in 1910 (only three years before the notorious Paris premiere of Stravinsky's *Rite of Spring*), the instrument was complex and mysterious: a large earth pit filled with resins and wood fragments and capped with rubber, and in the centre, a vertical hollow log partially filled with powdered mica, bone fragments and other materials, again capped by hard rubber.

Between 1961 and 1967, French ethnomusicologist Hugo Zemp found simpler terrene instruments — an earth drum, an earth bow, and an earth friction drum — during his time researching among the Dan of western Ivory Coast and Liberia. A photograph of the earth bow can be seen in Zemp's book, *Musique Dan*. A man squats and sings, plucking an ingenious version of what came to be known among African-American musicians as the diddley bow (though by fixing the string to a wall, the diddley bow uses a dwelling as resonator, rather than the earth itself). In this case, a sapling is bent over to form a bow. A string connects this to a sounding surface, a whole palm leaf fastened securely over a hole dug into the ground.

Zemp categorized the earth friction drum, rubbed fibres threaded through the bark cover of an earth-pit resonator, as the voice of a mask or supernatural being, hidden from the sight of women and children and destroyed after ceremonial use. Named guéyibeu, mask-that-eats-water, the otherworldly sound of this instrument could be heard on *Masques Dan*, a collection of Zemp's recordings of mask voices released by the Ocora label.

As we go deeper, darkness gathers. Animals of wells, pools and damp darkness croak and slither. Of the innocent frog, Seamus Heaney wrote: 'The slap and plop were obscene threats. Some sat / Poised like mud grenades, their blunt heads farting.' The childlike satisfaction of digging a hole (perhaps all the way to the other side of the world) may be followed by associations of burial, entrapment and the underworld. One interpretation of the sixteenth-century English nursery rhyme, 'Ding dong bell, pussy's in the well', hypothesizes that the 'pussy' of the rhyme described a woman accused of immorality; the sound of the bell may have referred to the 'rough music' of pots and pans played as the woman was paraded through the streets on the way to her torture by ducking stool in the village well. Holes in the ground can be disturbing, sinister regions of troglodytes, trolls and vampires, mythological places of punishment such as Tartarus, Hades the Abyss, created within the darker places of imagination and speculative fictions: Edgar Allan Poe's *Pit and the Pendulum* and other 'sepulchral terrors' such as *The Premature Burial*, and films in which pits, caves and deep holes entrap humans or disgorge monsters: Kaneto Shindo's *Onibaba*, Hiroshi Teshigahara's *Woman of the Dunes*, Bruce Hunt's *The Cave* (a less distinguished example of the genre), or Hideo Nakata's *Ringu* trilogy, in which a misshapen young woman crawls slowly, joints cracking, out of a deep well into the light.

When the young, somewhat hysterical Axel, narrator in Jules Verne's *Journey to the Centre of the Earth*, loses his way deep underground he is saved by a strange acoustic phenomenon, the same transmission of small sounds carried over distance that can be heard in the whispering galleries of St Paul's Cathedral in London or the Badshahi Mosque in Lahore. First, he experiences the shock of a violent noise, like thunder, hearing 'the waves of sound lose themselves, and die away in the distant depths of the abyss.' In the ensuing silence, he listens to his own heartbeat, then begins to sense other sounds: 'Suddenly my ear, which happened to touch the wall, was startled by a sound like distant, undistinguishable, inarticulate words. I trembled.' He asks himself if he is suffering from hallucinations, then realizes he can hear the conversation of his uncle and their Danish guide, transmitted along four miles of rock walls. 'Now that our voices meet it is by a purely acoustic phenomenon, and we cannot touch hands', says his uncle. 'But do not despair Axel! To hear one another is something!'

The uncanny associations of chthonic resonance may also apply on a smaller scale to domestic utensils. Ueda Akinari's eighteenth-century gothic tale, 'The Kibitsu Cauldron', tells the story of a haunting in which unpropitious omens are established from the outset by a Cauldron Purification ritual (Mikamabarai) held on the grounds of the Kibitsu Shrine, a Shinto shrine in Okayama, western Japan. For this divinatory rite, still extant, a fire of pine needles is lit under a water-filled kami, a large iron rice cauldron. 'It has long been the custom', wrote Ueda, 'for worshippers at the Kibitsu Shrine to make abundant offerings, present hot water to the god, and seek a divination of good or bad fortune. When the maidens complete their ritual prayers and the water comes to a boil, the cauldron will, if the prospects are good, produce a sound like the lowing of cattle. If the prospects are bad, the cauldron will make no sound.' Inevitably, the cauldron is silent and so the story ends with its villain hanging by his topknot from a roof beam, all other traces of his body other than hair obliterated save for a smear of blood.

A SIREN SONG

Louisiana Museum, Humlebaek, Denmark, April 2009: Max Ernst: Dream and Revolution. *Napoleon in the Wilderness*, 1941. Napoleon stands calcified, pillar of salt, carapaced in viral shell, peg-leg embedded into a tropic Elba. Plinthed on an adjacent rock, a naked woman leans in his direction, draped in seaweeds and shell growth. She holds a fantastic wind instrument, a gracefully curving, slender horn whose bell culminates in the head of a screaming green dragon. She and Napoleon are separated by a livid totem pole of balanced stones, beaked and encrusted with the kitsch outer flowerings of pink and green mosses and lichens. The woman holds the mouthpiece of the horn away from her lips, holds it with one hand, well away from the finger holes, yet it sounds in the still blue afternoon.

CHAMBER MUSIC

Two university friends wax philosophical in *The Lost Stradivarius*, J. Meade Falkner's late-nineteenth-century novel of musical bewitchment and occult obsession. They discuss the power of music and its contradictory propensity to awaken that which it aspires to transcend, a conflict between spirituality and sensuality. Music is capable of evil, one of them argues; piously, he quotes 'some beautiful verses by Mr. Keble' (John Keble, churchman and poet):

> Cease, stranger, cease those witching notes,
> The art of syren choirs;
> Hush the seductive voice that floats
> Across the trembling wires.

Given the masculine context of this discourse, set as it is within the rigid traditions of a pre-twentieth-century Oxford University, the personification of music's deadly propensities as a female seductress can only strike us more forcefully as yet another consequence of Eve biting the fruit of knowledge, good and evil. The male is vulnerable to witchery, arts and airs, floating, trembling and all other diaphanous, ethereal, soft seductions, or so Mr Keble would have us believe. Men must not allow themselves to be dissolved into dark sweetness by sound; instead, they must deploy it to draw down fire from heaven in order to purge themselves of impurity. Through laws of form, sound can be silenced.

And yet the sirens will never be silenced; their return is inevitable. 'Woman's song then is both beautiful and dangerous, pleasurable and disturbing, descriptions which link the female voice irrevocably with its mythological embodiments', writes Patricia Pulham in her study of Vernon Lee, Victorian-era author of supernatural fiction and essays on aesthetics. Even in our time, it is possible for a newspaper to return to such mythological embodiments for a headline — 'Sex-siren plot to lure victim to slaughter-house' — as if sirenic notes still draw us to that meadow of breathless calm described by Circe in *The Odyssey*, 'piled high with the mouldering skeletons of men, whose withered skin still hangs upon their bones.'

In episode 11 of *Ulysses*, James Joyce evokes the siren song of *The Odyssey* with a tour-de-force of writing so saturated in sound, music and sex that its close reading is almost narcotic in effect. The drunkenness that threatens the life or voice of certain characters who gather of a lunchtime in the Ormond Hotel bar rises off the pages in a heady fumigant brew. In parallel with alcoholic inspiration, lamentation, sentimentality and resignation run as threads through Sirens, a stage set for Joyce's famous love of the tenor voice and a yearning love song. Among the performers during that lunchtime in the Ormond bar is Simon Dedalus, who sings 'Appear To Me', 'M'Appari', Lionel's aria from Friedrich von Flotow's nineteenth-century opera, *Martha*. Again, a lamentation, a parting, joy ending in weeping, a 'dream too soon hath flown'. All memories of loss and pain, beauty and love, fuse in the long dying moment of a single note's flight. The chest-note — Come! — soars upward in the smokey air, avian 'in the effulgence symbolistic', the 'high vast irradiation', the 'endlessnessnessness . . .'

Whatever mathematical virtues of law and order might be embodied through the paradox of immaterial yet material sound, the carrier acts upon and through the body; no matter what the 'instrument', all music makes its impact primarily through the canal of the ear and owes some evolutionary debt to the original instrument, the voice. Joyce makes this connection repeatedly: the action of sound upon the drum of the tympanum, the booming voice, the warrior horn, the barroom innuendo of 'the organ like yours', that threatens to burst the female tympanum of the beloved who is the target of this ardent love song. A vulgar joke follows from Father Cowley — 'not to mention another membrane' — making explicit this analogy of forceful penetration. The ear is at once a drum whose head is vibrated by beatings, a rhythm — Tap, Tap, Tap, Tap — clock clack, jingling, the throbbing of buzzing prongs, the phallic penetration of the male tenor voice and the stealthy infiltration of calls long low and long in dying call, yet at the same time the ear is a shell, a cave, a room in which the roaring resonance of air in its containment suggests the infinity of ocean.

'Music is ascribed the power of being able to attain God's mercy and win the heart of one's beloved,' writes Mladen Dolar in *Opera's Second Death*, 'and this is also the place of its ineradicable ambiguity – music is at one and the same time the epitome of transcendence and of sensuality and eroticism.' Let us not forget that Circe, invaluable to Odysseus with her advice about the Sirens and their dangerous song, was herself a supremely dangerous singer, a web weaver and herbalist who lured men into her house with beautiful singing, then transformed them with her drugs into animals. Only when Odysseus threatens her with violence, then forces her to swear by the gods not to emasculate him when he is naked, is she subdued, seduced, pacified and ready to rat on other vocal sorcerers.

To judge from his early writing, Joyce was less fearful of the female voice. *Chamber Music*, his collection of poems first published in 1907, speaks frequently of those same floating voices, soft sighs of harps in the wind and siren choirs that Mr Keble found so alarmingly seductive, so sapping, yet he idealizes them, finds nothing but love and sweetness in their sound. Only in poem 'XXIV', 'Silently she's combing', does he resort to supplication, like Mr Keble pleading against the witchery of a woman who combs and combs her hair. Significantly, the woman who combs is said to be silent, though she combs 'with many a pretty air'; in the third stanza there is the suggestion that seduction comes from the repetitive spell of combing and the witchery that lies, 'under a pretty air.' Do we take the 'air' to be a song? Since Joyce modelled these poems on Elizabethan ayres and imagined them set to music (and Luciano Berio's settings of I, XXXV and IX, composed for the voice of Cathy Berberian in 1953, capture some of their pagan innocence), this seems likely, in which case the woman portrayed is an embodiment of Circe, who weaves and sings in order to charm, draw in, delay.

To linger once again for a moment with the sirens of ancient Ionia, there are anomalies in their story. Why, for example, does Circe think that Odysseus might wish to enjoy the singing of the Sirens? Perhaps because he has already 'mastered' Circe. Odysseus plugs the ears of his sailors with wax so that they will be deaf to the auditory charm of the Sirens, then while the workers toil he settles down in his chains to absorb pleasure from their unbearable sweetness. In other words, he makes himself immune so that music can be distanced and diminished to the level of music while you work, or background music. This was not dissimilar to Vladimir Jankélévitch's stern view in 1961, arguing against acoustic din that both diverts and perverts. 'For the Siren's music is more than distracting noise, more than noise that diverts or dissipates, preventing reflective thought,' he wrote in *Music and the Ineffable*. 'It is a fraudulent art of pleasing.'

In all of these stories, music calls up great longing. At heart, it is a lamentation. Music is of time, never quite in the moment of itself since it emerges before full hearing then decays before it can become an object, so its death, impending or lingering, is a constancy. Music can shake a room, pass through walls, fill the air, yet for all its magic, death is never far away (Joyce's Sirens section takes place after a funeral). Both in ancient China and Greece, music was considered too dangerous to be left unregulated. 'The mermaid sirens, enemies of the Muses, have only one goal,' wrote Jankélévitch, 'to reroute, mislead, and delay Odysseus. In other words, they derail the dialectic, the law of the itinerary that leads our mind toward duty and truth.' For this affront, there must be punishment. Often portrayed in paintings in the style of academic soft-porn — young voluptuous women rising naked out of the sea or posing on the beaches or meadows of their island — the Sirens, as we have seen before, were more accurately hybrid creatures, a fusion of flesh and feathers, claws and wings.

Sounds arc through the complex shift and flow of feelings, sensations, conversations, movements, sighs and songs of Joyce's Sirens. The section has been described as musical, which it is, and yet Joyce has passed through the specificity of this cultural category already, now placing music within its wider context of sound as nature. 'There's music everywhere,' he wrote (or his character, Leopold Bloom, thinks to himself), as if anticipating John Cage, but despite himself, Joyce was a musical conservative. Sea, wind, thunder, water, the sound of cows, hens and snakes, the racket of the cattle market are all music, though not 'Ruttledge's door: ee creaking', which Joyce decides is noise. He returns to the sylvan innocence of his *Chamber Music*, but older and wiser, the chamber music now 'a kind of music I thought when she.' The act from which tinkling ensues is left unsaid, a sentence chopped off, but we are left in no doubt that Joyce is gathering up theories of acoustics, Liszt's rhapsodies and the babytalk wordsounds of rain within the bowl of the lavatory: the piddling of pearls. Base and elevated, the movement flows between sounds of the spirit, of fire, of creaking shoes, the blind tap-tap of a cane, in finality expelled from Bloom's ciderous arse: 'Pprrpffrrppffff.' The end of an end.

Songbirds flit throughout this quiet cacophony, the whistle of uncle Richie (who earlier in the day had pursed his lips to sonorously outbreath Ferrando's *aria di sortita*) thrushing and throstling, echoed and lost. Long cries echo, calling, calling. Mr Dedalus brings from his coat a pipe and in his preparations for smoking blasts through the flue 'two husky fifenotes.' Later, as he seats himself at the piano, this 'lost-chord pipe' as it comes to be called, is laid side by side with the tuning fork whose buzzing prongs had called in yet another 'long in dying' call, a throbbing within the room. An architecture is mapped: sounds that fill, or come from within, or beyond a door. The pipe lies with the tuning fork above the obedient keys. Pat the hard-of-hearing waiter sets ajar the door of the bar so that sound may make its way with greater ease into the ears and hearts of those whose cheeks are touched with flame as the flow pours through their 'skin limbs human heart soul spine'.

For the architecture of the body is mapped also, its ins and outs, Joyce dwelling on the organs that emit and receive the physicality of sound, and its movement through space, syrupy liquor for the lips dealt by the siren who syrups with her voice. Miss Douce, that same siren, produces a shell, a seahorn, so that George Lidwell can listen. 'Her ear too is a shell,' wrote Joyce, 'the peeping lobe there . . . The sea they think they hear. Singing. A roar. The blood it is. Souse in the ear sometimes. Well it's a sea. Corpuscle islands.' Bodies are shells that hear themselves, instruments to resonate space. Instruments are rooms also: a blade of grass cupped in the shell of the hands, then blown through pursed lips. Sounds to wake the dead. Music of tiny chambers built from the body. The fractured inner thoughts of Bloom clatter and flit like birds, alighting on a female body who is herself a resonating vessel, an instrument: 'Play on her lip and blow, body of white woman, a flute alive. Blow gentle. Loud. Three holes all women.' Bodies are instruments and instruments are bodies: the double basses with gashes in their sides; the semigrand open piano whose music hath crocodile jaws, the deep, soft, open darkness of the self.

Despite these internal disquisitions on auditory phenomena, Bloom hypothesizes a music of nothing but numbers, a Musemathematics. 'And you think you're listening to the ethereal,' he says. But this rationalisation, this reduction to the law, won't do. As he admits, a numerical substitute for music will fall flat when set alongside the real thing, the song. 'It's on account of the sounds it is.' The tenor voices lament and keen, ribald in their restoration of masculinity yet perilously close in that register of pitch and high emotion to the domain of the Siren. Corpuscle islands, male or female, we graze our meadows, waiting for lonely sailors and through this barroom scene of sirens and sailors, of fluting notes and lamentations, we gain privileged insight not just into Joyce but into the polyphonic complexity of all minds, the ardent resonant depths of all bodies. The law is undone by shamanic birds, the carriers of souls who fly betwixt trees and underworld, souls gripped in their beaks, the flighting sounds of sensuality that rise to the callings of grief, love and comfort, plunge to the quiet tinkling of the toilet bowl, down to earth and what it is to be in a place and conscious of its vivid presence, then climb again to the endlessnessnessness.

THE LOST CHORD

What was this lost chord, the husky fifenote sound of Mr Dedalus' pipe? One of my earliest memories as a small child is of my father laughing at a 78 rpm record of 'The Lost Chord'; perhaps it was the antiquated sound of the music, or perhaps the comic potential of the title (exploited by Jimmy Durante in his song, 'The Guy Who Found the Lost Chord'). Yet the song, written by composer Arthur Sullivan at the bedside of his dying brother in 1877, struggles to articulate the ineffability of music, its hauntological transience, and the channel through which it connects humans to the unspeakable, the unsayable, the sound of the end of time. At a low ebb, the composer is sitting at the organ, idly running his fingers over the keys; by accident, he strikes a revelatory, mystic chord, by implication a harmony more transcendent than earthly:

> It linked all perplexed meanings
> Into one perfect peace,
> And trembled away into silence
> As if it were loath to cease.

For Joyce, the song would have been familiar. Sullivan's song was one of the earliest recordings of music ever made, used to illustrate the potential of Edison's phonograph to Londoners and sung by Caruso at the Metropolitan

Opera House in 1912, as part of a benefit concert for families of victims of the *Titanic* disaster.

THE VOICE OF GHOSTS TALKING

Bloom's speculation, that the tinkling of Molly's piss in the chamber pot is a kind of music, is not so wayward. Wooden boxes, cooking pots, cups, bowls, bottles, drainpipes, tin cans, jerry cans, plastic water jugs, matchboxes — throughout the literature of organology and ethnomusicology lies scattered evidence of these everyday vessels being transformed into musical instruments. The majority of the musical instruments that we call acoustic — piano, clarinet, guitar, violin, drum, and so on — derive their audible energy from being enclosed or semi-enclosed rooms, chambers, tunnels or vessels of marvellous shape, their equally fanciful apertures opening out onto the greater vessel of an external world. The crowded molecules of sound move about in these rooms, the equivalent of social beings, mixing and conversing, crowded or left alone, emptying out and filling up, speaking quietly or making noise. This movement is reminiscent of the architecture of the body and our sensitivity to sound moving within the body or escaping from the body. The story of Syrinx and her transformation into Pan's flute reminds us of the body's potential to become an instrument, and the absorption of music into and through the body. Jankélévitch describes this as an act of trespass: 'Music acts on human beings, on their nervous systems and their vital processes . . . By means of massive irruptions, music takes up residence in our intimate self and seemingly elects to make its home there. The man inhabited and possessed by this intruder, the man robbed of self, is no longer himself: he has become nothing more than a vibrating string, a sounding pipe.'

Stringed instruments sound out with more clarity and beauty when accurately tuned, and yet out-of-tune is not the same as detuned, a deliberate act of untuning, or untuned, a natural state of neglect that summons the uncanny aura of an abandoned house, even a haunted house. When a stringed instrument is untuned by age and natural forces, so that any sense of its original pitch relationships fades, then it prophesies its own decomposition. Wind whistling in reeds augurs a return of nature spirits, but the eerie sound of untuned piano strings activated by unknown agency (rats, ants, moths or wind) is a sibylline moan predicting human civilisation's entropy, as if despite his first defeat, Pan and his flute compete against the more orderly lyre music of Apollo, but this time, they triumph.

Whatever state of senescence has been reached, a ruined piano retains some vestige of its music, so encapsulating the ghostly aura associated with certain collapsed, broken or abandoned buildings and artefacts: a crumbling abbey, a broken doll, an umbrella left in a deserted house. For the enactment of Jean Tinguely's *Homage to New York* in March, 1960, a self-destructive machine tore itself to pieces in the sculpture garden of the Museum of Modern Art. Within this ramshackle towering construction of washing machine drums, stinking chemicals, metal tubing, a painting machine, bicycle wheels, a noisy Addressograph machine, a radio, a baby-cart, klaxons and a large orange meteorological balloon, Tinguely wedged in an antique upright piano, played by the forceful percussion of armatures fashioned from bicycle spokes. Not long after the machine began its auto-destruction, clouds of thick smoke were released from containers of titanium tetrachloride. 'Having waited half an hour to see the show,' Calvin Tomkins wrote, 'the spectators now found themselves enveloped in a choking cloud that completely obscured the view of the machine. They could hear it, though. Most of the percussion instruments were working splendidly, and the din was tremendous.' At one point, the radio turned itself on but nobody could hear it. 'Smoke and flames began to emerge from inside the piano,' Tomkins recalled, 'which continued to sound its melancholy three-note dirge . . . The piano was really blazing now. "There is something very odd about seeing a piano burn," George Staempfli has since said. "All your ideas about music are somehow involved."'

INSTRUMENT OF DEATH

In ancient Chinese literature, the motif of the abandoned musical instrument was used to symbolise a wider social decay, or the pathos of old customs in decline. Tang dynasty poet Po Chü-i's 'The Five-String' begins as rhapsody for the five-string lute and its player, 'The soft notes dying almost to nothing; / "Ch'ieh, ch'ieh," like the voice of ghosts talking.' The poem ends with a nostalgic coda:

> Alas, alas that the ears of common men
> Should love the modern and not love the old.

Thus it is that the lute in the green window
Day by day is covered deeper with dust.

Sometimes an instrument claims a form of autonomy, aspiring to automatism by sounding itself (the rattling snare drum, or resonating grand piano), like a house in which a chair creaks, no one sitting there, as if no longer needing any entity other than itself, as if haunted by the sounds and players that have activated its body in the past. In *The Lore of the Chinese Lute*, Robert Hans van Gulik gave the example of a Chinese ghost story in which the lute, the guqin (or ch'in), sounds without human agency: 'Ch'ên Ch'iu-yang fell ill and died. His father thought much of him, and placed his son's lute before his soul-tablet. Always after that in the middle of the night the tones of this lute would be heard; they could be heard even outside the house.'

Of all instruments, the piano is most conducive to this ghostly activation, its keys either visibly undisturbed or lowering and rising by themselves. As a piece of furniture it harbours disturbing undertones of uncanny automata, of innate violence (those scenes in films in which the lid is slammed down on the fingers of the pianist), even coffins and caskets. In *Bruges-la-Morte*, by Georges Rodenbach, the grieving widower, Hugues Viane, has moved to Bruges for its melancholy atmosphere of quiet decay. Dedicating his life to mourning, he surrounds himself with mementoes of his dead wife, including the long locks of her hair:

In order to be able to see them all the time, these locks that were still Her, he had placed them on the piano, silent from now on, in the large, never-changing drawing room. They simply lay there, a cut-off plait, a broken chain, a rope saved from the shipwreck. And to protect the hair from contamination, from the moist atmosphere that could have taken the colour out of it or oxidized its metal, he had had the idea, naïve if it had not been touching, of putting it under glass, a transparent casket, a crystal box, the resting place of the bare locks to which he paid homage every day. For him, as for the silent objects living around, this plait of hair seemed bound up with their existence, seemed the very soul of the house.

The piano never sounds during the novel but at the end, it is the hair that becomes (in English translation at least), 'the instrument of death'.

The idea that silent objects might be repositories of the soul of a house has great dramatic potential, since their auditory activation would suggest that the house itself has chosen to speak. Jack Clayton's 1961 film, *The Innocents*, based on *The Turn of the Screw* by Henry James, contains a key scene in which the governess, played by Deborah Kerr, experiences a ghostly visitation of sounds. She hears piano notes playing the music box melody of a tune that recurs throughout the film; the camera cuts away to the grand piano, but no one sits there. Voices whisper; laughter swirls around her. The scene shows nothing alarming — its elements are clichés of the genre — yet through effectively montaged sound design, a chilling sense of the uncanny is conveyed.

In the 1920s, the American composer Henry Cowell applied his overtone theories to a project that shifted the conceptualization of the grand piano into unknown territory. Extending Debussy's revolutionary notion of the piano as a sounding frame, he activated the instrument as if it were a resonant flat harp, an echo chamber of complex harmonic sensitivities (implicit in existing compositions by composers such as Scriabin and Schumann, perhaps, but otherwise left undisturbed as potentiality within the bowels of the instrument). In a number of Cowell's short works, the pianist sounds the strings by plucking, pressing, stroking, damping or rubbing them. Some of these 'string piano' pieces were given titles based on the atmospheres they evoke — *Aeolian Harp* or *Sinister Resonance* — while others drew on Cowell's Irish ancestry, or tales of Irish mythology interpreted by the mystic poet John Osborne Varian, then a member of a Californian Theosophical sect, The Temple of the People. One of Varian's obsessions was the importance of the harp in Irish mythology. For years he worked on developing a large harp with two sound chambers, loud enough to be used in outdoor settings. He hoped that Cowell would take over the responsibility of what seems to have been an impractical instrument. Instead, Cowell adapted the idea to his own music for piano interiors, composing pieces such as *The Banshee*, performed by two players, one holding down the damper pedal for maximum resonance and sustain, the other standing at the tail of the piano and either rubbing strings lengthwise or plucking them. Its eerie sound evokes the Irish spirit woman of myth, the messenger from the Otherworld who wails outside a house if an occupant is about to die, then flies away into the night. These ghostly properties housed within a piano proved to be seductive to American composers after Cowell: John Cage, whose adaptation of prepared piano inclined to more meditative atmospheres, and George Crumb, whose *Music of Shadows, Ghost Nocturne, The Phantom Gondolier,* and *Otherworldly Resonances* are unambiguous about such spectral associations. More recently, in his notes on Salvatore Sciarrino's *D'un Faune,* for alto flute and piano (1980), flautist Mario Caroli describes the transmogrification originally initiated by Cowell in terms that suggest an evolutionary process, a mutation from mechanical to organic and corporeal: 'The piano changes from an instrument with felt-covered hammers into an instrument with lungs with their particular characteristics of changeable dynamics and colour and light effects.' An instrument breathes.

SOUND AS APPARITION

When Joe Gillis steps into the over-decorated living room of washed-up silent movie star Norma Desmond's crumbling mansion in *Sunset Boulevard,* his entrance is greeted by the low aeolian moan of wind catching in the pipe organ that fills one corner of the room. 'I ought to have it taken out,' says Norma. 'Or teach it a better tune,' says Gillis. The sound — another kind of lost chord — swelling and fading in a moment, is symptomatic of the decay, physical and moral, that infects every part of the story. Gillis should heed this, the warning siren that sounds as he crosses a threshold, but some part of his nature — flip cynicism, curiosity or desperation — blunts his intuition. The house enfolds him; finally destroys him: three gunshots followed by a face-down splash into the pool, never to surface for air.

Space itself is an instrument in which the background sound of subtle auditory shifts, singing resonance and dead echoes fills the air so completely that this peripheral sound seems to personify the place itself, a ubiquity of such familiarity that it fades into nothing. 'Finally, we don't live in sealed containers', write the authors of *A Perfect Mess,* explaining that ambient background noise must be inserted back into the cleaned-up signals of mobile phone conversations for the callers to feel that they are connected and 'natural'.

We live in a world where things that make noises are constantly new to us, where in a sense even the space around us has a faint murmur to it. This noise feels right to us; at an unconscious level, it is reassuring.

The technical term for this type of background noise, in fact, is *comfort noise* — [telephone] engineers like [Frédéric] Bourget call it *CN* — and trying to talk to someone in the absence of it is a bit disorientating and even a little creepy. Our brains rebel at the unnatural neatness.

Without this ambience, a shared air, conversations can be extraordinarily stilted, each person stumbling over the other's beginnings and endings, or waiting too long before speaking because there is too little 'non-essential' information to indicate natural pauses.

Sounds surround the home in their own air, a ring of familiarity, changing with the seasons and change itself. James Knowlson's biography of Samuel Beckett, *Damned to Fame*, describes Beckett's 'extraordinarily acute sense of hearing' as a boy: 'He and [his brother] Frank used to lie in their beds listening to sounds that stayed with Beckett all his life: "the barking of the dogs, at night, in the clusters of hovels up in the hills, where the stone-cutters lived, like generations of stone-cutters before them"; the clanging of the iron gates in a storm at the end of the drive; the clatter of horses' hooves on the road beyond the garden, even the sighing of every tree close to the house.'

In every place that feels or becomes uncanny and unhomely, there is a sound that does not belong, an interloper. In their biography of the English composer, Elisabeth Lutyens, Meirion and Susie Harries describe Lutyens in her childhood. Her mother is reading aloud to the children but Elisabeth dislikes this reading so profoundly that she fidgets in the corner, her fingers in her ears. 'As she got older,' they write, 'her main desire was privacy and some territory of her own. Her most successful hideout was to be the cistern cupboard in a downstairs lavatory; she painted the walls glossy black in imitation of her father's colour schemes, laid in supplies of dog biscuits and retired from the fray. "To this day," she wrote in her autobiography, "I find the sound of running water soothing."'

Contrast this with Muhammad Ali's concept of the 'Near Room', the place whose door would swing open when a particularly heavy punch threatened to send him to the canvas: '. . . Bedlam . . .' was how George Plimpton described Ali's vision, 'a place to which, when he got in trouble in the ring, he imagined the door swung half open and inside he could see neon, orange and green lights blinking, and bats blowing trumpets and alligators playing trombones, and where he could hear snakes screaming.

Weird masks and actors' clothes hung on the wall, and if he stepped across the sill and reached for them, he knew that he was committing himself to his own destruction.'

FLOOR EE-CREAKS

I have been burgled twice. On the first occasion the burglar broke in through a window at the back of the house, looked into the bedroom of my friends downstairs as they slept, stole a bag and made an exit by the front door, leaving it wide open. This was winter, snow on the ground, a night of cold wind. Busy upstairs, I noticed a pressure shift in the house, a subtle modulation of sound in which the normal nocturnal resonance indoors was augmented by sounds from outside, muffled by snow. When the temperature fell, I looked out to the hallway and noticed our door was open. Even then, though disquieted by these slight variations in familiar states of sound and temperature, I failed to realize we had been burgled. Some years later I was woken during the night by a burglar who had sprung the lock on the front door and was at that moment stealing my wallet downstairs. Though I had no consciousness of hearing a sound I knew there was an alien presence within the familiarity and security of my private place, my home. I walked to the top of the stairs, not knowing why, and saw a man run out of the front door. Some mystery surrounds the question of why we wake when we do, not always the noise of a drunk in the street or the breaking of a window. A terse passage of dialogue from Cormac McCarthy's novel, *The Crossing*, encapsulates this mystery:

> What woke you? he said.
> You did.
> I didn't make a sound.
> I know it.

A creaking floor is heard one night in darkness, in a place, a home. As assonance and alphabet suggest — from within sleep, from within the sonic vocabulary of horror, terror, the supernatural — the creaking door opens onto the creaking floor. A moving body, or some other agent — pressure, cooling, movement within the greater structure of the building — passes over or through a flexible surface, causing audible friction in this quiet place. Sound radiates outward in all directions, feeling and probing its way both through the solid structure of a building and the interior channels of air space, entering finally the ears of a listener. 'The old house, for those who know how to listen,' wrote Gaston Bachelard, 'is a sort of geometry of echoes . . . Still farther it is possible to recover not merely the timbre of the voices, "the inflections of beloved voices now silent," but also the resonance of each room in the sound house.' This resonance speaks for the history, the memory of a house, venerable personal place, a rubbing of old boards; but perhaps at the source there is an intruder, and so a sound from another place, a place literally out of sight, acts as omen, a bringer of trespass, an agent of threat, unease, disturbance, fear. Anomalous sound enters in the way of an animal or insect: mouse, rat, spider, cockroach, fly, wasp, woodworm or the uncanny ticking of death-watch beetles, celebrating warm weather and desire by banging their heads against the tunnel walls they have bored through old church timbers. How much do such creatures violate the sanctity of the human domain? In *Let Us Now Praise Famous Men*, James Agee raised this question with his exquisite description of a wasp's auditory presence in the silence of a front bedroom of a house occupied, the summer of 1936, by a family of Alabama sharecroppers: 'Here also, his noise a long drawn nerve behind him, the violin wasp returns to his house in the angle of the roof, is silent a half minute, and streams out again beneath eaves upon broad light.' Then he answers, with a coda: 'But he: he is not unwelcome here: he is a builder; a tenant. He does not notice; he is no reader of signs.'

When sound invades a locked and secure dwelling, the initial effect may verge on comedy, a sound design cliché of suspense, spooks in a haunted house, but when it happens, that sudden hyperacusis that detects something unusual within the subtle audio flow of a complex bounded territory, then subaudition is a natural response: the act of mentally supplying whatever is missing in an auditory sequence.

A few years ago, our cat was dying of leukaemia and was restive in the night. Her familiar sounds, normally so familiar that we wouldn't wake, were becoming a fragile indicator of her condition. One night I was woken by the thinnest clicking, then repeated suction sounds. Painfully thin, the cat's movement across the bedroom floorboards was like the tapping of a spider too huge to contemplate; the suction sound was her drinking, now so impeded by the tumour in her jaw that to fight dehydration she had to dip her face completely into her water bowl in order to absorb even the smallest amount. In blind darkness, without seeing, these sounds seemed monstrous.

Stirred up by this experience, another memory, long buried, rose out of the swamp. I recall many occasions as a child, lying in bed at night in complete darkness, suddenly hearing sounds, tiny sounds, and by concentrating hard, going deeper and deeper into these sounds, they seemed to me like a kind of sonar reading that tracked the slow, infinitely careful progress of an intruder working his way around the edges of my bed. I would lie completely still, thinking that my absolute silence would banish the malevolent presence in the bedroom, or at least conceal my presence.

These are some of my earliest memories of sound, primal memories, no doubt linking elements of my personal aesthetic — my proclivity for audio-microscopy and haunted sound — to the fear that can attach itself to hearing sounds whose activation is unseen; noises in the dark; a silence which is not quite silent enough, a house that won't lie still. For the memory to be so tenacious, all of these elements have depended upon each other: the creaking floorboard, the house, the dark, the silence, and the vulnerable listener. Lacking an object, the imagination intercedes and supplies a ghost. 'Then how shall we see without hearing?' Gaston Bachelard asks, in his ruminations on the miniature. 'There exist complicated forms which, even when they are at rest, make a noise. Twisted things continue to make creaking contortions.'

As sound fades, its energy spent, its reputation as verifiable evidence diminishes, to be treated with circumspection as an unreliable witness to the past. Thomas Edison's poignant belief that sounds may linger as elusive auditory ghosts — physical clutter or memory residue that can be accessed by recording technology — is a haunting in itself, explored in the mediumistic pseudo-science of EVP (Electronic Voice Production) pioneered by Konstantin Raudive and Friedrich Jürgenson. Exploited for the plot of Geoffrey Sax's disappointing film, *White Noise*, the science-fiction of Nigel Kneale's television drama, *The Stone Tape*, and Alanté Kavaïté's 2006 film, *Ecoute le Temps (Listen to Time)*, EVP grew from a poignant belief, or at least a sublimated hope — that the voices of the dead speak to us and can be captured on a normal tape recorder.

Voice Transmissions with the Deceased, published in conjunction with the 2004 Frankfurt exhibition, Friedrich Jürgenson/Carl Michael von Hausswolff, is a diary of Jürgenson's experiments with the medium of the tape recorder. As he discovers phantom information within noise and hears unknown, seemingly random voices in tape recordings, noise itself becomes the field of grief, loss, longing, out of which particular signals offering solace may emerge. In 1960, Jürgenson noted one of his early successes, through which his own emotional needs were addressed directly by the 'voices':

> Out of old habit I kept the microphone in front of the open window and when I heard a finch starting his merry trills in front of the window I decided to record his song. I played back the recording immediately, and all of a sudden — in the middle of the birdsong — I heard a voice calling my name. It was my mother's voice. Her name was Helene and she had died in 1955 following a pelvic fracture. Unintentionally my mind jumped back to her last hour when I sat at her deathbed and held her soft warm hand in mine until her last weak pulse beat had ended.

J. G. Ballard's short stories, 'The Voices of Time' and 'The Sound-Sweep', and the work of a number of artists, including Susan Hiller, Louise K. Wilson, Scanner and Carl Michael von Hausswolff, also explore this hauntological aspect of sub-audible presence. 'The Sound-Sweep' was one of Ballard's earliest stories. First published in 1960, the narrative is built around the theme of a vacuum cleaner that can sweep up sonic waste. These sonovacs are operated by a caste of sound-sweeps. Like Mulk Raj Anand's untouchables, they are social pariahs — 'illiterate, mutes (the city authorities preferred these — their discretion could be relied upon) and social cripples' — who live in shacks on the edge of the city, close to the sonic dumps. These waste containers are filled with noise collected from the residue of sounds that cling to all solid structures. Damaged in childhood, lonely and mute, Mangon is particularly aurally sensitive. He has come to idolise an ageing opera diva, Madame Giaconda, whose career was ruined when a new fashion for ultrasonic music superseded all conventional forms of music making. Though inaudible to the human ear, ultrasonic music is experienced through direct neural connections between sounds and the auditory lobes. 'In the age of noise', Ballard wrote, 'the tranquillizing balms of silence began to be rediscovered.'

Written at a time when consumer capitalism was promising a leisured future for domesticity, with its utopian visions of labour-saving electronic technology, 'The Sound Sweep' overflows with prescient ideas. Ballard anticipates future problems of environmental damage and waste disposal (his vision of the sonic dump reserved for aircraft sounds is particularly prophetic, describing as it does 'the ceaseless mind-sapping roar that hangs like a vast umbrella over any metropolitan complex'), along with the potential crisis for musical professions in an electronic age. In this world of lingering sonic debris and inaudible music, there is rich potential for confusion between externally generated signals and auditory hallucinations. As Mangon sweeps the room of sounds that he knows exist only in Madame Mangon's fantasies, he accepts his complicity in her self-deception: 'Of course the cylinder was always empty, containing only the usual daily detritus — the sounds of a door slam, a partition collapsing somewhere or the kettle whistling, a grunt or two, and later, when the headaches began, Madame Giaconda's pitiful moanings.' Like unshredded bank details carelessly left out in the rubbish, the sonic dumps allow Mangon to eavesdrop on conversations from the past. Hungry for gossip, Madame Giaconda assumes that the air is filled with juicy morsels of compromising conversations, in her egotism failing to realize that Mangon is condemned to hear sonic history in its fragmented, randomized and insalubrious entirety: 'The sounds appeared to come from an apartment over a launderette. A battery of washing machines chuntered to themselves, a cash register slammed interminably, there was a dim almost sub-threshold echo of 60-cycle hum from an SP record-player.' Revisiting Ballard's early work is the eerie equivalent of reading a Nostradamus for the accelerated age of media — fifty years ahead of the event he imagined his own versions of Dubai, the Iraq war, the sinking of the Maldives and many other twenty-first-century phenomena. Similarly, the passage quoted above could be describing the recordings of 1990s German duo Microstoria, whose muffled, dreamy electronica — particularly tracks like 'Sleepy People/Network Down' — pull away from conventional definitions of music, sounding more like documentary recordings of atmospheres heard through the floor of an apartment over an office complex or scientific research facility.

THE SQUEAK OF A FLOORBOARD

When a door creaks or floorboards squeak together, sound enters in uncanny form. Though this may signal a burglary, the fear it engenders differs from the physical shock of confronting an intruder. I had assumed this fear was inextricably linked to human fictions of fright, deep memories of insecurity and invasion fed by our myths and stories. Then I discovered that a dog can exhibit anxious behaviour in a similar situation. This happened as I was waiting in our local vet's reception with our dog, seeing her nervous reaction to a door that slowly opened inward, creaking as it did so like the hammiest Hammer horror. Presumably, in her thinking some sort of threatening creature was about to enter, which is how it is for humans, more or less.

This is not just a job for lubricant. There is a history attached, exemplified by the famous Nightingale Floor still functioning in Nijo Castle, Kyoto. Built around 400 years ago by Tokugawa Ieyasu, the founder of the Japanese Edo shogunate, the floor is artfully designed to betray intruders by the squeaking of its boards against nails concealed underneath. Inspired by this unique architectural feature, and with the success in 2002 of her novel, *Across the Nightingale Floor: Tales of the Otori*, Lian Hearn (a pseudonym for children's author Gillian Rubenstein) has written a series of books in which the supernatural hearing of her central character, Otori Takeo, is both an aid to social progress and a liability: 'I knew I should not listen. It was a whispered conversation that no one could hear but me . . . But my ears had a longing for sound that I could not deny, and every word dropped clearly into them.' The squeaking of Nijo Castle's floor exaggerates and exploits one of the more commonly experienced negative attributes of sound, in which sound itself is a transgressor, passing through those obstacles and partitions that block vision and the passage of solid objects, contain odours and prevent physical contact, to invade private space. Sound can flow from public space into private place or the reverse. Frequently it lacks tangible or verifiable connection to a source, and this capacity to move as apparition into places uninvited, to cross the threshold of private territory, combines with its odourless, colourless, shapeless lack of visibility to be a subject of suspicion, fear and intrigue.

TAP-TAP-TAP

Memories of fear linger, yet there is a pleasure in recalling childhood fears at a remove. Stories written by specialists in horror, haunting and the supernatural, deploy sound and silence as agents, premonitions or signs of the uncanny, those meetings with whatever lies beyond death or the limits of this world. For M. R. James, this was deeply personal. When James lived in rooms above the classics tutor, Nathaniel Wedd, in King's College,

Cambridge, he would feel real horror each night when Wedd knocked out his pipe on the mantelpiece. Even though James knew the benign source of the sound from below, tap-tap-tap, he was convinced there was a ghost in his outer room.

This is curious, that he should be so unnerved in this way as to feel haunted by what he knows is familiar and real. Clearly, James was sensitive to the uncanny atmosphere that may rise unexpectedly out of some trivial incident, a room, or even a landscape. In his story, 'A Neighbour's Landmark', the narrator's curiosity is piqued by the riddle of two lines from a country song — 'That which walks in Betton Wood, knows why it walks or why it cries' — in a letter written by a clergyman. The wood has been stubbed up but he explores the countryside, which seems beautifully idyllic to the point of cliché. 'All at once I turned as if I had been stung', James wrote. 'There thrilled into my right ear and pierced my head a note of incredible sharpness, like the shriek of a bat, only ten times intensified the kind of thing that makes one wonder if something has not given way in one's brain.' All of the complacent images that he expects as a mental corollary of the clock bell striking seven are displaced by dusty beams, creeping spiders, savage owls, forgotten graves and creeping Time. Again, he hears the piercing sound this time in the left ear, and 'close as if lips had been put to within an inch of my head'. He decides that the sound has an external source and thinks of a line from Tennyson: 'With no language but a cry.' The effect of this emotionless scream is to drive him away from a place he later discovers to be the former site of Betton Wood. The story ends inconclusively, the atmosphere of the audible ghost who defines a troubled landscape clearly being of more interest to James than a neat resolution.

The conjecture that sounds can linger in a place for centuries, long after the decomposition of physical bodies, is a theme found in other stories written by James. In 'Canon Alberic's Scrap-book', the bookish, bachelor Englishman typical of this genre visits a French church and hears stories of strange sounds. As he examines the church and its paintings, the faint noises audible all day — muffled footfalls and distant talking voices — intensify, '. . . no doubt because of the fading light and the consequently quickened sense of hearing'. This sonic prelude to a haunting also features in 'Oh, Whistle, and I'll Come to You, My Lad', first published in 1904. Parkins, a Professor of Ontography (a subject that might, if it existed, describe reality), takes a short break on the coast of Suffolk, intending to improve his golf and work in seclusion on his ontographical studies.

Exploring a ruined Templars' church at the behest of a colleague of 'antiquarian pursuits', he pockets a small metal whistle, inscribed with Latin text that he interprets, on first reading, as 'Who is this who is coming?' As a test, he blows the whistle, not only raising a fierce wind, 'moaning and rushing past the house, at times rising to a cry so desolate that, as Parkins disinterestedly said, it might have made fanciful people feel quite uncomfortable', but also invoking the unshakeable mental image of a man pursued by a flickering, ill-defined figure in pale draperies. Amusingly, given the exclusively masculine milieu of James's unworldly dons, the apparition conjured by the whistle first manifests its presence by twisting and crumpling the spare sheets, as if the colleague due to occupy the empty bed in his room had arrived ahead of schedule, in the form of an erotic dream. The following night, as Parkins tries to sleep, he senses a movement in this empty bed: 'Tomorrow he would have it moved, for there must be rats or something playing about in it. It was quiet now. No! the commotion began again. There was a rustling and shaking: surely more than any rat could cause.' The ghost takes the form of crumpled linen, blind yet alert to sound. A 'cry of disgust' betrays Parkins and he almost suffers the ignominious fate of losing his life at the hands of a bed sheet.

A PHONOGRAPHIC GHOST

To hear the noises of another, from concealment or some unseen place, is to be unnerved, at some level to feel shame and desire, to become a body cleaved, split between two places, to become a spy, a voyeur, or more accurately, an eavesdropper. In Sir Arthur Conan Doyle's short story of 1899, 'The Japanned Box', a private tutor named Frank Colmore gains employment at Thorpe Place, the old ancestral home of a melancholy widower named Sir John Bollamore. One night, while the tutor is walking with the governess of Bollamore's daughter, the sound of a voice breaks into their conversation: 'It was a voice — the voice undoubtedly of a woman. It was low — so low that it was only in the still night air that we could have heard it, but, hushed as it was, there was no mistaking its feminine timbre. It spoke hurriedly, gaspingly for a few sentences, and then was silent — a piteous, breathless, imploring sort of voice.' Known as 'Devil' Bollamore for his reputation as a drunken debauchee, gambler and bruiser, Colmore's employer had been 'cured' of decadent intemperance by marriage to

Little Beryl Clare, a woman who then devoted herself to bringing him back to 'manhood and decency'. The silence of this brooding man is now compromised by the disembodied voice, explicable only as an audible sign of his return to debauchery, a ghost, or something more sinister still, an imprisoned woman or some occult manifestation conjured in Bollamore's secret room in the high turret. Suspicion falls upon a black japanned box kept locked in the room.

The nature of the secret is uncovered, quite literally, when the sleepless tutor treats his neuralgia with a dose of chlorodyne (a patent medicine containing laudanum, cannabis and chloroform) while indexing Bollamore's library. Overcome by sleep, he wakes in moonlight to see Bollamore seated at his table, unaware of the tutor's presence. Confused by his drugged state, he watches and listens in horror: 'He bent as I watched him, and I heard the sharp turning of a key and the rasping of metal upon metal. As if in a dream I was vaguely conscious that this was the japanned box which stood in front of him, and that he had drawn something out of it, something squat and uncouth which now lay before him on the table . And then, just as it rushed upon my horrified perceptions, and I had half risen to announce my presence, I heard a strange, crisp, metallic clicking, and then the voice.' All elements of the scene are impressively gothic to the point of parody: the dim radiance of moonlight; chlorodyne visions; hints of devilry, séance and orientalism; harsh metallic noises; the squat shape that suggests the incubus of Fuseli's eighteenth-century painting, *The Nightmare*; a strange rhythmic clicking and then the eerie apparition of a female voice, sounding in space yet lacking any visible form. Out of this hallucinatory melodrama emerges an explanation that is both prosaically rational and remarkable. Within the japanned box is a phonograph, a machine whose uncanny clicking mechanism gives access to the invisible world of the dead; the source of the voice is a phonograph recording of Beryl Clare. While Bollamore's account of his wife gasping a deathbed message into the machine with her last breath is suitably maudlin, the implications are affecting, since the voice is both a haunting and an object of stability, a repeatable reminder that the speaker and hearer will join each other in the afterlife. 'The technology that had at first suggested to the narrator a secret life of vice', writes John M. Picker, in *Victorian Soundscapes*, 'instead ends up facilitating a monotonous pattern of solitary sobriety.'

A SILENT ROOM

This work may have begun in a room, sitting, thinking, listening, writing, reading, dozing, and if so, then the room may have been quiet, and if that were the case, then that quiet room was not just one room, because quiet rooms accumulate throughout life, rooms within rooms within rooms, fragmented rooms of childhood and dreams, sharply defined rooms, now virtual chat rooms and online sites for social networking, all enfolded within unfamiliar rooms barely remembered or selectively forgotten: those rooms of pleasure and dread, action and boredom, safety and danger. Their atmosphere collects as dust, standing in relation to the feeling of being in rooms when something important was at stake: classroom, exam room, bedroom, doctor's surgery, interview room, hospital ward. Clocks once defined the feeling of otherwise silent rooms: clocks ticking, measuring time, slowly, quietly, a presence, an interior atmosphere, dividing time with their chimes, then resuming their steady plod through, what exactly? For those who grew up in the era of audible clocks, time has been measured out by the constancy of their ticking. 'Behind me, on the other side of where I'm lying down, the silence of the house touches infinity', wrote Fernando Pessoa in *The Book of Disquiet*. 'I hear time fall, drop by drop, and not one drop that falls can be heard.' If the clock stopped then the feeling of a room would change, a drama of sudden absence. Virginia Woolf ends a beautiful passage from *Jacob's Room* — the dramatic transformation of a landscape as snow falls, colour, temperature, sound, the dead severity of frozen matter, then light banished as the day goes out — with interior sound, the burden of measuring duration, 'The worn voices of clocks repeated the fact of the hour all night long.'

This occupation of a silent room, regulated and even articulated by a mechanical clock, was not silence at all of course. Tick and tock were paroxysms around which silence gathered, momentarily suspended in the pause of a pendulum at the top of its swing. Clocks, clock chimes and church bells granted people time, by glossing an auditory reality onto its constant but elusive existence. At the same time, time was sacrificed, every new sound subtracting from time remaining. The chimes of Big Ben strike out as a periodic structuring device in Virginia Woolf's *Mrs. Dalloway*: 'There! Out it boomed. First a warning, musical; then the hour, irrevocable. The leaden circles dissolved in the air.' As the stability of its measuring decomposes, each chime joins other sounds of beating whose mark of time is more free, or carefree — cricket bats and the hooves of ponies — and all these sounds are shadowed by a more ominous beating of drums, 'a rustling, regular thudding sound', as young men in uniform marched to war. The novel was written between 1922 and 1924, when memories of the Great War were still vivid, its catastrophic effects apparent. 'The Empire is perishing', Woolf thought, 'the bands are playing; the exhibition is in ruins.'

Even as time ran out, there was plenty of time to listen to all this time, the ticking, chiming and ringing; time's sounding acquired both pleasurable and sinister resonance, fluctuating from moment to moment. Time's immortal click will not stand still, whereas time's biological counterpart, the heartbeat, will eventually stop. As Woolf wrote in *Mrs Dalloway*:

> It is half-past eleven, she says, and the sound of St. Margaret's glides into the recesses of the heart and buries itself in ring after ring of sound, like something alive which wants to confide itself, to disperse itself, to be, with a tremor of delight, at rest . . . It is Clarissa herself, he thought, with a deep emotion, and an extraordinarily clear, yet puzzling recollection of her, as if this bell had come into the room years ago, where they sat at some moment of great intimacy, and had gone from one to the other and had left, like a bee with honey, laden with the moment. . . . Then, as the sound of St. Margaret's languished, he thought, she has been ill, and the sound expressed languor and suffering. It was her heart, he remembered; and the sudden loudness of the final stroke tolled for death that surprised in the midst of life . . .

Georges Rodenbach's late nineteenth-century novel, *Bruges-la-Morte*, was also punctuated by a constancy of bells, sounding out 'the death of the hours'. Rodenbach described the atmosphere of Bruges as an invasive dust — 'the dead ashes of time, the dust from the hourglass of the years' — or mist: 'Towns above all have a personality, a spirit of their own . . . Each town is a state of mind, a mood which, after only a short stay, communicates itself, spreads to us in an effluvium which impregnates us, which we absorb with the very air.' There are intimations of airborne disease here, and the solemn rhythms of bells from antiquity combine with rain, mists, granite and the veiled northern light 'to influence the colour of the air'. Sometimes the bell sounds are pale, far distant; sometimes their sound oozes like sludge: 'The sound of the bells also seems blackish. Muffled, blurred in the air, it arrives as a reverberation which, equally grey, moves along in sluggish, bobbing waves over the waters of the canals.'

Though this sound lives on as metaphor — the ticking of biological clocks and so on — we measure a more silent, precise, urgent version of time with digital clocks, small battery-operated clocks with a tick so fugitive that only paranoid listening in the middle of the night can search it out, and the visual noise but apparent audio silence of numerical displays on TVs, ovens, microwaves, computers and mobile phones. Quiet rooms and the people within them now float within a more continuous and subliminal form of air. All of these devices radiate electromagnetic emissions, so their silence is illusory. With the right inductive equipment, sound materializes, just like the things of the air, thronging H. P. Lovecraft's fiction.

Small sounds are too quick, too slight, to leave any sense of overcrowding air or imposing authority, yet they form wisps into solids, glue fragments into forms, keep people sane, or shield them from loneliness and the void. In *Life: A User's Manual*, Georges Perec wrote about Gaspard Winckler, the craftsman who in old age stared at nothing, his radio playing at such low volume that no one really knew if he could hear it, yet when Madame Nochère went to switch it off, he stopped her. He listened to the hit parade every night. That was his claim. In the Parisian apartment block imagined and meticulously described by Perec, Valène's bedroom is directly above Winckler's workshop, so for nearly forty years, 'his days had been accompanied by the thin noise of the craftsman's tiny files, the almost inaudible throb of his jigsaw, the creaking of his floorboards, the whistling of his kettle when he boiled water, not for making tea but for some glue or glaze he needed for his puzzles.'

BACKGROUND FEELINGS

A sensing of air and the steady existence of the self, what we call background sound or silence, has some relationship perhaps to what neurologist Antonio Damasio called 'background feelings'. 'The background feeling is our image of the body landscape when it is not shaken by emotion', he wrote in *Descartes' Error*. 'I submit that without them the very core of your representation of self would be broken. . . . background feeling is mostly about body states. Our individual identity is anchored on this island of illusory living sameness against which we can be aware of myriad other things that manifestly change around the organism.' In describing these background feelings, Damasio turned to music for an analogy which suits their discreet presence: 'It is not the Verdi of grand emotion, nor the Stravinsky of intellectualized emotion but rather a minimalist in tone and beat, the feeling of life itself, the sense of being.'

On its own, without leavening or levity, Verdi or Stravinsky, air can be too much of nothing. 'Your silence was effortless and windless, like the silence of clouds or plants', wrote Vladimir Nabokov in one of his earliest short stories, 'Sounds'. 'All silence is the recognition of a mystery.' Air in its undisturbed state triggers the hypothesis of silence. The elusive whiteness of the white whale in *Moby Dick* is counterbalanced by Ahab's invisibility at the beginning of the Pequod's voyage. Suddenly, he appears in the sight of his crew and as the ship progresses, takes to spending more and more time on deck, sometimes forgetting the noise made by the impact of another absence, the missing leg replaced by hard ivory, 'the reverberating crack and din of that bony step' that knocks on timber as he patrols the quarter-deck. Below decks is the tomb in prospect, a 'grave-dug berth'; when Stubb suggests a muffling of the ivory heel with a globe of tow, so that the men can sleep at night without their dreams being invaded by sounds like 'the crunching teeth of sharks', Ahab scorns him for his weakness: 'Below to thy nightly grave, where such as ye sleep between shrouds . . . Down, dog and kennel!' For The Cabin-Table section of the book, Melville revives childhood memories (children should be seen and not heard) of what he calls 'awful silence'. At meal times on the Pequod, Captain Ahab eats silently, like a 'mute, maned sea-lion'. Though not forbidden conversation, all the officers defer to his solemnity. Starbuck starts when a knife grazes against a plate, and Stubb, choking in the stilted hush, is relieved to hear a rat clattering in the hold below. This unhappy ritual contrasts with the physicality and gusto of gastronomic pleasures indulged elsewhere on board. 'While their masters, the mates, seemed afraid of the sound of the hinges of their own jaws,' wrote Melville, 'the harpooners chewed their food with such a relish that there was a report to it.' Those who face death and hope to survive dip into life with relish, whereas Ahab, obsessed with destroying the white whale even at the cost of his own life, denies himself pleasure from any form of orality, denies others respite from his aurality.

NIGHT SOUNDING FAST

'I have often thought I could distinctly hear the sound of the darkness as it stole over the horizon', wrote Edgar Allan Poe, in his notes to Part II of 'Al Aaraaf'. In this poem he spoke of passion's echo lingering like the murmur within a shell, darkness arriving with a rush of wings, and the 'sound of silence on the startled ear, / Which dreamy poets name "the music of the sphere."' Peter Ackroyd's biography, *Poe: A Life Cut Short*, is critical of Poe's poems, *Ulalume* and *The Bells*, for their insistence on sound. Poe's own account to journalists in Richmond is quoted — his desire 'to express in language the exact sound of bells to the ears.' He succeeds in his experiment in sound poetry, says Ackroyd, but at the cost of sense 'and perhaps of significance.' But do we read Poe for sense, for logic or probability, or for the thickened, uncanny atmospheres of which he was a master? In 'The Bells', Poe plays the sound of words as an instrument, an incantatory spell whose mellifluous repetition works the same magic as the bells themselves. The sense of what he says lies in the cumulative, associative affect of these sounds, penetrating the body with a direct, instantaneous force that circumvents rationality, stirring emotions of happiness, panic, terror, grief and pagan ecstasy according to the occasion. Ackroyd acknowledges a persistent Anglo-American prejudice against Poe and his 'juvenilia', his 'nonsense', his indefinite pleasures. 'Yet there was something more', he writes. 'There was also his statement that "the origin of Poetry lies in a thirst for a wilder Beauty than Earth supplies," for a "supernal Loveliness", be glimpsed in "the glories beyond the grave"; he is invoking the yearning for something irremediably lost, something missing for ever.'

Enduring fragments, survivors from the obscurity of a brief, tormented life, Poe's stories stir those fears generated by claustration, occult spaces, depths and absolute silence. In 'The Tell-Tale Heart', 'The Pit and the Pendulum', 'The Premature Burial', 'The Fall of the House of Usher' and 'The Narrative of Arthur Gordon Pym of Nantucket', characters are subjected to atmospheres of gloom and hyperacusis, their feeling of loneliness enclosed in webs of malignant, oppressive sound and silence. Spaces possess lives of their own. The beating heart that betrays its own killer, the hollow knocking and shrieking of the prematurely or unjustly incarcerated, suggest that Poe listened with fastidious concentration to all external and interior sounds.

'The Colloquy of Monos and Una' fantasizes a spirit conversation in which sensations of death and decay are described. Specific identities of the senses are randomized, even though still acute. After his breathing stops, Monos hears light as sound: 'The hearing at the same time, although excited in degree, was not irregular in action — estimating real sounds with an extravagance of precision, not less than of sensibility.' Darkness is heard as a continuous moaning sound, like the booming of distant surf, and when lamps are brought into the mourning room, this drone is interrupted by a 'melodious monotone' that trembles as the light flickers. In 'Al Aaraaf', Poe wrote of 'the murmur that springs from the growing of grass' as the music of things. In 'Silence', he described an encounter with a demon who takes him to Libya, a place of living profusion and sonorous abundance. 'And there is no quiet there,' says the demon, 'nor silence.' The narrator is guided through scenes of ecological complexity: rain, mud, sighing water-lilies that murmur like the 'rushing of subterrene water', unquiet shrubbery, the rustling heavens, and hippopotami that roar 'loudly and fearfully beneath the moon.' The teeming, incessantly sounding physicality of nature bears down on him, pitiless and overpowering. He spies on a man who is visibly disgusted with humankind, who longs for solitude, and in his angry reaction to this afflicted figure, condemns everything in this world with a curse of silence. On hearing utter silence fall on nature, the man turns away in terror. The sound of life may be excessive, Poe seems to be saying, yet its absence is intolerable.

This condition is embodied in the person of Roderick Usher, who suffers from 'a morbid acuteness of the senses', forcing him to restrict his environment to a narrow range of sensations: insipid food, no perfumed flowers, clothes only of a certain texture, and only 'peculiar sounds, and these from stringed instruments'. All other stimuli from the normal richness of life inspire him with horror, according to the narrator of 'The Fall of the House of Usher'. Like a Dutch vanitas painting, the house is littered with books and musical instruments, yet they fail to enliven the dismal scene. Usher's 'morbid condition of the auditory nerve' allows him to play only fervid impromptus on a guitar, wild fantasias accompanied by rhymed verbal improvisations. In one of these poems, 'The Haunted Palace', he describes a decayed and ghostly court, reduced to 'vast forms that move fantastically to a discordant melody.' During the narrator's stay in the house, Usher's sister dies. They entomb her in a coffin and leave her in a dungeon vault, waiting for a proper burial. After this, neither of them can rest. Finally, the realization of their crime is signalled by sound: 'I became aware of a distinct, hollow, metallic, and clangorous, yet apparently muffled reverberation.' They have buried her alive. 'Said I not that my senses were acute?' Usher murmurs. 'I now tell you that I heard her first feeble movements in the hollow coffin. I heard them — many, many days ago — yet I dared not speak.'

Poe returns obsessively to burial, both actual and metaphorical, where eyes are powerless in resonant, slippery, pungently decaying darkness. 'The Pit and the Pendulum' describes burial as a thought that steals into the narrator's mind, 'like a rich musical note'. In the novel *The Narrative of Arthur Gordon Pym of Nantucket*, the false narrator constructed by Poe tells of his incarceration in the hold of a ship, isolated and near to death from poisoning, starvation and dehydration, and moving through dangerous spaces in pitch darkness. Only sound can guide him and his rescuer to the same point in sightless space: the crash of a bottle on the floor, slight movements that grow less distinct, then again less so, and still less, then the speaking of his name. 'As I fell,' he says, 'the carving knife was shaken out from the waistband of my pantaloons, and dropped with a rattling sound to the floor. Never did the strain of the richest melody come so sweetly to my ears.' Poe's air, a toxic anti-air, is not transparent nothingness. As the story progresses, it accumulates a texture of compacted charcoal, pitch, coal dust, soot, liquorice, ash, ink wash, pencil shading, sump oil, volcanic sand, all mixed with ditch water and black bile then poured to capacity into restrictive volumes.

Listening through the impenetrable muck of such darkness carries its own dangers of delusion and reprisal. Set on board a packet ship bound for New York, 'The Oblong Box' is a story in which the dubious morality of eavesdropping comes to exact an auditory revenge. Beginning the story in a moody, inquisitive frame of mind, the narrator is curious about the arrangement of state rooms on the ship and the contents of an oblong box stored in the rooms of an artist who shares the journey. This, he believes, contains a copy of Leonardo's *Last Supper*. Again, the air is toxic. The tar used for lettering on the box gives off a disagreeable and 'peculiarly disgusting odor.' Kept awake by strong green tea and his curiosity, the narrator is attracted by 'cautious, subdued' sounds from the next room. Listening with thoughtful intention, he succeeds in mapping these sounds into spatially exact visual images and actions. The artist is prying open the oblong box with a chisel and mallet, he realizes, 'the latter being apparently muffled, or deadened, by some soft woollen or cotton substance in which its head was enveloped.' His listening intensifies:

In this manner I fancied I could distinguish the precise moment when he fairly disengaged the lid — also, that I could determine when he removed it altogether, and when he deposited it upon the lower berth in his room; this latter point I knew, for example, by certain slight taps which the lid made in striking against the wooden edges of the berth, as he endeavoured to lay it down very gently — there being no room for it on the floor. After this there was a dead stillness, and I heard nothing more, upon either occasion, until nearly daybreak; unless perhaps, I may mention a low sobbing, or murmuring sound, so very much suppressed as to be nearly inaudible — if, indeed, the whole of this latter noise were not rather produced by my own imagination. I say it seemed to resemble sobbing or sighing — but, of course, it could not have been either. I rather think it was a ringing in my own ears.

He ascribes this indeterminate sound to the distempering effects of green tea — a reminder of Sheridan Le Fanu's story, 'Green Tea', in which the hallucinating tea drinker sits in a darkening room, in uncanny silence: 'The stillness, too, was utter; not a distant wheel, or bark, or whistle from without; and within, the depressing stillness of an invalid bachelor's house.'

Later, as the ship founders in a storm, the artist ropes himself to the box and plunges into the sea. Man and box sink beneath the waves, where they will stay, says the captain, until the salt melts. As the shape of the box suggests, the artist has been travelling with the embalmed corpse of his recently deceased wife, packed in salt and disguised as merchandise. Despite the precision of his listening, the narrator realizes his inquisitive temperament has led him to intrude on the morbid rites of a very private grief, only to draw mistaken conclusions from auditory signs. Too open to interpretation, those sounds he failed to identify return in a melodramatic version of tinnitus, an appropriate chastisement for an eavesdropper: 'But of late, it is a rare thing that I sleep soundly at night. There is a countenance which haunts me, turn as I will. There is an hysterical laugh which will for ever ring in my ears.'

The most remarkable of Poe's microauditory stories is 'The Tell-Tale Heart', first published in Boston in 1843. Succinct and mysterious, it retains a sinister power. In late 2008, 'The Tell-Tale Heart' was cited (by inference, implicated) in the case of Robert Napper, a British serial rapist and murderer, who was said to be so deeply affected when he heard 'The Tell-Tale Heart' read aloud at school that he was thought to be suffering a seizure. 'Remember the story of the beating heart?' wrote one newspaper journalist at the end of a prolonged description of one of Napper's most disturbingly violent crimes.

Much of Poe's work was addressed directly to the reader through a narrator, but 'The Tell-Tale Heart' begins by interrupting a conversation or confession, either between the perpetrator and himself (or herself), or with an unnamed listener. Again, a neurotic condition of 'nerves', of exaggerated acuity, establishes a context of microsonic hearing: 'Above all was the sense of hearing acute. I heard many things in the heaven and in the earth. I heard many things in hell. How then am I mad?' For reasons unknown to himself, the narrator has decided that the old man who shares his dwelling must be killed. His eye has settled the issue, 'the eye of a vulture', and so this prelude to murder progresses in silence by degrees of time and darkness 'black as pitch', its object revealed to vision by a dark lantern whose thin ray of light is released cautiously each night for seven nights, each night falling on the closed eye of the old man. On the eighth night, moving with painful slowness in the thick darkness, the perpetrator chuckles. The old man moves on his bed. The narrator's thumb slips on the tin fastening of the lantern and the old man springs up in bed, crying out, 'Who's there?' For one hour the murderer stands motionless, saying nothing, conscious that the old man is still alert, sitting up, listening, 'just as I have done, night after night, hearkening to the death watches in the wall.' Then a slight groan of terror, 'the low stifled sound that arises from the bottom of the soul when overcharged with awe', and the narrator knows that that the old man has been listening since that first slight sound: 'His fears had been ever since growing upon him. He had been trying to fancy them causeless, but could not. He had been saying to himself — "It is nothing but the wind in the chimney — it is only a mouse crossing the floor," or "it is merely a cricket which has made a single chirp." Yes, he had been trying to comfort himself with these suppositions: but he had found all in vain.'

He opens the lantern, shines it onto the eye, then hears 'a low, dull, quick sound, such as a watch makes when enveloped in cotton.' The pulse grows louder, faster, the thud of the old man's heart, increasing his fury, 'as the beating of a drum stimulates the soldier into courage.' As if a steady crescendo within the silent dark, the pulsations grow louder still, loud enough for a neighbour to hear; the murderer shouts, the old man shrieks and is suffocated. Even after his death, the heart pumps on with a muffled beat, then like a decaying echo of sound haunting its original self, gradually fades until sunk into silence. He dismembers the corpse and buries it under the floorboards. At four o'clock in the morning, there is knocking at the door, policemen investigating reports of a suspicious noise. The murderer greets them with confidence, shows them the house, seats them exactly over the spot where the old man's remains have been hidden, but as time passes, he begins to hear a ringing in his ears. Throughout the story, the narrator has meticulously drawn a distinction between madness and the hypersensitivity to external sounds that he claims to suffer. Now the question of what is generated from within or without reaches a point of crisis: 'I found that the noise was not within my ears.' What he hears is the 'low, dull, quick sound — much such a sound as a watch makes when enveloped in cotton', increasing and increasing, too insistent to mask by pacing across the floorboards, raving and swearing, or scraping his chair. In the end he admits his crime, no longer able to tolerate the return of the sound he sought to still: the beating of the old man's hideous heart.

THE PAGES WILL TURN SILENTLY

John E. Reilly's essay, 'The Lesser Death-Watch and "The Tell-Tale Heart"', first published in *The American Transcendental Quarterly* in 1969 (later revised for the website of the Edgar Allan Poe Society of Baltimore), attempts to resolve the mysterious presence of fluctuating sounds in Poe's story. He proposes a rational interpretation based on clues buried within the text. Like the narrator with his thin beam of light, Reilly focuses on a single passing remark: the description of the terrified old man bolt upright in bed, listening just as the narrator had listened night after night, hearing death watches in the wall. These death-watch beetles, he suggests, are the source of the heartbeat heard by the narrator, even distinguishing between the greater death-watch, which raps its head on whatever surface it stands on, and the lesser death-watch, which makes a faint ticking sound with its stridulatory organs. Reilly documents superstitions associated with the ticking sound of the death-watch, said to predict a death in the family within the house infested by the insects. He quotes from John Keats, whose 'Ode to Melancholy' warns against the influence of death-watch beetles and other natural associations of melancholy: 'Make not your rosary of yew-berries, / Nor let the beetle, nor the death-moth be / Your mournful Psyche'. Other death-watch references include Mark Twain's *Tom Sawyer*, who listens to scarcely perceptible noises emphasising themselves in the stillness of night, particularly the 'ghastly ticking of a death-watch in the wall at the bed's head', which made Tom shudder because 'it meant that somebody's days were numbered', and Henry David Thoreau's 'A Natural History of Massachusetts', published, Reilly conjectures, shortly before Poe wrote 'The Tell-Tale Heart'. 'Nor can all the vanities that vex the world alter one whit the measure that night has chosen,' wrote Thoreau. 'Every pulse-beat is in exact time with the cricket's chant and the tickings of the death-watch in the wall. Alternate with these if you can.'

Reilly situates Poe's depiction of the narrator's hyperacusis within early nineteenth-century theories of psychopathological disorders, quoting Joseph Mason Cox's *Practical Observations on Insanity* of 1811, which listed among the symptoms of approaching insanity, 'listening to fancied whispers or obscure noises.' If we assume this significance of the lesser death-watch beetle in Poe's story to be plausible, then Reilly's conclusion adds even greater moral and allegorical depth to a highly suggestive narrative. 'Much of Poe's fiction and poetry participates in the romantic complaint against Time,' he writes, 'the lament that the spirit of man is the victim of corruption and death. In 'The Tell-Tale Heart', the innocuous sound of an insect becomes a measure of time under the aspect of death, a kind of metaphor binding together three tokens of man's mortality: the process of nature, the beating of the human heart, and the ticking of a watch. And it is the agony of Poe's deranged and superstitious narrator to have hearkened to the sound, to have been driven to homicidal frenzy by a metaphor.'

Poe's inventions of those fictional forms we now categorize within the established genres of mystery, science-fiction, horror and the macabre were based originally on his prophetic insights into the psychology of perception, the symptoms of psychopathology, and the limitless scope of the imagination. His listeners unravel in the intensity of their own listening. They move through a world of indecipherable sound, lost in the psychological complexities of inner voices cohabiting with those sounds too faint and ambiguous to belong in the material world. Are they bodies invaded by external sounds, or does their neurasthenic listening break through into auditory territories that lie beyond normal perception? Marcel Proust described sound as an aggressive, colonising force; an invader. A lengthy contemplation of sonic properties in *The Guermantes Way* begins with the uncertainty of hearing sounds without visible confirmation of their source. He stops outside a closed door, hears movement inside. Something moved, something dropped: 'I could feel that the room was not empty, that there was someone in it. But it was merely the recently lighted fire burning away. It could not keep quiet . . . And even when it was still, as common people do, it made constant noises, which from the moment I saw the flames rising, revealed themselves as the noises that come from a fire, whereas if I had been on the other side of the wall I should have thought that they came from someone who was blowing his nose and walking about.'

In the same passage, Proust wrote of a sick man with plugged ears, reading in a silence so profound that the pages of his book seemed to be turned by the fingers of a god: 'The withdrawal of sound, its dilution, robs it of any aggressive power it may have over us . . . we play games of patience with cards we cannot hear, so much so that we imagine we have not shuffled them, that they are moving of their own accord and, anticipating our desire to play with them, have begun to play with us.' For Proust, sound is necessary for a full understanding of reality. From the intimate connection of hearing with seeing, we interpret the meaning of events. Sound is a source of regret, and of beauty, and yet the elimination of that beauty reveals another beautiful world hidden behind its screen, an Eden in which sound has not yet been created: 'Since sound was for him, before his deafness, the perceptible form which the cause of movement assumed, objects moved now without sound seem to be moved without cause; stripped of all qualities of sound, they display a spontaneous activity, they seem to be alive; they move, remain static, burst into flames of their own accord.'

For a small child, sensitive to the shifting tides of consciousness and open to possibilities of supernatural meddling, sickness and fever can exacerbate this suspicion that sound in its unpredictable states of flux and disproportionate affect is an invisible finger reaching out from an extra-human world. The fire settles and dies, roaring heat exhausted, falling slowly into darkness, fading warmth and the whispers of soft ash. Sensual tremors — the logs shifting in the fireplace — are perceived as ghosting borders, flickers around the edges of solid experience, alive in the language of poets though elsewhere largely unnoticed: the silent white world of Samuel Beckett's play, *Embers*, in which only the dying fire is heard in a silent house: '(*Pause.*) Embers. (*Pause.*) Shifting, lapsing, furtive like, dreadful sound . . . white world, great trouble, not a sound, only the embers, sound of dying, dying glow'; and Fernando Pessoa: 'Silence emerges from the sound of the rain and spreads in a crescendo of grey monotony over the narrow street I contemplate'; and Tom Raworth: 'hearing the paper hearing the sound of the pen / like a séance: i will dictate these words'.

THE LISTENER

Closer to thoughts, emotions, memories and fleeting, peripheral sensations than to tangible objects and reassurances of the known world, sound slips into the territory of the mind to settle at unknown depths, to stir up intimations of other futures. For certain writers of supernatural fiction, this capacity to broach bodily defences begins by unsettling beliefs. The listener's sense of self is destabilized in the initial stages of a transition from materialism and rationalism to the world of ghosts, spirits and demons. Along with other late nineteenth-century writers and artists who were interested in esoteric philosophies — Arthur Machen, Dion Fortune, William Thomas Horton, Evelyn Underhill, Charles Williams, Sax Rohmer and W. B. Yeats — Algernon Blackwood was involved briefly with The Hermetic Order of the Golden Dawn, a Victorian-era occult group notorious for its internal struggle for control between one of the founder members, Samuel Liddel MacGregor Mathers, and his former acolyte, Aleister Crowley.

Born into a strictly Christian family and educated by the Moravian Brotherhood in Germany, Blackwood began his career as a writer when living in poverty in a New York boarding house. His best stories were set either in baleful rooms within haunted houses, or in wilderness, where the spirits of nature reveal themselves to those who underestimate its forms. His rooms and houses are refuges, yet they symbolize the debilitating effects of contemporary urban life. Whatever plot device explains to the reader the cause of a haunting, Blackwood leaves an underlying impression that civilization's toxins are the real source of malign psychic phenomena.

First published in 1906, 'A Case of Eavesdropping' describes events in the life of Shorthouse, a man who succeeds in drawing himself into 'the atmosphere of peculiar circumstances and strange happenings.' As is customary in these domiciliary hauntings, he takes lodgings which suit a low income and irregular habits, a set of conditions which offers only the most dismal, isolated dwellings. 'A cheap hole', to use Blackwood's description. Overhearing a noisy conversation between two German speakers in the adjacent room to his own, he finds himself overcome by lassitude, a sense of dreaminess in the head, a withdrawal of vitality yet simultaneously a sharpening of his senses. As he listens he hears a sequence of actions, an argument, then what can only be a murder. In a material equivalent of the sonic intrusion into his room, a thick, sluggish worm of blood advances toward him across the floor. When he breaks in to the room next door, he finds nothing but black, cold, silent, empty space. In another story, 'The Empty House', Blackwood dealt explicitly with the fear that can emanate from listening and silence. 'Inside the house the silence became awful', he wrote. 'Awful, he thought, because any minute now it might be broken by sounds pretending terror . . . he heard the blood singing in his veins. It sometimes seemed so loud that he fancied it prevented his hearing properly other sounds that were beginning very faintly to make themselves audible in the depths of the house. Every time he fastened his attention on these sounds, they instantly ceased.'

Of all the interior stories, 'The Listener' is the most detailed in its exploitation of those ambiguities lying between excessive sensitivities of sensory perception, a vivid imagination and the prospect of a recurring history, a haunting of susceptible spaces and vulnerable subjects. Following the form of the narrator's diary, the story records his physical and mental decline, caused largely by inexplicable sounds. They originate in darkness, from the wind and its tricks: 'Down this funnel the wind dropped, and puffed and shouted. Such noises I never heard before.' Not only troubled by unfamiliar sounds, the narrator is irritated by noises of more mundane origin. The landlady's little boy plays in the alley, dragging his broken wooden cart over the cobbles. Between noise and silence there is no settled, median condition. 'These rooms are very quiet,' Blackwood wrote, 'almost too quiet sometimes. On windless nights they are silent as the grave, and the house might be miles in the country. The roar of London's traffic reaches me only in heavy, distant vibrations. It holds an ominous note sometimes, like that of an approaching army, or an immense tidal-wave very far away thundering in the night.' He begins to suffer what we might call paranoid delusions: he experiences violent thoughts, 'as if the words were not my own, but had been spoken into my ear'; in the night he wakes in the darkness 'with the impression that someone was standing outside my bedroom door listening.' He senses that people are staring at him, catches himself looking into mirrors, begins to catch sight of another man, to smell a fetid odour. Gradually the listener of the story is doubled, materialising as a previous occupant of the house. In an infinite recession of sounding and hearing, listener listens to listener. All of these stories are flawed, in the sense that their denouement cuts through the carefully constructed atmospheres, grounding the unimaginable in a melodramatic history of murder, suicide, cruelty, disease, or, more simply, the pain of loss. The depressing reality of a ghost, summoned back from the spirit world for endless revivals of an insalubrious past, is far less chilling than the mysterious first signs of spectral intervention into the territory of corporeal space.

Significantly, given his obsession with auditory atmospheres, Blackwood wrote six stories featuring a 'psychic detective' named Dr John Silence. In the first of his cases, 'A Psychical Invasion', Silence is consulted by a woman seeking help for Felix Pender, a young writer of humorous stories. Pender still writes but his livelihood is threatened by a failure of the humour that made his success. Something in the house has 'prevented his feeling funny.' Pender has experimented with unadulterated liquid tincture of Cannabis indica. Taken over by uncontrollable laughter, then dark visions of an intruder, he finds that whatever he writes after this experiment is full of sinister amusement, innuendo and 'horror disguised as merriment'. From the second dose of cannabis, taken three nights later, he experiences synaesthesia: 'Those red bindings I heard in deep sounds, and the yellow covers of the French bindings next to them made a shrill, piercing note not unlike the chattering of starlings.'

According to the doctor's diagnosis, the cannabis has heightened Pender's senses (this was 1908). Quickening his responses to 'an increased rate of vibration', hypersensitivity has opened him up to what Silence describes as psychical invasion by a 'singular class of Invisible' from the Outer World. He sends the writer and his wife away to another house and mounts a nocturnal vigil, accompanied by two animals — his dog and cat — in order to flush out this invader. Gradually, fog fills the room in which he sits; a silence descends upon the room: 'Only the breathing of the dog upon the mat came through the deep stillness, like the pulse of time marking the minutes; and the steady drip, drip of the fog outside upon the window-ledges dismally testified to the inclemency of the night beyond.' Like Beckett's embers, the sinking of the fire is a decrescendo of faint sounds, ushering in deeper and deeper levels of silence, until the house feels entirely shrouded from the outside world. Most of what transpires when the spirit arrives is enacted by the animals, more sensitive to invisible forces, as they confront what is perceived by Dr Silence as a tangible nothingness. Blackwood's personal conviction — that phenomena we name as supernatural are simply revelations of ubiquitous natural energies — are expressed here. Perhaps he drew upon his exposure to the rituals of the Golden Dawn to describe Silence raising his voice to impose harmony and order on what is termed (using the eighteenth-century meaning of enchantment or charm) 'the glamour': 'In a deep modulated voice he began to utter certain rhythmical sounds that slowly rolled through the air like a rising sea, filling the room with powerful vibratory activities that whelmed all irregularities of lesser vibrations in its own swelling tone.' The dog survives, but is blinded by the struggle.

Blackwood's deeply felt belief in what might be described as an animist philosophy is what brings intensity and conviction to his wilderness stories: 'The Willows', 'The Wendigo' and 'The Camp of the Dog'. The sensitivity of description reveals his own deep listening. 'A wall of silence wrapped them in,' he wrote in 'The Wendigo', 'for the snow, though not thick, was sufficient to deaden any noise, and the frost held things pretty tight besides. No sound but their voices and the soft roar of the flames made itself felt. Only, from time to time, something soft as the flutter of a pine-moth's wings went past them through the air.' Blackwood was known to his friends as Pan; his story, 'The Touch of Pan', contrasts the pagan enchantment latent in sentient nature with what Blackwood perceived to be the immorality and self-indulgence of modernity. 'For a wind passed through the branches with a sound that is the oldest in the world and so the youngest', he wrote. 'Above it there rose the shrill, faint piping of a little reed . . .' For the romantic imagination, the sound of wind is the perfect expression of remorseless nature, a timeless world whose energies are beyond the transience and artificiality of human affairs. In 'The Willows', Blackwood transforms an ordinary adventure, two companions paddling along the Hungarian Danube in a Canadian canoe, into a vivid conjuration of place. 'I watched the whispering willows', says the narrator. 'I heard the ceaseless beating of the tireless wind; and one and all, each in its own way, stirred in me this sensation of a strange distress. But the willows especially: for ever they went on chattering and talking among themselves, laughing a little, shrilly crying out, sometimes sighing — but what it was they made so much to do about belonged to the secret life of the great plain they inhabited.'

SIGHS FROM THE DEPTHS

Thomas De Quincey's *Suspiria de Profundis* (sighs from the depths), was first published in 1845 as a sequel to his more celebrated *Confessions of an*

English Opium-Eater. Recounting feelings connected with the death of his sister, De Quincey describes the sound of a mournful wind: 'Mournful! That is saying nothing It was a wind that had swept the fields of mortality for a hundred centuries. Many times since, upon a summer day, when the sun is about the hottest, I have remarked the same wind arising and uttering the same hollow, solemn, Memnonian, but saintly swell: it is in this world the one sole audible symbol of eternity.' A trance fell upon him, whenever he heard the sound he called 'this vast Aeolian intonation'. De Quincey alludes to the Colossi of Memnon, the two huge statues erected to guard the mortuary temple of Pharaoh Amenhotep III, sited on the West Bank at Luxor. Constructed in the fourteenth century BC, the temple's collapse in an earthquake in 27 BC ran a fissure through one of the statues. From this point until its repair, the statue would emit a sound every morning at dawn, a 'singing' that led to the myth of Memnonian oracular powers.

Such sounds — howling wind, ghostly echoes, the moaning, whistling and rumbling of meteorological phenomena and geological formations — reverberate through myth, religions and the arts, symbolising the inchoate beginnings of existence, a time before the evolution of our animal selves, before the massing of coherent forms. Like Pan's flute, their uncanny, edgeless tones insinuate themselves into otherwise ordered lives as omens, disruptions, reminders that despite sciences and social mores, some aspects of life remain unknowable. In 2008, a BBC television adaptation of Thomas Hardy's *Tess of the D'Urbervilles* demonstrated a contemporary inability to understand the significance of such auditory metaphors. In the televized version, Tess and Angel Clare wander into Stonehenge in broad daylight, Tess draping herself tragically on one of the stones shortly before the police arrive to arrest her for murder. In the book, they stumble into the stone circle at night, unaware of what they have found but overwhelmed by its sudden massive presence within the landscape:

'It hums,' said she. 'Hearken!'
He listened. The wind playing upon the edifice, produced a booming tune, like the note of some gigantic one-stringed harp . . .
'A very Temple of the Winds,' he said.

Sound matters in Thomas Hardy's novels because critical moments of narrative turn upon what is left unsaid: the repressions, evasions and missed opportunities for openness that so often prove excruciating to a modern reader. What should be spoken is left silent, cannot be voiced, or by accident, is overlooked. The misunderstandings that follow invariably blossom into grim tragedies. At the climax of *Tess of the D'Urbervilles*, Tess and Angel emerge out of darkness into the humming drone of Stonehenge. They stay and listen 'to the wind among the pillars', like two pagans momentarily isolated from the strictures of the world. As light comes with the dawn so society returns. The romantic idea of Stonehenge as a 'heathen temple', and the uncanny natural wildness of the sounds produced by aeolian harps combine to haunting effect, echoing Coleridge's poem of 1795, 'The Eolian Harp', in which the sound of the harp floats softly as a spell, 'a soft floating witchery of sound / As twilight Elfins make . . .' In a passage from one of his John Silence stories, 'Ancient Sorceries', Algernon Blackwood's narrator recounts a story of hearing bewitching music that makes him think of 'trees swept by the wind, of night breezes singing among wires and chimney-stacks, or in the rigging of invisible ships.' Despite the odd intervals and discords of half-broken instruments, he is charmed. 'He recognized nothing that they played, and it sounded as though they were simply improvising without a conductor. No definitely marked time ran through the pieces, which ended and began oddly after the fashion of wind through an Aeolian harp.' These were still powerful ideas in the late nineteenth and early twentieth century. To ignore them not only misses the drama of Hardy's scene, but loses the contrast between this eerie sounding of stones in the landscape and the disastrous calcifying silences of the past.

Disturbing a moment of silences and mutters, 'all lost in thought' in Chekhov's *The Cherry Orchard*, a distant sound is heard, 'as if from the sky: the sound of a breaking string — dying away, sad.' What was that? asks Ranyevskaya. 'I don't know', Lopakhin answers. 'Somewhere a long way off, in the mines, a winding cable has parted. But a long, long way off.' The others speculate; perhaps a heron or some kind of owl? Ranyevskaya shivers. 'Horrible', she says. 'I don't know why.'

Shingo, the sixty-two-year-old man at the centre of Yasunari Kawabata's *The Sound of the Mountain*, listens to the rasping screech of locusts in his Kamakura garden, wonders if they are troubled with nightmares, thinks he can detect the dripping of dew from leaf to leaf, then hears the sound of the mountain, like wind, faraway, but with depth, like a rumbling of the earth. He questions his own perception: could it be the wind, the sea, or within himself, a ringing in his ears? No, it was the mountain: 'It was if a demon had passed, making the mountain sound out . . . He did not wake his wife to tell her of the fear that had come over him on hearing the sound of the mountain.' Later, Shingo is shocked to be reminded of a previous occasion when the mountain roared, shortly before the death of his sister-in-law. Again, like the death-watch beetle, the calls of the little owl, or Lady Macbeth hearing the hoot of an owl that shrieked, 'the fatal bellman which gives the stern'st good night', these uncanny sounds are unsettling enough to portend impending death.

In *A Passage To India*, E. M. Forster wrote about interiors, the way in which no Indian animal had any respect for an interior, as soon nesting inside a house as out. Later, during a visit to the Marabar Caves twenty miles from Chandrapore, two English women who wish to see 'the real India' are affected by the echo of the cave. One of them experiences the echo as 'terrifying', whereas Professor Godbole, a Hindu, hears only a monotonous 'boum': 'Hope, politeness, the blowing of a nose, the squeak of a boot, all produce "boum". Even the striking of a match starts a little worm coiling, which is too small to complete a circle, but is eternally watchful. And if several people talk at once an overlapping howling noise begins, echoes generate echoes, and the cave is stuffed with a snake composed of small snakes, which writhe independently.' And yet, like the bat or wasp who builds a nest inside a house, the echo within the cave threatens to dissolve the fragile boundaries between the outwardly regulated, social-ized, de-sexualized body and some deeper intuition of the self: '. . . the echo began in some indescribable way to undermine her hold on life.' As the scandal of the story breaks, the possibility that a young Muslim doctor has in some way assaulted the younger of the two women, the echo is implicated as an accessory to the crime:

'There was an echo that appears to have frightened her. Did you go into those caves?'
'I saw one of them. There was an echo. Did it get on her nerves?'

Whether writing critically of sexual repression, social conformity or the institutional racism of the British in India, Forster returned often to these mysterious sounds, their metaphorical power contrasting vividly with the fraught complacency of his subjects and their nerves. Sound performs upon the social and physiological body as a subversive element, a Janus-faced agent of invasive disruption and vital force. 'From the new campanile there burst a flood of sound to which the copper vessels vibrated responsively', he wrote in 'The Eternal Moment'. 'Miss Raby lifted her hands, not to her ears but to her eyes. In her enfeebled state, the throbbing note of the bell had the curious effect of blood returning into frozen veins.' In *Chaos, Territory, Art*, Elizabeth Grosz builds upon a theme of Deleuze and Guattari: architecture and all arts that follow it are linked to birdsong and other territorial displays that define space in the natural world. Art is a practice of sensations, intensities and affects derived from chaos and framing chaos to become territory. The body shields itself from chaos, 'in habit, cliché and doxa', as a way of containing sensations to render them predictable. 'I hope to understand music as a becoming,' she writes, 'the becoming-other of cosmic chaotic forces that link the lived, sexually specific body to the forces of the earth.'

Air in motion, resistant to containment and the architectural impulses of humans, epitomizes the human sense of what is unheimlich. As Charles Dickens suggested in *The Chimes*, ghost stories work their magic when the reader is settled by a fire within the security of home, a cold wind whistling in darkness outside as an audible reminder of unknown night. In the 1939 film of *The Wizard of Oz*, a deafening wind twists through the landscape, drowning out speech and destroying human dwellings. Dorothy and her dog Toto are hurled out of sepia Kansas into the Technicolor dream world of Oz. After a series of ordeals in which she defeats the forces of darkness (including strange flying monkeys whose flight is heard as an eerie aeolian wail) she wakes up back in bed in Kansas. Her final words of the film are: 'There's no place like home.'

For author John Cowper Powys, the wind was an unknowable breath, playing upon trees as if they were instruments fixed into landscape for that purpose. In a passage of sustained power in *A Glastonbury Romance*, published in 1933, he described the sound as a 'portentous requiem', a choir whose orchestration is familiar enough to be connected to human music, yet vast and alien, the sound of mythic beings for whom Cowper Powys experienced the nostalgia of a passing world:

> And then Cordelia, gazing directly into the wide-flung branches of the biggest of the two giant trees, was aware of something else upon the wind. Those enormous branches seemed to have begun an orchestral monotone, composed of the notes of many instruments gathered up into one. It was a cumulative and rustling sigh that came to the woman's ears, as if a group of sorrowful Titans had lifted their united voices in one lamentable dirge over the downfall of their race.

PART IV

Interior Resonance

10 Snow falling on snow (fragments in a history of not-listening)

Excited as he was by tempestuous phenomena, John Cowper Powys showed an equal appreciation for fugitive sounds barely perceptible to human senses, as intangible as Marcel Duchamp's concept of the infra-slim. 'The words were almost as faint as the sub-human breathings of the plants in the conservatory', Powys wrote in *A Glastonbury Romance*. 'They were like the creakings of chairs after people have left a room for hours. They were like the open and shutting of a door in an empty house. They were like the groan of a dead branch in an unfrequented shrubbery at the edge of a forsaken garden. They were like the whistle of the wind in a ruined clock-tower, a clock-tower without bell or balustrade, bare to the rainy sky, white with the droppings of jackdaws and starlings, forgetful of its past, without a future save that of anonymous dissolution.' Of the many epiphanies of sensation and their fusion of eroticism, masochism, pagan mysticism, neurosis, personalized mythology, and natural sensitivity that teem within Powys's 1929 novel, *Wolf Solent*, one of the most haunting images is of silence descending like a great bird of death: 'After he had rung the bell he was struck by the curious silence that always falls down on the thresholds of houses, like the feathers of some vast overshadowing bird when house bells are rung.' The author enjoys this deathly avian shadowing so much that he writes two versions (admittedly separated by more than four hundred pages): '. . . and silence seemed to fall down upon that place like large grey feathers from some inaccessible height.' For Powys, any environment, sacramental, excremental or exalted, was potentiality: a place in which mundane perceptions might become sufficiently intense to dissolve the familiar boundaries of experience: 'This was what he wanted to cry out; but he did not dare to utter a whisper. The room had become enchanted. It was a dedicated place — set apart.'

All silences are uncanny, because we have become estranged from absences of sound. An uncanny silence falls when it envelops or drifts down into a sounding world, like snowfall muting an otherwise noisy city, as if the presence of nothing can soak up noise, a white blotter that retains its whiteness no matter how much ink is absorbed. Then silence is heard more clearly, like fog, through whatever faint shapes can be discerned within. No silence out there; no silence in here either; though there are many species of silence.

There is a private silence, the drift of consciousness that murmurs at the edges of awareness. If I listen in to this drift, I hear what I may choose to conceal from others, perhaps even from myself. Lying on the floor, on my back, eyes closed and empty-minded though trying to dispel a headache, I fall into a drift of hypnagogic narrative that is suddenly wiped away by the intrusion of a single voice, saying (no, not saying, because saying demands a speaker, an activation), so an audible emanation, then, whose words are: 'Go to Toop'. Any connection between this cryptic instruction and the narrative is impossible to trace, because the voice clears out all that came before it. I lie there, hearing the high frequency fizzing of my ears, a stomach gurgle, little else. Though hard to place, the voice is not a complete stranger to me. A constant, familiar flow of thought, the so-called inner dialogue that disciplines such as meditation seek to quiet, is not heard so much as felt — a complex of emanations — whereas this 'other' voice is always heard, as if through a miniature radio buried within the black emptiness that corresponds spatially to the volume of my brain. 'David', it says, or to be more accurate, she says, because the voice is always female. The tonal quality is familiar; a composite, I would say, of certain women who have been significant to me, now absent in different ways. If I were mystical, mad or religious, a spiritualist, or believed unequivocally in an afterlife, then the presence of the voice would be quite logical.

But I am not mystical, mad, religious, or a spiritualist, nor am I persuaded by heaven or hell except as metaphors and symbols, so the voice is not logical or easily explicable. What it seems to be is a clear memory, a revisitation so vivid that its clarity separates it from thoughts I identify as my own. No ears are involved; the voice utters distinctly in a void, a small yet infinite place between the ears giving me some indication of what it might be like to hear the voice of god, demonic voices, malicious voices, voices instructing me to kill, and any other incidents of internal speech that may or may not be auditory hallucinations. 'Daddy, I hear the voices again, waaagh, s-s-s-s-sss, I even hear the foot-tracks,' sang Screamin' Jay Hawkins on his 1962 recording of 'I Hear Voices'. There is no single silence; there is no one voice. That entreaty to Daddy (a Daddy now beyond the grave, we presume) is revealing. Can the absent father salvage the collapsing identity under attack by unravelling this tangle of voices, by differentiating this confusion of senses?

STUCK IN THE MIDDLE WITH YOU

In the late 1960s, the Secretary of the British Board of Film Censors, John Trevelyan, gave a public lecture in London. Held in a prestigious venue, the event was quite an occasion, and as far as I can recall he discussed the limits of censorship and the ways in which those limits were flaunted and so pushed further into previously taboo areas by filmmakers. To illustrate his point, Trevelyan showed short clips from films that would never be shown uncut in the UK (or so he believed at the time). One of them, disturbing in its violent misogyny though far less gory than a twenty-first-century horror comedy like *Shaun of the Dead*, was Japanese. In the clip, a woman lies in the bath. A man walks into the bathroom, stands behind her and slashes off her ear with a cutthroat razor.

Maybe the ear (and I am speaking generally here, rather than in reference to brutalized women in Japanese cinema) asks to be cut off, in the way that the design of the nose asks Roman Polanski in *Chinatown* to stick his knife up into Jack Nicholson's nostril and slash sideways. Perhaps that sudden severing influenced Michael Madsen's notorious ear amputation scene in Quentin Tarantino's *Reservoir Dogs* (Tarantino is, after all, scholar without peer when it comes to malicious surgery in Asian cinema), but the Bible holds precedence in its story of Malchus, a servant of the high priest, whose ear was struck off by the sword of Simon Peter. Jesus touches Malchus's ear and heals him, though the miracle is only noted in one of the gospels, in Luke 22.51.

Mad Detective, a Hong Kong film co-directed in 2007 by Johnny To and Wai Ka Fai, features a clairvoyant/clairaudient policeman as its central character. This gift, or burden, of extrasensory perception allows the detective to solve cases by re-enacting them, or by seeing inner personali-ties and hearing sounds that are inaudible to normal sensory capabilities. Early in the film, he cuts off his right ear, presents it as a leaving gift to his superintendent, then for the rest of the film wears a plastic false ear. His reasons for this brutal self-immolation are never made explicit; for the other characters it serves as one more example of what they perceive to be his mental instability. Yet as the story develops, the corrosive effects of possessing such faculties become apparent, and so his sacrifice symbolizes what he relinquishes, the protective limitations of the outer senses, in order to exercise his extrasensory perception.

ENTOMBMENT

A high-jumper at the Beijing Olympic Games completes the jump that will gain him a silver medal, stands up, turns to the crowd and with an expect-ant look on his face, cups his hand to his ear. 'Hark! Hark! What shout is that?' Agamemnon asks in Shakespeare's *Troilus and Cressida*. 'Peace, drums.' Calling for sound, calling for hearing, gathering in audio approba-tion — I can't hear you, make some noise — his gesture is the antithesis of the 'shhh', the hush.

We can see seeing, but we can't hear hearing. To speak about hear-ing requires qualifiers, supplementary words, appendages, elucidations, approximations. The equivalence of a gaze is intensive listening; peering is straining to hear; a stare is somewhere between eavesdropping and listen-ing avidly, yet not quite. As for pictures of nothing (to borrow the title of Kirk Varnedoe's famous lectures on abstract art) . . .

For Henri Lefebvre, our emphasis on seeing has resulted in complex phenomena being reduced to the simplified state of images. The social existence of space is repressively visualized. 'In the course of the process whereby the visual gains the upper hand over the other senses, all impres-sions derived from taste, smell, touch and even hearing first lose clarity, then fade away altogether,' he wrote in *The Production of Space*, 'leaving the field to line, colour and light. In this way a part of the object and what it offers comes to be taken for the whole.'

Within the history of Western thought, seeing has been regarded as the most active sense, the king of senses; seeing is often categorized as masculine, hearing feminine, as if in the most stereotypical gendering of perception, seeing goes out to penetrate — phallic, the hunter, the warrior — whereas hearing gathers in, enfolds, receives, gestates. Ears are the instruments of darkness. Leonardo da Vinci believed that losing sight was a form of incarceration, an entombment (the dark senses): 'Whoso loses his eyes leaves his soul in a dark prison without hope of ever again seeing the sun, light of all the world.' Though all these polarisations are crude, there is no doubt that eyes are the reflective lights of the exterior self, giving off signs of interiority, whereas ears burrow into a dark, concealed unknown ('All dark and comfortless,' is Gloucester's response in King Lear, when asked by Cornwall, 'Where is thy lustre now?'). Eyes are open, shut, active, moving, eyelids blinking and closing, the eyes reflecting what they see, face working with or against the eyes, lashes fluttering, eyebrows raised or narrowed.

Metaphorically, eyes run over somebody's body, scrutinize a face, search, mist over, shine, squint, cloud over, harden, soften, flicker, narrow, widen; eyelids flutter, droop and close. An eyebrow can be quizzical; the forehead can crease into a frown. A look can be piercing, searching, dirty, hard, sharp, questioning, pitying. There are bedroom eyes, sorrowful eyes, and any number of other eyes: wide, bright, sad, cold, soulful, clouded, roving, lazy, sleepy, baggy, rheumy, watery, dry, dead, peeled, bug, glass, one, wild, shifty, unseeing, eagle, x-ray, beady, dim, downcast, wall, cross, and this is without the colours. There are fleeting glances, penetrating stares, averted gazes, eye to eye contact. In The Last of the Mohicans, there was Hawk-eye. In cartoons, eyes can suddenly pop out of the body, on stalks or springs, usually accompanied by a boiiing! Let's take a closer look. Since Lacan, we have the Gaze and the Mirror Phase. Eyes can be masked. Make-up accentuates the eyes; spectacles can be a fashion item, a statement; contact lens can change the colour of the eyes. Eyes are vulnerable: they can be scooped out, bashed in, slashed, blackened, blinded. 'Pluck out his eyes', says Goneril, and after the first of Gloucester's eyes is plucked, Cornwall despatches the second, 'Out, vile jelly.'

Surprisingly few of these terms, metaphors and functions can be applied to the ears, though despite their curvaceous form, ears may be described as sharp. They can also be pierced. Prying eyes will usually be augmented by prying ears — though the former sounds correct, the latter does not. Keep your eyes and ears open seems a logical way of telling somebody to stay alert, except for the fact that ears are always open unless stopped with hands (as in Caravaggio), fingers or plugs. Shivering through and through his nervous system with the strange sensations of school, the lighting of gas lamps that 'in burning made a light noise like a little song', homesick Stephen Dedalus longs to be home and laying his head on his mother's lap. James Joyce, in *A Portrait of the Artist as a Young Man*, has Stephen leaning his elbows on the refectory table, shutting and opening the flaps of his ears. The roaring noise of the refectory reminds him of a train at night, and when he shuts the flaps he thinks of the train at Dalkey going into a tunnel, the roaring suddenly stopped. The coming and going of the sound and the memory it evokes is a comfort to his distress.

The eye observes the eye, loving or despising itself, judging all other organs and forms according to the moist colourful lustre and depths of itself. In their external form (to the eye), ears are dull and passive, immobile and technical, shells of shells; cloth-eared, jug-eared, cauliflower-eared; Big Ears, Dumbo. Handles on a soup tureen, they are conveniently placed as secure symmetrical rests for spectacles and sunglasses. A theorist of intelligent design might argue that such economic functionalism was planned in anticipation of these inventions, but just how intelligent is it to design defective eyes?

Just as the bull's-eye is at the centre, the oculus admits the light of reason. If the eyes are windows to the soul, then ears must be tunnels to some other place, some darker zone of unreason, or simply a channelling of inner feelings described, by implication, in common sayings, as too subtle and elusive for the rationalism of seeing. An old song by The Stylistics fused this idea with the neatness of a phrase devised to educate children in road safety: 'It's never too late, too late to stop, look, listen to your heart, hear what it's saying.' Not only listen to your heart, which is logical, but listen to your instincts, listen to your inner voice (and that egregious invention of new age psychobabble: listen to your inner child). For this mode of hearing the ears must be turned in, tuned to an inner darkness that will also suggest activities such as prayer. For those who are believers, the inner self opens out to an auditory plane encompassing the entire theological universe, though there is another inner auditory reality, explored by Tom Rice in his short story, 'The Doctor'. Dr Francis, a cardiologist whose relationship to stethoscopes borders on fetishism, hires a prostitute to visit him at home. Instructing her to undress to the waist, he derives erotic pleasure (or finds release from insomnia caused by hyperacusis) from listening to her heartbeat through the 'heavy alloy headpiece' of an Allen Gemini stethoscope: 'Then suddenly he seemed to clinch, to seize the sound he was seeking out.

His ears gathered up the beat, dusting and polishing it, until each round thump resonated strongly and colourfully. It was as though someone was beating a huge drum. A clean powerful sound. This was the beat to which the human race marched, the rhythm to which all life was played out — the sinus rhythm.'

'The patient's pulse was a hundred and twenty,' wrote Vladimir Nabokov in *Laughter in the Dark*, 'the chest over the seat of the pain was dull on percussion, and the stethoscope revealed fine crepitation.' All hearing animals can audit the body's sonic expulsions of vocalisations, vomiting, sneezes, snores, wheezes, belches and farts, but close listening also reveals a close and interior sound world of corporeal functioning: the beating heart; breath entering and exiting the nostrils; clicking eyelids and jaw; the chewing of food (now recognized as being an important component of taste); contractions of the throat; saliva in the mouth; the gnathosonics of teeth clashing or grinding during sleep (the latter known as nocturnal bruxism); otoacoustic emissions from the ears; bones, joints and ligaments clicking and creaking; the crunching, bubbling sounds of crepitation or rales, heard from diseased lungs; the wonderfully named borborygmi, which are the sounds given off by food and digestive juices passing through the intestines; and the continuous hum and intermittent crackle given off by muscles. These latter noises were first documented by a seventeenth-century scientist and Jesuit priest from Italy, Francesco Maria Grimaldi, who found that by placing his thumbs in his ears and then clenching his fists, he could hear a quiet rumbling. This is reminiscent of a Chinese Qigong exercise, Kou ji yu zhen, or knock and beat the jade pillow, in which the ears are covered by the palms. The index and middle fingers are then snapped down on the cavity areas underneath the external occipital protuberance, producing a loud rejuvenating drumming that fills the head.

Some of these sounds, such as teeth grinding, breathing, chewing and borborygmi, are clearly audible to others, but all of them can be heard externally, given the right conditions and instruments. To say that a person is silent is simply a figure of speech; to sense a presence in a room is actually to hear the combined audio activity of a body at rest. Most uncanny of all are the sounds emitted by bodies after death. 'The Countess was stretched on her bed', wrote Wilkie Collins in *The Haunted Hotel*. 'The doctor on one side, and the chambermaid on the other, were standing looking at her. From time to time, she drew a heavy stertorous breath, like a person oppressed in sleeping. "Is she likely to die?" Henry asked. "She is dead," the doctor answered. "Dead of the rupture of a blood-vessel on the brain. Those sounds that you hear are purely mechanical — they may go on for hours."'

FIGURES OF SPEECH

I'm all ears, as if hearing can engulf the other senses, become the body as receptor. This expression has great potential for irony, or outright sarcasm: fill me up with your worthless sound.

'You guys can talk the ears right offa my head,' says actor Ed Begley, in Sidney Lumet's 1957 film, *12 Angry Men*. What he means is, go so far as to amputate my ears with your sharp chatter but even then I won't listen.

An ear to the ground (the Indian scout dismounts, presses his ear to the earth, senses a distant vibration of hooves, stands, gravely informs the cavalry troop that a large war party of Apache is heading their way).

Pin your ears back, as if in normal circumstances ears are folded forward, like shutters, obstructing the free flow of sound.

Ears prick up, metaphorically speaking, though not in the expressive directional pantomime of dogs or cats.

One minute the ears are unlovely, faintly ridiculous, then love can change everything, the intricate shape and curve and folding and interior pathway of an ear explored through touch of finger and tongue, breath and whisper, privacy and seclusion. Secrets and intimacies are passed, person-to-person, with the same sensation of merging as any other sexual exchange. The razor hiss of a whisper becomes a caress. 'My baby whispers in my ear, mmmmh, sweet nothings,' sang Brenda Lee in 1960, sotto voce not an option for her fabulous blowtorch voice. 'Things he wouldn't tell [pause] nobody else [pause] secret baby, I keep 'em to myself'.

FLESH HORNS

In a metaphorical sense, or in cartoons, ears can grow into open flesh-horns or trumpets. Leonora Carrington's drawings for her novel, *The Hearing Trumpet*, depict the listening device as an extendable sinuous cone — elephant trunk, phonograph horn, spiritualist ectoplasm — that can insinuate its way into spaces in order to hear things otherwise inaudible. As with large-eared nocturnal creatures such as the Fennec fox, jerboa and bat, her enhanced ears swivel and expand in their collection of audio data. 'People under seventy and over seven are very unreliable if they are not cats', says her friend Carmella. 'You can't be too careful. Besides, think of the exhilarating power of listening to others talk when they think you cannot hear.'

'Father was listening', wrote Bruno Schulz in *The Night of the Great Season*. 'In the silence of the night his ear seemed to grow larger and to reach beyond the window: a fantastic coral, a red polypus watching the chaos of the night.' This conception of the ear as a gathering device or reversed trumpet, a prosthetic supplement to the main body, extends to the notion of detachability, hence one of the most familiar passages from Shakespeare, Antony's address to Rome's citizens after the murder of Caesar: 'Friends, Romans, countrymen, lend me your ears.' Hence, also, the famous wartime phrase, 'walls have ears', which suggests that ears may grow within the fabric of a building, like the fungi they resemble. In Florian Henckel von Donnersmarck's film, *The Lives of Others*, listening devices (bugs, rather than fungi) are embedded into walls, light fittings, and beneath wallpaper in order to eavesdrop on the private sounds of suspect citizens. These continue to nest silently under their domestic camouflage, even when the paranoid regime that implanted them has long since disintegrated, even when the brain connected to the ears has ceased to exist.

THE BUTCHERED EAR

Sun is the enemy of the ear. On a sunny day in Leiden, birthplace of Rembrandt van Rijn, Gabriel Metsu, Gerrit Dou, Jan Steen and Lucas van Leyden, everybody is sitting outside to take their lunch in the spring warmth, everybody except saxophonist John Butcher. As I get older, I tend to avoid hot sun, and besides, I enjoy John's company so I join him. We talk about this avoidance of direct sunlight and he tells me that in 2007 he was diagnosed with a malignant melanoma on the top of his right ear. This was cut away but he has to stay in the shade to protect against further outbreaks. His ears are now slightly different shapes. Embarrassed to stare so closely, I study them and begin to see what I had missed before: his right ear is smaller than his left. We talk about the effect this operation may have had on his hearing. John's playing is as focussed on the minutiae of differ-ence in frequencies and tonal aggregations as any saxophonist anywhere, so he had been listening for a change in subtleties of sound heard from right to left. In practical situations nothing had altered in his sonic perception, but having suffered from tinnitus for twenty years, he discovered an online hearing test called Tone Tester. If the subject is listening on headphones, the software moves an identical sine wave signal back and forth between the two ears. What he discovered at frequencies below one kilohertz was a difference between the 'colour' perceived by each ear, and in some ranges a slight difference in his perception of the fundamental pitch, a common condition called binaural diplacusis, that is resolved into an average frequency by the brain (the English composer and suffragette Ethel Smyth had to cope not only with deafness, but with a semitone difference between the hearing in her right and left ears).

Later, he sent me this note: 'I guess the earphones and pinna [the outer part of the ear] generate some overtones, and you have ear canal resonances and who knows what going on in the inner ear. Anyway, when I tried this after the operation, I thought the effect was more pronounced but it could be my imagination. It's hard to compare subjective things over a period of time, especially when you weren't expecting the change.' What I find intriguing about this story, aside from the provocative iconography of the (butchered) ear, is the evident subjectivity of hearing. Even for professionals such as John and myself, changes in hearing, loss of hearing and psychoacoustic phenomena can be difficult to monitor accurately. Every year I go to professionals to test the state of my teeth and eyesight, yet I have never had a test on my hearing, despite knowing that once teenage years are over, hearing begins to decline. Commonly experienced psychoacoustic phenomena such as the phantom effect, in which the brain builds coherent patterns of sound from noise or very weak and even non-existent signals, or the hypersonic effect of inaudible high frequency signals on brain activity, call into question the shared reality of what we hear. A progressive loss of sight is quickly noticed, but hearing loss is only measured by the vague and unreliable method of comparing elusive memories across time, or from the feedback of others. What is it that we don't know of ourselves? What do we know of what we hear; what is absent from our hearing? What? I can't hear you? You'll have to speak louder.

The most famous ear in the art of the Netherlands is a lacerated ear, that of Vincent van Gogh. Like the sliced eye that opens interior vision at the beginning of the Bunuel/Dali film, *La Chien Andalou*, or the eyes of Georges Bataille's *Histoire de l'Oeil*, Van Gogh's attack on his ear goes beyond his own madness. The true circumstances or reasons for this act of self-harm are unclear — perhaps an escalation of tension between him and Gauguin — but the ear was wrapped in newspaper and given to a prostitute named Rachel for safekeeping. In *The Yellow House*, Martin Gayford's account of the nine weeks when Van Gogh and Gauguin shared a home in Arles, two narratives are identified as focal points for obsession, as Van Gogh became increasingly tormented by voices. One was Zola's novel, *The Sin of Father Mouret*, in which one of the characters chops off a friar's ear, the other being the story of Christ's agony in the Garden of Gethsemane, when one of the disciples chops off the ear of the high priest's servant. After the incident Van Gogh was unable to say why he had maimed himself in so specific a manner. 'However, there were some clues', Gayford writes. 'It seemed that Vincent, who could not normally sing, had sung in his madness. He had sung "an old nurse's song," because he was "dreaming of the song that the woman rocking the cradle sang to rock the sailors to sleep." That was, he explained to Gauguin, the same subject "for which I was searching in an arrangement of colours before I fell ill."'

Van Gogh's 1889 *Self-Portrait with Bandaged Ear*, in the Courtauld collection, shows him gaunt, cold, haunted, his eyes fixed on some part of himself between brush and painting. On the wall behind him, strangely angled as if attached to the left side of his head, like a rectangular ear, is a Japanese print showing two women wearing kimono, Mt Fuji in the background. The bandage on his right ear muffles sound, perhaps serves to block out voices, disturbance, everything other than the seeing of a great painter. 'For my part I don't need Japanese pictures here,' he wrote to his sister, 'for I am always telling myself that I am here in Japan. Which means that I have only to open my eyes and paint what is right in front of me, if I only think it effective.' Seeing and imagination are his only necessities; the rest is immaterial. In 1930, Bataille devoted a short essay — 'Sacrificial Mutilation and the Severed Ear of Vincent Van Gogh' — to the subject of this wounding. The act is characterized as a sacrifice, 'a drive revealed by an inner experience', in the context of Van Gogh's solar obsession. For Bataille, the ear was a 'relatively unimportant' part of the body to lose by comparison with that most unthinkable of sacrifices, 'the Oedipal enucleation' (Oedipus blinded himself after discovering that Jocasta, his wife and mother, has committed suicide). 'The one who sacrifices', he wrote, 'is free . . . free to throw himself suddenly *outside of himself . . .*'

Another Dutch painting of an ear that would be notorious had it not been lost is noted by Polish writer Zbigniew Herbert in his essay on the seventeenth-century painter known as Johannes Torrentius. Convicted of a long list of moral offences and crimes including heresy, Torrentius was liberated from his prison sentence in Haarlem after the King of England, Charles I, sent a letter of appeal to the Prince of Orange. Torrentius was released in 1630 and sent to England, where he is known to have painted a number of works. Included in the inventory of the collection of Charles I is a painting of 'a woman pissing in a man's eare'. This, along with all but one Torrentius painting — the *Emblematic still life with flagon, glass, jug and bridle* of 1614, in Amsterdam's Rijksmuseum — is now either lost or hidden away in secret collections. But in the self-mythologizing of Torrentius, his paintings were not material creations. 'He was surrounded by an aura of mystery', wrote Herbert, 'and legends circulated about what took place in his atelier, tales about supernatural forces he brought into his work. Probably Torrentius thought a certain dose of charlatanism did not harm art . . . he used to say he did not in fact paint but only placed paints on the floor next to his canvases; under the influence of musical sounds they arranged themselves in colourful harmonies.'

On this subject of missing ears, Lafcadio Hearn's *Kwaidan* included his translation of a supernatural tale from Japan, 'The Story of Mimi-Nashi-Hoichi'. A young blind monk, Hoichi, is persuaded by ghosts to play his stringed biwa every night to what he believes to be a large, illustrious company. In fact, he has been performing alone in the cemetery. To protect him from the persistent attentions of these ghosts, the priest of the temple paints his body with texts from the holy sutra Hannya-Shin-Kyo, the Doctrine of the Emptiness of Forms. When the ghost returns that night, Hoichi is invisible to him except for his ears. 'Here's the biwa', he says, 'but of the biwa-player I see — only two ears! . . . So that explains why he did not answer: he had no mouth to answer with — there's nothing left of him but his ears . . . Now to my lord those ears I will take — in proof that the august commands have been obeyed, so far as was possible . . .' He then grips the ears and tears them off. The priest had given his acolyte the job of painting Hoichi's ears, but they were forgotten. At the end of the story, Hoichi's misfortune leads to wealth and fame — many people travel to the temple to give him gifts in exchange for a recital — but the lasting impression for the reader is conveyed by the inadequacy of ears and the terrible punishment visited upon them. Without sight, a person is vulnerable to supernatural forces. Invisible and immaterial, ghosts are more at home in the domain of hearing.

OPEN MOUTH

7 November 2008. Lying in the dark at 1.00 am, waiting for sleep, I hear somebody roaring in the street. Looking out of our bedroom window I see what seems to be an ordinary man, probably in his early thirties, walking along the centre of the road between parked cars. He is moving quickly but after every few paces he stops, throws back his head and roars loudly, like an angry, wounded beast. Each roar is slightly different but his actions appear to be entirely unselfconscious, as if they come from some deep and violent derangement. He looks and sounds bestial, enraged, so engorged with these sounds that he can only let them loose on our sleeping neighbourhood.

SEETHES UNDER MY SKIN

One moment, by a wooden railing, sky and sea swirling in waves of energy, their force flowing from a white ghost head that clutches and covers its ears, the sides of its skull, as if to hold the head securely to a body that waves in attractive sympathy toward the sweeping sound waves shrieking from an open O mouth of an unseen horror. This is Edvard Munch's *Skriket*, *The Scream*, first painted in 1893, one of the most famous, influential and frequently stolen paintings of the modern period, a work whose violent shout broke into the homely quietude of what Munch described as 'interiors and people reading and women knitting'. This insight came to him in a bar, as Romanian music carried him off into his own thoughts, as he watched a man whisper into a woman's ear, her eyes shut, her lips open. 'What we cannot see is whether it is an internal or an external pressure that is the cause of the horror', writes Poul Erik Tojner in his monograph on Munch. 'The sound rises and falls like blood pulsing through the picture. It is as if the person is trying to press the plasmatic magma out of his body, yet at the same time, it appears as if he might implode. There is an exchange of traffic, not on the road but between eye and ear.'

Like his Norwegian contemporary, Knut Hamsun, Munch listened with such heightened intensity and introspection that he came to realize that the body generates sound within silence. Quiet is a complex of many sounds. 'I lie at night and listen to my heart beating', he wrote. 'I hear the blood roaring in my ears — it fills my head — it seethes under my skin and in the tips of my fingers and toes. My skin tingles.

'How they buzz, those billions of worlds that stream along from the skin to the heart — rhythmically steered by the beating of the heart. Billions of worlds push forward. They wish to find a path out of their confinement. Yet they have to return over and over again. It gushes in the canals of my ear — it vibrates in my limbs — those billions of worlds.'

The belief that vibrations of light and sound could transmit powerful energies was fundamental to his work. As an example of how such vibrations might intersect with propitious circumstances to produce dramatic effects, Munch wrote this brief narrative: 'A gentleman enters and sits down at a table. A woman stands stiffly — cold and pale behind him — she speaks a tiny word — seemingly indifferent, the man immediately collapses, grabs a revolver and shoots himself.' Along with speculations on correspondences between sound, light and colour, telegraphy, ether and electrical vibrations, Munch made a number of notes describing the events that led to his first version of *The Scream*. 'That shrill bloody red', he wrote in the most vivid of these recollections. 'On the road and the fence. The faces of my comrades became a garish yellow-white. I felt a huge scream welling up inside me — and I really did hear a huge scream. The colours in nature — broke the lines in nature. The lines and colours quivered with movement. These vibrations of light caused not only the oscillation of my eyes. My ears were also affected and began to vibrate. So I actually heard a scream. Then I painted *The Scream*.' And in another, written in block capitals, each word, even letter, a different colour: 'The sky turned suddenly to blood and I felt nature utter a huge scream.'

Spreading and merging into the ambient scream of nature, the scream of this transfigured man resonated through the twentieth century. In his essay on Mark Rothko, 'The World in a Frame', David Anfam hears it reverberating, 'an emotional tide flooding from the self into its surroundings', in compositions by the young Rothko, even in the Seagram murals of the late 1950s, which '. . . immerse the beholder in a wilderness of empty, though deeply tinted or shadowed, mirrors.' We hear it also in the paintings of Francis Bacon, howls, snarls and screams reverberating in non-spaces, from *Man in a Cap* from 1943, the various Heads painted from 1947, *Fragment of a Crucifixion* and *Study After Velázquez* from 1950, *Study of a Baboon* from 1953, *Chimpanzee* from 1955, *Three Studies for Figures at the Base of a Crucifixion* from 1944, right up to the 1988 version of *Triptych*. Always a gaping maw, bared teeth, a sightless scream to confront whatever is out there. We know that Bacon drew from sources such as the screaming nurse from Sergei Eisenstein's *Battleship Potemkin*, from studies of animals, and from photographs of Nazis, but the silent scream rises over this archaeology of the visual. *Head II*, from 1949, unveils a grey, tortured bird-beast, a swollen lump fading or falling into the rhinoceros hide curtains of its darkened rooming. A croak in the gloom. *Head I*, painted between 1947–48, auditions another voice raging from tormented flesh, melting and fusing in anticipation of the cinematic body-horror monsters of John Carpenter's *The Thing* and Ridley Scott's *Alien*. As if listening in appalled curiosity, a disproportionate ear swivels toward the noise of its fellow orifice, an equally disproportionate mouth of vampire teeth and torn lip. The neck slides away to puddle into the floor of a room without room.

Simultaneously bestial, terrorized and sexual, these scraps and screams echo as unresolved stories, the 'fragments of narrative' identified within Bacon's work by David Lynch. Imagination can do its work of filling in whatever is absent, assisted by the condemnatory silences of those photographs that reveal to us the inhumanity of our time: a naked man pushed to the floor by a soldier, smear of blood wiped across the concrete from his taped knee, mouth stretched open in agonized scream. In the same prison, Abu Ghraib, in Iraq, the scream of a naked man terrorized by dogs, hands over his ears (a Caravaggio scene), attempting to shield himself from their murderous noise, then from an earlier era, screaming, open mouthed, naked Vietnamese children, burned by napalm jelly and running for cover, surrounded by soldiers. In all cases, the contrast between uniforms and nakedness, between insouciance and terror, between quiet calm and involuntary screaming, is where we learn more about the depths of our depravity.

CLOSED MOUTHS

Francis Bacon spoke about opening up the valves of sensation. This is what deep listening means: to go beyond a shielded, inattentive state (Stravinsky's distinction between hearing and listening); to allow sensation to enter and flood the body; to relinquish the manufacture of sound, if only momentarily; to hear the details of inaudibility. In his book, *Rhythmanalysis: Space, Time and Everyday Life*, Henri Lefebvre described the human body as a reduction, an image of an entity that is reduced to manageability from the complex workings of many rhythmic processes. 'We contain ourselves by concealing the diversity of our rhythms', he wrote, 'to ourselves, body and flesh, we are almost objects. Not completely, however. But what does a midge perceive, whose body has almost nothing in common with ours, and whose wings beat to the rhythm of a thousand times per second? The insect makes us hear a high-pitched sound, we perceive a threatening, little winged cloud that seeks our blood. In short, rhythms escape logic, and nevertheless contain a logic, a possible calculus of number and numerical relations.' Listening to the rhythmic beating of a bee's wings, we hear a buzz at around 200 Hz; listening to the faster rhythms of a mosquito's wings, we hear a higher whine, at around 1000 Hz. Within these apparently continuous sounds there are rhythms. In *Views From a Tuft of Grass*, Swedish author Harry Martinson's description of a dragonfly overpowering a robber fly emphasizes the auditory significance of the event: 'Often this happens so quickly that you can't detect it except by ear. First you hear the robber fly's muffled sound like a bow drawn lightly across the strings of a double bass. Then you hear the wings of the dragonfly rustle against each other as it turns and it enters into its attacking curve. That's the end of the robber fly. It goes dead silent and becomes a quick lunch al fresco. You listen for it but can't hear it anymore.' What we can understand of the world is reduced by the nature and limitations of our senses, then again by our restriction of their true potential. What Lefebvre proposed as a counter to 'thingification' or reification in modern thought was a new science, a new field of knowledge — the analysis of rhythms — with its practitioner, the rhythmanalyst, a person for whom nothing is immobile. 'He will listen to the world,' he wrote, 'and above all to what are disdainfully called noises, which are said without meaning, and to murmurs [rumeurs], full of meaning — and finally he will listen to silences.'

INTIMACY

'Before entering the cabin I stood still listening in the lobby at the foot of the stairs. A faint snore came through the closed door of the chief mate's room. The second mate's door was on the hook, but the darkness in there was absolutely soundless.' This passage from Joseph Conrad's short story of 1910, 'The Secret Sharer', is striking for a number of reasons: an auditory tension that pivots upon eavesdropping and the fragility of a silent condition; then the characterisation of darkness as an equivalent or manifestation of absolute silence.

The story's narrator is a young sailor promoted recently to his first command as captain. Feeling the loneliness of isolation common to many of
Conrad's central protagonists, he discovers a swimmer close to his ship. As
it transpires, the swimmer — a man named Leggatt — murdered a man on
his own ship, the *Sephora*, then escaped confinement, determined to sink
and drown rather than answer the consequences of his actions. Similar
in height and hair colour, trained at the same school, the two men then
collude within the captain's quarters in a complex theatre of concealment,
the unfolding and refolding of an eerie doubling. The two share claustrophobic, private spaces and a common secret. Often, they must do so in
complete silence: 'It would not have been prudent to talk in daytime; and
I could not have stood the excitement of that queer sense of whispering
to myself. Now and then, glancing over my shoulder, I saw him far back
there, sitting rigidly on the low stool, his bare feet close together, his arms
folded, his head hanging on his breast — and perfectly still. Anybody would
have taken him for me.' Conrad's description of this second self as silent
corpse double, enfolded and silent like a bat, reinforces the desperate role
of sound. One waits to be activated by the other, yet they must move in
well-drilled collusion. They whisper, they murmur; one eavesdrops upon
the other, and on others.

The story emerges from stillness, 'very still in an immense stillness', as
Conrad wrote, the ship 'anchored at the head of the Gulf of Siam.' This
doubled stillness is so immense, the quiet communion so comforting, that
only a cosmic event, the sudden appearance of stars in the tropical night
sky, can disrupt its serenity. Following the cosmic comes the earthbound,
the human: 'And there were also disturbing sounds by this time — voices,
footsteps forward; the steward flitted along the maindeck, a busily minister-
ing spirit; a hand-bell tinkled urgently under the poop-deck . . .'

At the level of sensation, the story turns upon stillness agitated, or
emptiness filled. Bodies are mirrored or ghosted; the volatility of sound is
so acute that its audition, suppression or amplification becomes vital to the
containment of the secret shared. Conrad wrote of a 'profound silence' only
disturbed by a 'quiet, trustful sigh of some sleeper inside', then, in the next
breath, contrasting the security of the sea with the unrest of the land. This is
a momentary silence, however, since the naked, piscine body of the swimmer emerges phosphorescent (suddenly, unexpectedly, like depression,
phobia, a violent act, a natural force) from the 'darkling glassy shimmer'
of the sea. Again, absolute stillness is punctured by the hiss of the captain's

cigar as it falls with an audible plop and short hiss into the water. No void can endure, Conrad seems to be saying, and ensuing events bear this out. What remains of the story is conducted under circumstances of extreme auditory and bodily restraint: earnest whispers, breathless whispers, fingers to the lips and similar silent admonitory signs, silences, exhalations, slight noises, desperate and hurried whispers, low bitter murmurs, words emitted with a hesitating effort, deadened voices, voices so subdued they become monotonous, slipping and stealth, bare feet making no sound, speech uttered under the breath, whispers that grow fainter and fainter. At one point the captain's double breathes anxiously into his ear. An implication, surely unintentional on Conrad's part, of closeted homoerotic intimacy grows from this painful subjugation of the sounding body, the present body. During a visit from the suspicious captain of the *Sephora*, shouting becomes necessary to help Leggatt eavesdrop on the conversation. When important information is mumbled, the host captain feigns deafness. In moments of crisis, the swimmer becomes as 'noiseless as a ghost' whereas the captain begins to lose control. He 'thunders' at the steward: 'My nerves were so shaken that I could not govern my voice and conceal my agitation.' This intense interweaving of dangerous voices, cultivated silences and rogue sounds is expressed through extreme pressures on bodies and vessels: 'At the sound of my voice he nearly jumped out of his skin, as the saying is, and incidentally broke a cup.'

Neither the captain nor the swimmer will ever hear each other's natural voice, though there are conciliatory aspects to this exercise in suppressed vocalism. 'The whispering communion of the narrator and his double — of the seaman-self and some darker, more interior, and outlaw self', writes Albert J. Guerard in his critical study, *Conrad: The Novelist*, 'must have been necessary and rewarding, since the story ends as positively as it does. But it is obvious to both men that the arrangement cannot be permanent.' Finally, as they sail desperately close under the looming black mass of Koh-ring Island to ensure the swimmer's silent exit back into the deep from which he first emerged, Conrad invokes Erebus, son of Chaos, whose name means shadow and darkness: 'Then stillness again, with the great shadow gliding closer, towering higher, without light, without sound. Such a hush had fallen on the ship that she might have been a bark of the dead floating in slowly under the very gate of Erebus.' In this ritualistic setting, the swimmer returns to the water, leaving only a hat floating on the surface as a visible trace. As he was on first emergence, Leggatt is headless (a precursor of Bataille's Acéphale, the secret society and its review that declared in 1936, Bataille writing in a little cold house by the sea, hearing dogs barking in the night, Andre Masson singing in the kitchen, putting a recording of the overture to Don Giovanni on the gramophone, 'Human life is exhausted from serving as the head of, or the reason for, the universe.' As if then, reason and unreason have engaged in secret dialogue, of necessity in whispers, so unreason plunges back into chaos from whence it came.

ONE FINAL SILENCE

Conrad described many silences: offended silence, profound silence, private silence, a silence of reproach, the jungle silence of *Heart of Darkness*, that 'did not in the least resemble a peace' and *The Lagoon*, with its silent forests and still air, in which 'every tree, every leaf, every bough, every tendril of creeper and every petal of minute blossoms seemed to have been bewitched into an immobility perfect and final'; then in *The Shadow-Line*, ship becalmed in an 'atmosphere which had turned to soot', a blackness that threatened to 'overwhelm silently the bit of starlight falling upon the ship, and the end of things would come without a sigh, stir or murmur of any kind and all our hearts would cease to beat like run-down clocks', the crew waits for the onset of a squall, preparing for the worst as 'all the time the black universe made no sound'. Through an aching jaw, the narrator becomes aware that he has been grinding his teeth in this tension, and is astonished that he failed to hear himself doing so. At that moment, the raindrops begin, 'Tap. Tap. Tap. . . .' but then cease, leaving an intolerable suspense, which breaks, not as he expected, with the first crash turning him into dust, but in the most uncanny fashion: 'A heavy shower, a downpour, comes along, making a noise. You hear its approach on the sea, in the air too, I verily believe. But this was different. With no preliminary whisper or rustle, without a splash, and even without the ghost of impact, I became instantaneously soaked to the skin.'

At the conclusion of *The Secret Sharer*, silence becomes a vanishing — submerged; the underworld; utter black. To be silenced; a euphemism for murder. The auditory tension of the story, in which all sound is treated as an unnatural, if inevitable rupture of stillness (the cup before it breaks), questions the notion of silence as a possible absolute yet emerges out of the base condition of a hypothetical space in which sound and light are completely absent, a darkness that is absolutely soundless. The polyphony of quietus resonates, at rest, and in the word's further senses of a final discharge of debt, the silencing of a claim, or death. 'When he himself might his quietus make with a bare bodkin,' says Hamlet, the release from suffering easily achieved through suicide by naked blade, but for the uncertainty of what lies beyond in the silence of death. Nothing moves.

This silence is a void that we have come to conceive as an impossibility. Through the influence of his writings, published lectures, and the conceptual milestone of his so-called 'silent' composition, 4'33", John Cage's twentieth-century redefinition of silence has resulted in an orthodoxy of belief: silence no longer exists. 'There is always something to see, something to hear', Cage wrote in *Silence*. 'In fact, try as we might to make a silence, we cannot.' Through their intensification of perception, modernist writers heard no silence. 'The sound of the bees diminished, sustained yet,' wrote William Faulkner in 1929, in *The Sound and the Fury*, 'as though instead of sinking into silence, silence merely increased between us, as water rises.' Virginia Woolf had explored similar territory in 1922, in *Jacob's Room*: '"There's no such thing as silence," he said positively. "I can hear twenty different sounds on a night like this without counting your voices."' Typically for Woolf, clues to the rationale behind this seemingly random remark glimmer only faintly in the preceding conversation: a deaf old man, reciting the names of the constellations; a passing comment about 'the silent young man'. Mr Erskine, who made the observation, is challenged to give examples. He begins his list — the sea, the wind, a dog — but swiftly loses his audience. Silence is just silence for some people; nothing more nor less. Woolf recognized that silence, for her somewhere between a state of mind and an intensity, must be allowed to rise through an obscuring murk. In a prescient passage from *To the Lighthouse*, published in 1927, silence is submerged beneath 'busy' everyday images of cleaning, tidying and farming.

And now as if the cleaning and the scrubbing and the scything and the mowing has drowned it there rose that half-heard melody, that intermittent music which the ear half catches but lets fall; a bark, a bleat; irregular, intermittent, yet somehow related; the hum of an insect, the tremor of cut grass, dissevered yet somehow belonging; the jar of a dor beetle, the squeak of a wheel, loud, low but mysteriously related; which the ear strains to bring together and is always on the verge of harmonizing but they are never quite heard, never fully harmonized, and at last, in the evening, one after another the sounds die out, and the harmony falters, and silence falls.

Centuries earlier, the Chinese poet, Po Chü-i, gave an example of the body's sounding (tinnitus induced by that terrible intersection of drunkenness crossing over into a hangover, perhaps) in his poem, *After Getting Drunk, Becoming Sober in the Night,* written in the year AD 824, or thereabouts:

All the time till dawn came, still my thoughts were muddled;
    And in my ears something sounded like the music of flutes and strings.

Silence might be described as a paradox — an amplification of slight events within a low-level auditory environment. The audible evidence of this can be heard in Philip Gröning's film, *Into Great Silence,* a document without commentary showing life inside the monastery of Grand Chartreuse, where monks of the Carthusian Order have taken a vow of silence. Yet the vacuum of their speechlessness is filled by a sounding out of movement, breath, the turning of book pages, footsteps on stairs, sighs, scissors, throat noise, creaks, air, bells, bodies moving, chairs, fabric, echoes, an electric razor, singing, poured water, floorboards, a plate rocking on a table, keys, cart wheels, bird song, melting ice and snow thaw, the shovelling of snow, squeaks, a wood saw, falling wood, an axe, and in a most general sense of life in motion the contact of materials both soft and hard echoing in otherwise quiet, reverberant spaces or dispersing through open air. The emptier the space of sound, the greater the apparent volume of sounds within it; the lower the level of auditory background, the more intense the listener's awareness of minimal interferences. Quiet becomes loud. This is the basis of the uncanny atmosphere of many supernatural stories — silences into which anomalous, inexplicable noises intrude to shatter all rational belief for those who hear them, the beauty that precedes terror, as Rilke wrote.

In *The Woman in White* by Wilkie Collins (more of a 'sensation' novel than a ghost story), the moribund central space around which events circulate and develop is the soundproof, lightproof room of Mr Fairlie, an enfeebled, dictatorially fastidious man who shields himself from external disturbances. The normal volume of a speaking voice, the movement of a chair (even though muted by thick carpet), the suspicion of what he calls 'some horrid children heard in his private garden, all upset his over-refined sensibilities. Collins's satire of Fairlie, directed perhaps at those Victorian men who sought to remove themselves from the distractions and nuisance of society (those horrid children, or the urban poor, trying to earn money by playing musical instruments in the street) by building soundproof rooms in their homes, establishes a context of hyperacusis, into which each barely perceptible sound signals a spreading entrapment: the breathing of an injured dog, light footsteps, rustling silk, overheard conversations, the scraping and scratching of a quill pen.

Sound is the villain, shifting in its allegiances, deceiving, spreading instability, yet silence is equally unreliable. At times, this becomes a contest of the microsonic. The familiar representation of women's quiet domesticity and virtue is twisted into a deadly struggle of near-silences, nothing on nothingness, of who can produce the quietest quiet: 'The sound had not caught my ears. But I was then deeply absorbed in my letters; and I write with a heavy hand, and a quill pen, scraping and scratching noisily over the paper. It was more likely that Madame Fosco would hear the scraping of my pen than that I should hear the rustling of her dress.' The most ingenious villain of the book, Count Fosco, is large and loquacious, yet his most unsettling quality is an uncanny capacity to move without sound. 'I heard his sympathetic voice travelling away from me by degrees', writes Frederick Fairlie, one of the multiple narrators of the story, 'but large as he was, I never heard him. He had the negative merit of being absolutely noiseless. I ventured to make use of my eyes again, after an interval of silence — and he was gone.' This is ironic, considering Fairlie's obsession with noise, yet the engine of the story runs on these nuanced contradictions and oppositions, through which sensibilities, emotions and bodies are stretched to breaking point.

Eavesdropping is a weapon deployed by adversaries on both sides of this muted struggle: '. . . silence is safe — and we have need of safety in this house', says Marian to Laura, mindful of eavesdropping and a deepening sense of threat. Silence is also an opportunity, a portal, as when Count Fosco is overheard exercising his canaries: 'I waited a little while, and the singing and the whistling ceased. "Come, kiss me, my pretties!" said the deep voice. There was a responsive twittering and chirping — a low oily laugh — a silence of a minute or two — and then I heard the opening of the house door. I turned, and retraced my steps. The magnificent melody of the prayer in Rossini's "Moses," sung in a sonorous bass voice, rose grandly through the suburban silence of the place. The front gate opened and closed. The Count had come out.'

In such a world, silence can only be realized within the interstices of fullness, though that fullness may itself be another level of stillness or silence. A creeping sense of the uncanny derived from the impossibility of silence is the contradiction upon which Conrad so effectively constructed his strange, strained tale of a secret shared, and through which Collins built an atmosphere of instability and helplessness. Yet without the conception of a symbolic condition called silence we are unable to fully articulate or express many profound passages and extreme states of existence: the familiar definitions of peace, tranquillity, stillness, absence, emptiness, nothingness, withdrawal, blankness, unconsciousness, isolation, solitude, alienation and deafness, but also rejection, erasure, oblivion, incommunicado, solitary confinement, grief, repression, suppression, death, genocide, extermination, total destruction, the abyss. Rachel Carson's influential polemic on environmental destruction, *Silent Spring*, Shusako Endo's *Silence*, a novel depicting the persecution of Christians in seventeenth-century Japan, or Orlando Figes's *The Whisperers: Private Lives in Stalin's Russia*, illustrate the potency and concision of this metaphor, if metaphor it is, as shorthand for oppression, catastrophe, and in the case of Endo's novel, the troubling question for Christians of God's silence. Silence may be a loss of language in a literal sense, as in Susan Hiller's *The Last Silent Movie*, 2008, a projected work in which the screen remains black for 20 minutes, other than subtitles, but the projection room is filled with the sound of voices speaking languages either extinct or endangered: Ngarrindjeri, K'ora, Kulkhassi, Nganasan, Welsh Romany, Silbo Gomera (the whistled language of La Gomera in the Canary Islands), and nineteen others. 'So if this is such an unusual collection of sounds, what is the word "silent" doing in the title, its presence there so paradoxically loud?' asks Mark Godfrey in his catalogue essay. 'The word "silent" encourages us to question the processes through which these languages have been silenced, to question, for instance, whether these languages have become silent because people stopped speaking them, or whether they were silenced as other refused to listen? Did colonizers force people to stop speaking their languages, or have cultural groups take up English for economic reasons, and in the process, silenced their own languages the better to communicate in a "modern" world? Can the anthropologists who gather and record languages actually end up silencing languages by leaving recordings in rarely-visited sound archives?'

Contradictory and conflicted, silence has many meanings in contemporary society. One minute's silence measures an amount of not-sounding, a marker of falling quiet long enough to denote respect and sacrifice in relation to a tragedy, yet, in theory, not too long to create unease or encourage disruption. This fear of disruption (anxious enough in certain circumstances to warrant the replacement of respectful silence with applause) allows that silence is not necessarily respected, appreciated, or easily tolerated. For many people, silence is an alien condition, only approachable as an artificial, self-conscious pause that interrupts normal life. Seeking isolation in New Zealand, Jenny Diski took a boat trip on Doubtful Sound: 'The high point of the trip came when, in the middle of the captain's broadcast commentary, he told us that the high point had come. Now we were going to hear the "sound of silence", the sound of Doubtful Sound. He asked for all camera clicking and conversation to stop. He turned off the engine. For a full two minutes there was — silence . . . Unfortunately, there was the sound of listening — a kind of buzz of people not doing anything in order to hear what people not doing anything was like, and the sound of expectation, of folk appreciating nature. The silent scream of appreciation gradually transmuted into a silent anticipation of the breaking of the silence.'

An ignorance of language enforces silence: to walk in a foreign city, not understanding the simplest conversation, unable to ask for food or drink without mime, enclosed within a bubble of detachment. During the early days of his stay in Germany in 1936, Samuel Beckett wrote about the pain of being isolated from society as he learned to speak German: 'How absurd, the struggle to learn to be silent in another language! I am altogether absurd and inconsequential. The struggle to be master of another silence! Like a deaf man investing his substance in Schallplatten [gramophone records], or a blind man with a Leica.'

There are few guilty pleasures in a liberal democracy these days, but even so, how often do you hear somebody say that their favourite art form is mime? The art of soundless acting, mime still has a few old favourites: Harpo Marx and Jacques Tati, Benny Hill (in some quarters), the violent wing of the movement — Clint Eastwood and Takeshi Kitano — and then the greats of silent cinema, Charlie Chaplin and Buster Keaton (Beckett and Keaton collaborated in New York in 1965, for the shooting of Beckett's *Film*, but their first meeting was a silent disaster: Keaton preoccupied with drinking beer and watching the ball game on television; Beckett too reticent to break the ice).

The absurdity of mime is nicely parodied by film director Sylvain Chomet in his Tour Eiffel section of *Paris, Je T'Aime*: a young boy humiliated by having to grow up with miming parents. Mime-Boy, the local kids call him, but he refuses to use the invisible car. There have been rumours that Harpo Marx named himself after Harpocrates, misnamed god of silence, but this seems unlikely. One of my favourite Harpo scenes comes from a lesser Marx Brothers film, *Love Happy*. Harpo stands with his mouth open as two men pull an increasingly improbable collection of objects from inside his raincoat: the leg of a dummy, a dog, a block of ice, a toboggan. Then they try to make him talk by using various forms of torture. All this gets them nowhere, so finally they eavesdrop on him as he phones Chico. At first, Harpo uses whistles and a car horn to communicate to his brother. 'Some sort of code' the eavesdroppers agree. Then Chico 'reads his mind', at one point telling Harpo to clean it out; Harpo responds by passing a handkerchief through one ear and out the other. All the time Chico is asking for quiet so he can hear what Harpo is 'saying'. This paradoxical hyperactivity of mimed silence is noted by Michel Chion in his book on Jacques Tati and his famous character, Monsieur Hulot: 'Hulot's notorious silence is not the mime's natural state . . . Tati chooses, however, to make Hulot, in spite of his silenced voice, an extremely talkative character. We notice this in his behaviour, gestures, and even in his immobility. Hulot is constantly correcting his actions, coming back to what he had strayed from.'

Mime can induce a kind of hatred, perhaps best expressed by Billy Crystal's performance as Morty the Miming Waiter, in *This is Spinal Tap*. His memorably cynical line, 'mime is money', is funnier for its breaking of a silence (mimes are annoying for their refusal of speech, but even more annoying when they do speak). For reasons of his success as much as anything else, the symbolic victim of mime's descent into bathos was Marcel Marceau, the French mime whose Walking Against the Wind routine inspired Michael Jackson's moonwalk. His history argues for a reconsideration. Marceau learned the art of silent entertainment while hidden with other Jewish children in German occupied France during World War II. His father, a kosher butcher, died in Auschwitz concentration camp in 1944. 'The people who came back from the camps, couldn't talk about it, they didn't know how to express it,' Marceau once said. 'Maybe that has counted, subconsciously, in my choice of silence.' After Marceau's death in 2007, somebody wrote a letter to a newspaper, suggesting a minute's noise, as a mark of respect. Another suggested a performance of John Cage's *4'33"*, by way of tribute.

BURROWING

Architect Peter Eisenman, who designed Berlin's Holocaust Memorial to the Murdered Jews in Europe, has talked about the concrete slabs of the memorial in terms of silence. 'I had the idea of silence,' he said. 'What was taken away from people was their ability to speak. I wanted a memorial that spoke without speaking.'

'The art of our time is noisy with appeals for silence', wrote Susan Sontag in her essay, 'The Aesthetics of Silence'. Equally, she could have argued that the art of our time is noisy, period, but there is evidence to suggest that silence as an art statement was anticipated in the late nineteenth century, long before Cage. In 1897, for example, the French humorist Alphonse Allais published *Funeral March for the Obsequies of a Deaf Man*. Though far too literal in its humour to have the impact of Duchamp's later, more sophisticated games with art (or to be humorous), this 'score' of nine blank measures is an early marker of the twentieth-century quest for the white whale of silence, for creation through destruction, for reduction, even for an erasure of history. The gesture was not isolated. Allais belonged to a Parisian prankster group, the Incoherents. In 1885, another member of the Incoherents, caricaturist and filmmaker Emile Cohl, photographed an ear filled with cotton. Noise grew louder, so the choice was evident: to speak out, to scream, to block out, to withdraw into silence?

'Father is gone,' Kafka wrote in a diary sketch called 'Great Noise', 'now begins the more delicate, scattered, hopeless variety of noise, headed by the voices of the two canaries. Not for the first time — the canaries remind me now — I think of opening my door a crack, crawling next door like a snake, and from a position prone on my belly begging my sister and her maid for a little quiet.' To justify his nocturnal writing schedule, he had sent this fragment to his fiancée, Felice Bauer, in 1912. 'The Burrow', written in the penultimate year of his life, fictionalizes Kafka's deep aversion to noise. The story begins by describing an elaborate retreat into security, invisibility and silence within a highly rationalized underground network of passages and chambers. As a sense of complacency accrues, the creature of the story (some kind of mole, we assume, though this is never stated) begins to hear a whistling sound within the deep silence and emptiness of his retreat. 'I did not hear it at all when I first arrived,' says the narrator, 'although it must certainly have been there; I must first feel quite at home before I could hear it; it is, so to speak, audible only to the ear of the householder.'

This is a distinctive characteristic of peripheral or fugitive sounds heard as introjections: suddenly a sound penetrates and disturbs that which feels safe and still. Again, this returns us to Freud's analysis of the uncanny, and the unheimlich. In the disjunctions between homely and unhomely, in doubling and doppelgangers, automata and animate life, between what was once familiar but long repressed and estranged, lurks the uncanny.

The narrator of Kafka's 'The Burrow' is confronted with an unpalatable truth about the homely, the undisturbed, perfect isolation, stillness and silence — that security is the architect of its own vulnerability. As security increases so freedoms contract. 'I must have silence in my passages', he says, demanding perfection that can only be compromised. He becomes haunted and obsessed with an invasive whistling: 'Sometimes I fancy that the noise has stopped, for it makes long pauses; sometimes such a faint whistling escapes one, one's own blood is pounding all too loudly in one's ears; then two pauses come one after another, and for a while one thinks that the whistling has stopped forever.' Uncertainty lodges itself in his mind, though the narrator's uncertainty is not identical to that of the reader. The burrower grows uncertain about the location of the noise, its source, whether he can trust another creature, whether he was right to design the burrow as he did, whether he can afford to make changes. The reader, on the other hand, grows uncertain about the origin of the whistle. Is it produced by air holes created by small tunnelling creatures or by the digging of a great beast, as the narrator believes, or does it emanate from within the narrator himself? Though considered virtually finished, the end of the story was lost, ending without either resolution or a full stop.

'Everyone carries a room about inside him', Kafka wrote in the first notebook of his posthumous papers. 'This fact can even be proved by means of the sense of hearing. If someone walks fast and one pricks up one's ears and listens, say in the night, when everything round about is quiet, one hears, for instance, the rattling of a mirror not quite firmly fastened to the wall.' This room within a space is critical to the idea of the auditory void of silence. The uncanny silence is not a place of repose, as some audio theorists seem to believe. 'Space, in contemporary discourse,' writes Anthony Vidler in *The Architectural Uncanny*, 'as in lived experience, has taken on an almost palpable existence. . . . Equally, space is assumed to hide, in its darkest recesses and forgotten margins, all the objects of fear and phobia that have returned with such insistency to haunt the imaginations of those who have tried to stake out spaces to protect their health and happiness.' Experiments

SINISTER RESONANCE

with sensory deprivation reveal another aspect of this paradox. In 1968, artists Robert Irwin, James Turrell and Dr Ed Wortz (at that time head of the life sciences laboratory at Garrett Aerospace Corporation) spent long periods of time isolated from sensory stimulation in the anechoic chamber of UCLA. 'You had no visual or audio input at all,' Irwin has said, 'other than what you might do yourself. You might begin to have some retinal replay or hear your own body, hear the electrical energy of your brain, the beat of your heart, all that sort of thing.' What was most striking about these experiments was the richness of material generated mentally within such a void, and the engulfing hypersensitivity that the participants experienced on emerging back into a more familiar environment. They claimed to have found, for example, that the best conditions for drinking Carlsberg Elephant Beer was when listening to a 650 Hz audio tone. Any slight variations of the tone's frequency would make the beer almost undrinkable. 'Confronted with a severe diminution of activity,' writes Adrian Kohn, 'the ravenous senses recalibrate to detect something, anything, from the dark silent stillness.'

These experiments conducted by Irwin, Tenney and Wortz are reminiscent of John Cage's now over-familiar story of the short time he spent inside one of the anechoic chambers in use at Harvard in 1951, in which he heard two sounds, despite the total absence of reverberation in the room. One was a low pulse, the other a high-pitched singing tone. Being disturbed by these, he was told by the engineer that they were the sounds of his circulation and nervous system respectively. This is so close to the experience of the mole creature in Kafka's 'The Burrow' as to be uncanny, as if Kafka had struggled with the perpetual disturbance of these same externalisations of interior body processes. One of the key texts of twentieth-century music, sound art, and American minimalism, the anechoic chamber story is almost certainly misleading. Cage may have been hearing symptoms of tinnitus, or spontaneous otoacoustic emissions from his own ears, rather than the sound of his brain at work (or as Susan Sontag put it, confusing the issue still further, the blood in his head). These faint sounds of otoacoustics, produced by the expansion and contractions of hair cells within the outer cochlea, could not be measured until the development of sufficiently sensitive low noise microphones in the late 1970s, so the Harvard engineer (and Cage) would have been unaware of their existence.

The physical origins of the sounds heard by Cage do not affect the sense or impact of the story, but these uncertainties point to an estrangement from the body. We are left with the suspicion that Cage, ever cheerful and rarely self-analytical, was a less diligent listener to his own body than gloomier, more introverted souls like Kafka, Conrad, Poe, Woolf, Joyce, Beckett and Melville. The conception of silence as an external phenomenon that can be heard (as opposed to 'meaningful' silences that are behavioural, metaphorical, mystical, philosophical or political) presupposes an absence of the body, a neutralisation of space as an active presence. Silence coalesces, aerial yet substantial, from within absorption, a flowing across boundaries: the sound of the listener; the sound of space and the air with which it is filled.

CONDEMNED TO SILENCE

Sound can be treacherous, rising up despite all suppressive efforts. An infuriating formula applies to quiet sounds: every attempt to create a silence seems to provoke counterattacks of invasive sound. In *Hubbub*, Emily Cockayne quotes a mid-seventeenth-century tutor, who suggested that the optimum environment for lute music was 'a Wainscote Roome where there is noe furniture if you can not let the Company exceed the number three or fewer for the noise of a Mouse is a hinderance to that Musicke.' As Mr Fairlie discovered in *The Woman in White*, what begins as sensitivity to sound can easily become neurotic; elimination only generates more information. In *Gargantua and Pantagruel*, a two part work published between 1532–34, Francois Rabelais wrote of '. . . an example of a philosopher who thought he was in solitude, and that, having departed from the crowd, he could now theorize, reason, and write; and yet all around him dogs were barking, wolves howling, lions roaring, horses neighing, elephants trumpeting, serpents hissing, asses braying, grasshoppers chirping, and turtle-doves cooing. In fact, he was in more turmoil than if he had been at the fair of Fontenay or of Niort.'

The solution would seem to be the intensely private soundproof room beloved of the Victorian gentleman, yet such an extreme social withdrawal simply opens the door to ambiguous inner phantoms of microsonic hallucination. Alcoholic adventurer, author and occultist William Seabrook drew attention to these irrepressible peripheral phenomena in his zealously gossipy exploitation book, *Witchcraft*. The newspaper mogul, Joseph Pulitzer, suffered from near-blindness and extreme sensitivity to sound. In his forties he cocooned himself in retreats such as the 'Tower of Silence' in Maine and a soundproof vault in his Manhattan brownstone. 'The elder Pulitzer spent thousands of dollars to have a room cork-lined and wound with silk, cocooned (walls packed too, they say, with mineral wool),' wrote Seabrook, 'but he still heard, or imagined he heard, church bells ringing. And even if he didn't hear outside sounds, it was still a noisy place. His pen sounded like cats scratching, and when he dropped a pencil on the rug it sounded like a depth bomb with a retarded explosion. A vacuum is the only thing that will blank sound completely, and you can't live in a vacuum.' This was the same Seabrook whose autobiography, *No Hiding Place*, describes the persistence of early auditory memories in its first paragraph: 'The sounds were faint yet near. They were the first my memory-conscious ears had ever heard. I had become alive to everything at once — sitting on a warm green lawn, eating bread spread with brown sugar, and hearing the sounds. I liked the sounds best and started crawling toward them.'

Seabrook's sadomasochistic games were described in Man Ray's auto-biography, *Self Portrait*. Visiting Seabrook's New York apartment for lunch in the 1930s, Man Ray arrived to find, in Seabrook's words, something interesting. 'In the middle of the floor sat a statuesque woman,' he wrote, 'like an odalisque, quite nude and decorated with strings of pearls, bracelets and rings. He introduced her as his secretary, but she did not move or speak. He informed me that she was condemned to silence for twenty-four hours but functioned otherwise like any normal being.' Later, when Seabrook's attention was diverted, she confided in May Ray, saying in a low voice that she would tell the bastard what she thought of him when her time was up. In *Witchcraft*, Seabrook documented an experiment with Aleister Crowley. In 1920, after a conversation about Trappist monks and their vows of silence, they both agreed to suspend normal verbal communication and limit themselves to one prearranged monosyllable for a week. After trying a variety of animal sounds, such as 'urr', 'woof', 'moo' and 'baa', they settled for 'wow' and found that even lengthy, deep philosophical conversations were possible, albeit with the assistance of a gallon of moonshine corn liquor. Based on this experience, Seabrook wrote a short story, 'Wow!', set in ancient China, in which people discover peace and contentment through replacing human language with the word 'wow'; eventually, a second fac-tion emerges, those who spread dissent by using 'wo'. In consequence, two great armies fight to the death over 'wow' and 'wo', leaving nothing but 'a few empty bubbles floating on a river of blood.'

DEAD AIR

Air and sound are much the same: we breathe sound and listen to air. Does air persist through time? Can sound transmute into other forms, like fog or condensation? In Georges Rodenbach's 1897 novel, *The Bells of Bruges*, bells are said to sleep: 'They were not entirely at rest, just as virgins are never completely at rest. Their sleep was visited by dreams. He felt as if they were about to move, stretch, moan like sleepwalkers. The incessant murmuring among the bells! A noise that persists, like the sound of the sea in shells! They never empty themselves entirely. Sound forming like beads of sweat! A condensation of music on the bronze . . .'

In *A Matter of Life and Death*, Powell and Pressburger's film from 1946, an angel messenger from the other side stops time. With stasis comes absolute silence. David Niven, in limbo between life and death yet functioning in the living world, rings a bell and viewers of the film realize that sound is absent, the air itself is held in limbo, the universe paused.

TREMBLING AIR

Rodenbach spoke about bare, empty rooms as 'granaries of silence'. Air is something, not nothing; more than one kind of air, more than one state of silence. 'After a moment I fired the second barrel too', Knut Hamsun wrote in *Pan*, 'the air trembled at the salute, and the echo flung the noise out into the wide world; it was as if all the hills had united in a shout for the vessel sailing away.'

LISTLESS AIR

'Listless is the air in an empty room,' wrote Virginia Woolf in her novel of the early 1920s, *Jacob's Room*, 'just swelling the curtain; the flowers in the jar shift. One fibre in the wicker armchair creaks, though no one sits there.'

PUTTY AIR

Mark Rothko had thoughts about air that are relevant to this reading of silence as a texture, a substance that can tremble or thicken, an event or noise out of which all forms emerge. 'Tactile space, or for the sake of simplicity, let us call it air, which exists between objects or shapes in the picture, is painted so that it gives the sensation of a solid', he wrote. 'That is, air in a tactile painting is represented as an actual substance rather than as an emptiness. We might more readily conceive it if we picture a plate of jelly or, perhaps, soft putty, into which a series of objects are impressed at various depths.'

HISSING AIR

Describing, with some distaste, the reptilian character of the Galapagos Islands, Herman Melville wrote, 'No Voice, no low, no howl is heard — the chief sound of life here is a hiss.' The bereft image could also serve as an evocation of the suburban sitting room, its undisturbed air that allows the hissing of the ears to rise up into consciousness. To record such an empty, still room, then play back the recording in the same space, will produce an approximation of Melville's Galapagos hiss. The elegant conceptual economy of Alvin Lucier's composition of 1971, *I Am Sitting in a Room*, explored the transformative characteristics of acoustic space by a process of repeatedly playing, recording, replaying, and rerecording a spoken text until the nature of the acoustics (the background) overtakes the foreground of the text. Lucier's articulation of what philosopher Edward Casey called 'the ancient dialectic of place and space' suggests that the phenomenon of cumulative reverberation will happen in any given space, a cloud of echoes inferring infinite space, yet his example begins and ends with himself, seated in a specific place of known provenance, also impregnated with secret history. As David Lynch said, interviewed by Chris Rodley, architecture itself is 'a recording instrument'. In 2005, Danish/German artist Jacob Kirkegaard applied a similar technical process to empty rooms in Chernobyl, Ukraine. These spaces were left abandoned after an explosion in the nuclear power plant in 1986 rendered the area uninhabitable. Rather than add any sound, Kirkegaard simply recorded empty, silent interiors. He then played back the recording into the same room, recording it again as he did so, then played this new recording back, repeating the process up to ten times. On each repetition, the room hears its own history, fills up with its own intangible volume in a cumulative haunting. Pieces such as *Auditorium* vibrate with luminescent, pulsing density, as if some entity previously indiscernible from the silence of evacuation and radiation had clustered, finally to manifest itself during this absence of human life.

DAMPENED AIR

'I wish to search out that single sound which is in itself so strong that it can confront silence', wrote Tōru Takemitsu. 'It is then that my own personal insignificance will cease to trouble me.' This might be the single, inarticulate screams of Munch and Bacon, the visceral response of human beings to a godless world, or, the breathing resonance of flutes made from the wing bones of birds, mute swan and griffon vulture (fragments of Pan), discovered in 2009 within the dark granaries of silence of the Hohle Fels caves in southwestern Germany, and estimated to be between 35,000 and 40,000 years old. Music is assumed to begin and end with silence, stated or tacit, emerge out of silence, articulate through silence, and because of this confrontation with the construct of silence, its need to be other, music itself refuses silence. Few musical compositions or performances consist of a single sound, unless that sound is extended through time to become a kind of time or textured air itself. 'Silence is the name of a book by John Cage,' composer Tom Johnson has written, 'and many composers talk about the importance of silence in music, but one does not actually hear much of it in the classical repertoire, or any other repertoire. In fact, silences longer than three seconds are extremely rare in all kinds of music.' Johnson has consciously incorporated periods of silence into pieces such as *Long Decays*, for piano, and *Organ and Silence*. Though clearly related to the repose of Cage compositions like *Prelude for Meditation*, they are more intimately connected to the work of Johnson's teacher, Morton Feldman, and join a lineage that might include Claude Debussy, Maurice Ravel, Erik Satie, Alexander Scriabin, Kaikhosru Shapurji Sorabji, Federico Mompou, George Crumb and Tōru Takemitsu, a secret society devoted to pauses, inhalations, murmurs, implicit and stated silence. 'Silence also inhabits and dampens audible music', wrote Vladimir Jankélévitch in *Music and the Ineffable*.

'Laconic tendencies, reticence, and the pianissimo are like silences within silence. In effect, brachylogy — brevity, concision of diction — is a form of silence in the music of Satie or Mompou. The pièce brève is a silence not in that it emerges from silence, but indirectly, in that it expresses a desire to retighten the grip, a will to concentration. Concision harbours the wish to disturb silence as little as possible.'

In notes accompanying his recording of Federico Mompou's piano cycle of short works composed between 1915 and 1967, *Música Callada*, pianist Herbert Henck emphasis the silence at the core of these 28 pieces: 'Mompou cites the Spanish mystic St. John of the Cross, who invoked the idea of "La Música Callada, la Soledad Sonora" in one of his poems, to express the idea of music that is the voice of silence itself.' This is the complexity of silence, a perpetual evasion of fixity, a constant play of contradiction expressed through shades of difference in every medium, every scene of life. 'I would claim that musical silence is not the void,' wrote Jankélévitch, 'and in effect it is also not only "cessation." Instead, it is "attenuation." Like reticence, or interrupted development, it expresses the wish to return to silence as soon as possible; an attenuation of intensity, it is at the threshold of the inaudible, a game played with almost nothing.'

In early piano pieces, such as *Intermission 6*, from 1953, or *Piano Piece 1964*, Feldman's method was to place sounds within empty space, as if their existence were preordained as sculptural objects, then allow their ebbing presence to linger and melt into air. Tonal gradations, or the echoing impact of a single note in silence, is what matters, as if the music belongs in silence, returning to silence, and what we call the 'music' is simply a degree of colouration dominated more by instrument tone than by the creak, the hiss, the empty room sound. To illustrate what interested him, Feldman invoked Ad Reinhardt, not as a painter of ultra-minimalist, so-called 'black' paintings, but as a master of gradation: '. . . the gradation of grays, you see, I'm very into that. This is like Ad Reinhardt. You see the gradation. Do you hear it? Are you focussed enough?'

In Yasunari Kawabata's novel *The Old Capital*, set in Kyoto after the American occupation, Sosuke, a weaver, is talking business with a customer. The customer, Takichiro, has brought in a design which he wants Sosuke to weave into an obi. The design, colourful, modern, yet restrained, is influenced by Paul Klee, and this provokes a discussion of the way in which English words such as 'sense' or 'idea', or Western terms for colour, have slipped into Japanese vocabulary. 'I hate it that Western words have

come into such use', says Takichiro. 'Haven't there been splendid elegant colours in Japan since ancient times?'
'Even black has various subtle shades,' Sosuke replies.

AN EFFECT OF SILENCE

Writing in his *Manifesto For Silence*, a polemic to confront the political and cultural implications of noise, Stuart Sim considers twentieth-century monochrome paintings by artists such as Kasimir Malevich, Alexander Rodchenko, Robert Rauschenberg, Robert Ryman and Ad Reinhardt as visual counterparts of audible silence. The monochrome tradition, he claims, is a return to purity in art, an expression of Kandinsky's idea that abstraction equals spirituality, which in turn suggests silence. 'Reinhardt represents the logical extension of this idealisation of silence with his move to black, but the lack of distraction in any of the monochrome paintings, whatever the colour used, is capable of creating an effect of silence.'

Manifesto for Silence was published shortly after another protest against our increasingly noisy world, *The Spirit of Silence*, by John Lane. Noise grows, as does the case against it, since research studies demonstrate clear links between damaged physical and mental health and the excessive, incessant levels of noise now present in society. 'The enemies of silence are twofold', writes Lane. 'First there are the external interruptions to one's peace of mind. . . . the second and more insidious is internal; it is the Trojan horse we have invited into our own lives. . . . the baggage of ideas, beliefs and assumptions we carry around in our minds.' Again, the mirage of silence as purity, a clean slate, yet we need not depend upon the elevated sources with which Lane builds an argument to realize that silence can never be unequivocally on the side of innocence. 'These things'll kill you,' says George C. Scott, talking about cigarettes in William Peter Blatty's film, *Exorcist III*. 'They're quiet,' says the priest. Silence may also be oblivious, indifferent, detached. Max Ernst's *Quiétude*, one of the collages from *La Femme 100 Têtes*, from 1929, shows a man reclining in an armchair. Dozing and dreaming, he floats on a raging flood. Behind him, a sea spout envelops a lighthouse, and by the arm of his chair, the naked arm of La Femme is raised out of the waves.

We may think, with justification, that the twenty-first century is the noisiest era in history, but manifestos for silence are not recent phenomena.

In 1916, an early twentieth-century anti-noise campaigner named Dan McKenzie published *The City of Din: A Tirade Against Noise*. The contradiction of his subtitle highlights one of the problems of such manifestos: though the concepts of noise and silence are valuable as markers of hypothetical absolutes and descriptions of relative states, they remain highly subjective, and so resist adequate definition or placement in any ethical scale. 'Too young to bring about change,' writes Lavinia Greenlaw in her memoir, *The Importance of Music to Girls*, 'we brought about disturbance. Heavy metal was our engine noise — it was trucks on the cricket pitch, bulldozers tearing up the green, boots stomping on flowerbeds, cars driven through hedges, the only thing that could tear a hole in the silence of a Sunday afternoon.' Urgent needs for outward expression, liberty, disorder, sociability and the release of energy all press on silence. Noise may be violent but its interruption raises an otherwise subjugated existence: Iggy Pop's 'I'm Bored', or Public Enemy's 'Bring The Noise'. Noise is so often central to social belonging, the shaping of identity, or protests and injustice, that pleas for silence seem one step from a joyless slide into conformity, passivity, living death. On the one hand, noise is just one of many collateral damages resulting from transportation, construction and manufacturing, all central to the destructive demands of economic growth; on the other hand, noise remains a potent symbol of rebellion and resistance. Given this perpetual conflict, the anti-noise activist faces an onerous task.

FEAR AND TREMBLING

During my last years at primary school I was persuaded to join the local church choir. Religion held little interest for me at that time, but certain aspects of ceremony could be affecting. The most enjoyable aspect of my short time as a choirboy was the opportunity for collective singing. Most of the hymns were ponderously dull; I preferred the austerity of psalms, sung at Evensong on Sundays, and even the bleak Good Friday service in which music was replaced by plain recitative. The only hymn that made me think about music in relation to the sentiments expressed was 'Let All Mortal Flesh Keep Silence' — an intriguingly slow and sombre melody of seventeenth-century French origins (given a new arrangement in 1906 by Ralph Vaughan Williams) whose words are taken from the ancient Liturgy of Saint James: 'Let all mortal flesh keep silence, and with fear and

trembling stand.' This image of trembling flesh, combined with the obliga-
tion to be fearful and silent in the presence of a terrifying God, might have
shaken my faith had I actually believed in God. As it was, it appealed to
my nascent Gothic tendencies, adding to a suspicion that the dark side had
more bite than the light. It seems I am not sole carrier of this particular
memory; web research indicates that John Cale performed his version of
'Let All Mortal Flesh Keep Silence' live at the Emerald City Club in New
Jersey in 1980. No doubt bootlegs exist, but New Jersey's reaction to this
intimidating dirge is best left to the imagination.

MY OWN SILENCE

'I want to write a book about Silence [. . .] the things people don't say',
says Terence Hewett, the writer in Virginia Woolf's novel, *The Voyage Out*.
'But the difficulty is immense.' Books that appeal for silence, struggle with
silence or try to speak of silence, usually confront the problem by calling
down reinforcements from those religions that give a high value to silence.
In *A Book of Silence*, by Sara Maitland, prayer is a constant thread. Accounts
of the Desert Fathers and other religious hermits are considered alongside
the journals of mountaineers, explorers and lone sailors. She spends time
in search of silence on the island of Skye, in Glen Affric forest, in the Sinai
desert, at Quaker worship and a Zen monastery in County Durham, then
in an isolated house in the south-west of Scotland. Early in her book, she
acknowledges the bias toward religion in writings on silence: 'Before the
mid eighteenth century I can find no detailed reports of voluntary silence
whatsoever that are not directed by a religious impulse; even when Daniel
Defoe wrote *Robinson Crusoe*, based on the real experience of Alexander
Selkirk, he took a totally secular event and turned it into a religious work.
All the early accounts share a set of particular expectations, rewards and
goals, which are bound to slew both the experience itself and the way it
is reported.' By the end of the book she is praying for three hours a day,
grounding herself in biblical meditation, the discipline of the psalms and
other relevant texts. 'I do it for myself, in truth,' she writes, 'but I also pray for
others and pray that my silence may be useful somehow in the noisy world.'

There is no doubt that such ardent withdrawing into a dedicated
spiritual silence is both inspirational and aspirational for many people who
feel overwhelmed by whatever noisy version of contemporary life they

are living. The urge to escape is a complex and paradoxically inescapable component of human nature. In the end, Maitland's book seems more a turbulent account of solitude and its challenges rather than an exploration of silence. Listening is not considered in great detail except as an occasional epiphany. Once again, we must accept that silence has many meanings, not all of which have much to do with sound, listening, or hearing.

'God is silent', wrote Fernando Pessoa. 'That is why we can love the saint but cannot love God.' Lacking religious belief myself, I find there are serious obstacles to accepting the proposition that religion owns the last word on silence. Religions have been silent too often, and on the other hand too ardent in their silencing of dissident views and proscribed behaviour. The illustration on the back cover of Alberto Manguel's *A History of Reading* shows light from the Izaak Walton memorial window in the Prior Silstede Chapel of Winchester Cathedral. Underneath the image of Walton reading by a riverbank, an inscription reads: 'Study to be quiet'. This may be the accepted view of studious reading, the ideal presented by Vermeer, Rembrandt and Maes — a silent, private experience that internalizes the text — and yet as Manguel points out, regulations demanding that scribes should be silent in monastic scriptoriums date only from the ninth century. Before then they had worked from dictation and by reading aloud. 'Some dogmatists became wary of the new trend', writes Manguel, 'in their minds, silent reading allowed for day-dreaming, for the danger of accidie — the sin of idleness, "the destruction that wasteth at noonday". But silent reading brought with it another danger the Christian fathers had not foreseen. A book that can be read privately, reflected upon as the eye unravels the sense of the words, is no longer subject to immediate clarification or guidance, condemnation or censorship by a listener. Silent reading allows unwitnessed communication between the book and the reader, and the singular "refreshing of the mind", in Augustine's happy phrase.'

Religious silences may be instructive but they can never be definitive except for believers. This is why I find Thomas Merton an uneasy read, his piety alienating, even when the charged atmosphere of his close listening is affecting. 'Late afternoon', he wrote in *Dialogues with Silence*. 'The quiet of the afternoon is filled with an altogether different tonality. . . . For about eight minutes I stayed silent and did not move and listened to my watch and wondered if I might not understand something of the work Our Lady is preparing. It is an hour of tremendous expectation.' If I am going to read reports from the far recesses of Christian silence, then I prefer Patrick Leigh

Fermor's *A Time to Keep Silence*, first published in 1957. Through a number of pragmatic, temporary engagements with monastic retreat, Fermor enters with great humility and curiosity into a world he finds both puzzling and beautiful. He writes exquisitely of the sensations aroused by these encounters: 'Their footfalls made no noise and only the ring of the crosier's butt on the flags and the clanging of the censer could be heard across the Gregorian. . . . The anthem was followed by a long stillness which seemed to be scooped out of the very heart of sound. After long minutes, a small bell rang and then the great bell from the tower which told of the rites that were being celebrated and the mysterious events taking place; and the heads of the monks fell as if one blow had scythed them away.' With a discretion that now seems endearingly quaint, Fermor insists that his appreciation of monastic life was limited by some personal perplexity; he lives in dread of any direct enquiry into his own spiritual convictions, describing himself as a possible giaour (a Turkish term for unbeliever). Despite what we can only assume to be his lack of religious faith, he finds the monasteries peaceful repositories of learning in which 'the troubled waters of the mind grow still and clear, and much that is hidden away and all that clouds it floats to the surface and can be skimmed away.'

There are silences of peace, and then there are silences of complacency, stasis, regulation, piety, submissiveness, secrecy, ostracism, excommunication, the status quo, a deserted town centre after dark, gloomy Sunday, a gated community, suburbia, a cold church pew, people living quiet, respectable lives or suffocating under ennui, shame, embarrassment, inhibition, blankness, boredom. In George Eliot's *Silas Marner*, the linen-weaver, Marner, is suspended from church membership after being falsely accused of a theft. His faith shaken, he moves to another town and lives a solitary life of toil, deriving his only pleasure from hoarding the money he earns from his weaving. Ear filled with the monotony of his loom, both body and soul wither; 'Old Master Marner' the children call him, even though he is only 40 years old. Eliot, always sensitive to hearing in her novels, suggests that the loom's sound is as socially problematic as the weaver himself: 'The questionable sound of Silas's loom, so unlike the natural cheerful trotting of the winnowing-machine, or the simpler rhythm of the flail, had a half-fearful fascination for the Raveloe boys, who would often leave off their nutting or birds'-nesting to peep in at the window of the stone cottage, counterbalancing a certain awe at the mysterious action of the loom, by a pleasant sense of scornful superiority, drawn from the mockery of its alternating noises, along with the bent, tread-mill attitude of the weaver.'

There are silences of the self, some insupportable. 'The silence depressed me', wrote Sylvia Plath in *The Bell Jar*. 'It wasn't the silence of silence. It was my own silence.'

Resonating loudly within the politics of silence, there are silences of the self, supportable, barely supportable, perhaps insupportable for others, or imposed by others: 'Silent, but . . .' was written by the twentieth-century poet Tsuboi Shigeji, imprisoned twice by the Japanese pre-war government for his left-wing views and tortured until he promised to silence his own antiwar writings:

> I may be silent, but
> I'm thinking.
> I may not talk, but
> Don't mistake me for a wall.

Torture can enforce an outer silence, but discourse may continue within.

THE SILENCE OF FORGETTING

Cheryl Kaplan: 'Ilya, you said that you "cannot look at a painting in silence; inside I am always talking to myself at the moment I am viewing it." . . .'

Ilya Kabakov: 'The artist doesn't come first, the viewer does [. . .] every space has its own strong aura. I feel like a dog, sniffing around, trying to understand the atmosphere. How does the aura speak? It's like a ghost.'

THE SILENCE OF REMEMBERING

A loss of memory is a silence, often accompanied in old people by a loss of hearing, so as events of the past speak only intermittently, scattered by the cold winds of age, sonic events of the present grow fainter. Loss of cultural memory is a silence, also — the so-called failed states and collapsed ideologies that are treated as mute spectres gathered at the global feast. Ilya Kabakov's work, *School No. 6*, created in 1993 on the site of Donald Judd's Chinati Foundation in Marfa, Texas, is a silent reminder of how memory survives in scraps of nostalgia and sharp shards of memory, incomplete scenes and conscious forgetting. In desolate, abandoned school rooms, a dusty violin lies on a bench. As if the children had left music practice one afternoon, then never returned, four red music stands wait for students, along with a flute, a trumpet, a violin bow, faded sheet music, a mandolin fixed to the wall, a backboard leaning against the wall, sheet music on a stand. A guitar lies on the floor in the dust, one more scrap among paper scraps. In the intensity of their silence, a faint music asks to be heard, like the slow heartbeat of a hibernating creature buried under snow.

SPEAKING TO A GHOST

Like many other prominent Japanese novelists of the twentieth century — Akutagawa and Mishima, for example — Yasunari Kawabata ensured his own silence by the definitive measure of suicide. He left no note after killing himself in 1972, but in an obituary he was quoted with this prophetic statement: 'A silent death is an endless word.' Silences are pervasive in his novels, though they are rarely the silences of stereotypical Japanese tranquillity. 'The night scene was severe,' he wrote in 'Gleanings from Snow Country', 'as if the sound of the expanse of snow freezing were echoing deep within the earth.' His characters confront the shades and increments of existence with varying degrees of precision:

> 'I don't know . . . You can't tell whether it's rain or raindrops just from hearing that it's water, and that it's making noise right now.'
> 'If rain makes noise it's raindrops.'
> 'That's not true. The sound of rain and the sound of raindrops aren't the same.'

As with his contemporary, filmmaker Yasujiro Ozu, the placid surface of Kawabata's stories is a thin crust covering emotional turbulence, onerous duty, conflict, and the melancholy of age and loneliness. In 'Love Suicides', one of his masterpieces of concision known as palm-of-the-hand stories, a letter comes to a woman from the husband who deserted her. Don't let our child bounce her rubber ball, he asks, because the sound strikes at my heart. Another letter arrives: their daughter shouldn't wear shoes to school, because they trample on his heart. Then the next letter: she shouldn't eat from a porcelain bowl, because the sound breaks his heart. The woman breaks the bowl, breaks her own bowl, throws the kitchen table out into the garden, flings herself through the paper wall of the house. 'What about this sound?' she asks. The final letter arrives with equally final demands: 'Don't make any sound at all. Don't open or close the doors or sliding partitions. Don't breathe. The two of you mustn't even let the clocks in the house make a sound.' At this moment, the mother and daughter die: 'They ceased eternally to make even the faintest sound.' The husband then dies, his selfish aim to suffocate what he has denied himself accomplished.

Kawabata's 'Silence', first published in 1958, is a Chinese box of a story, in which successive versions of silence replace each other, snow falling upon snow. At the beginning of the story, a writer plans to visit Omiya Akifusa, an old friend and author who can no longer speak and whose writing hand is paralysed. The narrator wonders why Akifusa won't make more effort to communicate his needs by using some simple code: 'The single letter "w" or "t" might be worth more than all the flood, the truly tremendous flood of words and letters he has written in his life. That single letter might be a more eloquent statement, a more important work.' Taking a taxi for the journey, he asks the driver about rumours of a ghost, a woman who suddenly appears in a car as it passes the crematorium, then sits silently in the back seat and fades out by the time they reach downtown Kamakura. At Akifusa's house, he encounters the difficulties of communicating with a person who understands what he is saying but can't respond:

'[. . .] Even when people are talking like I am now, the present instant is just a sound — "I" or "a" or "m"– it's still just meaningless silence, isn't it?'

'. . . . .'

'No. Silence is certainly not meaningless, as you yourself have . . . I think that sometime before I die I would like to get inside silence, at least for a while.'

'. . . . .'

Tomiko, Akifusa's daughter, tells him about a novel of her father's, in which a young man with ambitions to be a writer goes insane and is sent off to a sanatorium. All potentially dangerous sharp objects such as writing implements are denied him. All he is allowed is manuscript paper, so every day he writes: 'Apparently he was always there in front of that paper, writing

. . . at least he thought he was writing. But the paper stayed white.' When his mother visited, he would ask her to read aloud what he had written. Despairing, it occurred to her to tell him stories of her own, as if she was reading from the manuscript: 'She remembers things she had forgotten. And the son's memories grow more beautiful. The son is drawing the mother's story out, helping her, changing the story — there's no way of telling whose story it is, whether it's the mother's or the son's.'

Tomiko finds a parallel between this story and her own situation, in which she has become a mouthpiece for her father. 'But if Akifusa was to continue in silence', the narrator asks, 'if his words were to come from Tomiko — wouldn't that be one of the powers of silence, too? If one uses no words oneself, other people speak in one's place. Everything speaks.' At the end of the story, during his journey back home, the ghost appears in the taxi. She is sitting next to him, yet only the driver can see her. He feels a chill from her presence and asks if he should speak to her. Don't even joke about it, says the driver. 'You get cursed if you speak to a ghost. You'll be possessed. It's a terrifying idea — don't. Everything will be fine if we just keep quiet until we've taken her as far as Kamakura.'

SHADES OF BLACK

In Ad Reinhardt's beautifully handwritten notes, he returned again and again to words such as 'silence', 'soundless', 'stillness' — in *Twelve Rules for a New Academy* he wrote 'No noise. "The brush should pass over the surface lightly and smoothly" and silently.' But then again, he said elsewhere, 'No such thing as emptiness or invisibility, silence.' Is it possible to say that his black paintings are 'silent', and if so, how can all monochromatic paintings, white, black and all shades between, be equally silent? Standing for a long time in front of Reinhardt's *Abstract Painting, 1963*, in New York's MoMA, staring into its depths, I felt myself passing into an abyss, was forced eventually to look away. The black is not simple black but a grid of squares, a reddish tone in the corners, a cross made up of a blueish-black vertical and a greenish black horizontal; prolonged looking releases this formal structure to the eye, yet the darkness of the painting still induced a form of vertigo. The falling was not a literal feeling, like falling down a well, more passing through the surface into something more complex and infinitely rich. I came away feeling dizzy.

Looking at other monochromes in MoMA's collection — Yves Klein's *French*, Brice Marden's *Grove Group*, or Robert Ryman's horizontal *Pace* — is, in each case, a distinctly different experience. This is also true for comparisons between the varied white surfaces of Piero Manzoni's *Achrome* series, made in the late 1950s and early 1960s. All of them convey varying degrees of activity or energy. His materials shape the beholder's engagement, in one case bread rolls dipped in kaolin, looking at once like a baker's tray but also the faces of worn Neolithic figurines. 'In extending the reach of the achromes in 1960,' wrote Matthew Gale in his essay, *From Alphabet to Zone*, 'Manzoni adopted a variety of materials that were inherently white and thus fulfilled the requirement of neutrality. Cotton was one of these as he aligned square pads, wads or cottonwool balls. Just as with the kaolin achromes, cotton afforded subliminal medical associations.' Whatever these inevitable associations of white dough, white flour, a white apron, white tiles, white uniforms and the silence of kneading or sickness, Manzoni was thinking of white that is nothing but white, a state of pure becoming.

Perhaps because the shadows and dust that passed across Robert Rauschenberg's six white canvases of 1951 influenced John Cage, even opening the way for the active silence of Cage's *4'33"* and Nam June Paik's 1964 projection of a roll of clear leader film in 1964, *Zen for Film*, there is an irresistible temptation to draw parallels between monochrome paintings and music. Robert Ryman, who has devoted most of his life to variations on white paintings, illustrates the dangers of this temptation. As a jazz saxophonist, Ryman was attracted to New York by the music scene of the early 1950s. Subtle but busy textures, gradations and an overall simplicity contained within discreet framing devices might imply that he responded favourably to the music of Cecil Taylor, Sun Ra and Ornette Coleman. In fact, what he played and listened to was the tightly organized virtuosity of Bebop. 'They played something you never heard', he has said. 'It was different. It wasn't predictable. [But] I was never interested in free jazz. I was interested in jazz with a structure. It definitely had to have structure.' This is unsurprising, given Ryman's preoccupation with framing devices. His paintings are not spirit, nor voids; his avoidance of colour allows for the sensuality of surfaces to be repeatedly worked, framed and differentiated from the walls on which they are hung in much the same way that bebop framed the expressive variety of its solos, the ingenious substitution of chords and the interpenetrative complexity of its accompaniments within unyielding structures derived from popular songs of the day.

As a silence, white is suspect. 'Insane, enraged white', wrote Henri Michaux, 'screaming with whiteness. Fanatical, furious, riddling the victim. Horrible electric white, implacable, murderous. White in bursts of white. God of "white." No, not a god, a howler monkey.' White returns us again to the scream. Yves Klein's *Monotone Symphony — Silence*, originally composed in 1949, acknowledged the possibility that a monochrome could be both reductionism (as little as nothing) and expansionism (the filling of all available space). Once Klein had become known as Yves — Le Monochrome, he used a musical analogy to explain his work. 'The artist used to recount an ancient Persian tale', writes Hannah Weitemeier in *Klein*. 'There was once a flute player who, one day, began to play nothing but a single, sustained, uninterrupted note. After he had continued to do so for about twenty years, his wife suggested that other flute players were capable of producing not only a range of harmonious notes, but even entire melodies, and that this might make for more variety. But the monotonous flute player replied that it was no fault of his if he had already found the note which everybody else was still searching for.' The *Monotone Symphony* was performed on a number of occasions: in 1957 a tape version was played by electronic composer Pierre Henry for the Blue Epoch exhibition at Gallery Iris Clert in Paris, then a few years later by a small string ensemble during a performance of Klein's celebrated *Anthropométries*, held in 1960 at the Galerie d'Art Contemporain in Paris. Directed closely by Klein, naked female models smeared in blue pigment pressed themselves against paper lining the walls, or were dragged across the floor. Seated at one side of the stage (though dressed formally for a concert, rather than naked) the musicians played first a single note drone for twenty minutes, then twenty minutes of silence. This basic formulation of a single noise followed by a single silence mirrored the paintings, in which the white paper was impressed, like those cave painting in which pigment was blown onto an outstretched hand, inscribing both the presence and absence of the human body.

TO KEEP ME FROM HEARING

Ad Reinhardt was born in New York in 1913. This was the same year that Kasimir Malevich painted *Black Square*, a year before Mondrian began his plus-minus paintings, five years before Aleksandr Rodchenko sent his *Black on Black* canvas to Moscow's Tenth State Exhibition. As a student of art history and philosophy at Columbia College, Reinhardt met the poet, Robert Lax, and the writer Thomas Merton. They became friends, and though very different personalities, their work shared common interests. For Thomas Merton, Christian devotion was silence itself. At the age of 26, he became a Trappist monk, joining the monastic community at the Abbey of Gethsemani in Kentucky in 1941, though Reinhardt tried to dissuade him. All of them contemplated silence and gave expression to their findings through their chosen forms: Reinhardt through painting, Lax through poetry, Merton through writing and prayer. In *End*, Reinhardt wrote:

> Nonsensuous, formless, shapeless, colorless, soundless, odorless
> No sounds, sights, sensing, sensations
> No intensity

For Lax, the white page was silence: 'Let the language fall to ashes and poetry will arise', he wrote, and then in *Psalm*:

> I listen at night. I listen through
> the day. I can't always listen, especial-
> ly through the day. There are too many
> other sounds to keep me from hearing.

Descriptions of Reinhardt or Lax as minimalists obscure their intentions. Rupert Loydell has suggested 'Intimist' as a better option for Lax. 'Quietist' has also been proposed, though Reinhardt's character hardly conformed to this description. Lax certainly valued silence. Having left New York for Greece in 1962, he tried to re-establish himself in Kalymnos in 1976, but found himself under adverse pressure from the authorities and a minority within the community ('the silent few') in the aftermath of the Greek military junta's collapse. These notes (all written in lower case) were made at that time in his journal: 'big booms today that sounded like fireworks; but they were bombs or cannonades, fired from one hillside to another, making tests. the first sound, or second, made me again decide to pack up & leave, but with the ensuing silence, comparative calm.' As much as quiet, the effect of his work depends upon placement and repetition. Lax's poem for Ad Reinhardt is language reduced to whatever resounds in the reader's thoughts as one word succeeds another in a falling litany, a gentle invocation, and as the eye follows the column of black outlined words down the white page as if tracing the verticality of a tall skyscraper silhouetted against a winter sky from roof to street level:

> Black
> Black
> Black
>
> Blue
> Blue
> Blue
>
> Black
> Black
> Black
> Black
>
> Blue
> Blue
> Blue

TRANSITIONS TO NIGHT

Encapsulating the combinatory image that is nocturnal darkness, a place and non-place of not-seeing in which no words can be spoken, an underworld of silence, the following lines come from *Hymns to the Night*, first published in 1800, written by the eighteenth-century German romantic poet Novalis:

> Downwards I turn
> To the holy, unspeakable
> The mysterious Night.

Stephanie Rosenthal has described the black paintings of Reinhardt, Rothko, Rauschenberg and Frank Stella as doors, transitions, thresholds, or rites of passage that can lead us to the limits of the visible (just as silence can lead us to the limits of the audible). In *Black Paintings*, she writes:

For Sigmund Freud disorientation was the final paradigm of the uncanny, 'the feeling of not knowing exactly what is before us and what not, or whether the place we are heading for might not be where we have been imprisoned all along.' Much earlier, in his treatise *Vom Erhabenen* (*On the Sublime*, 1795), Friedrich Schiller had described darkness as 'terrible because it hides objects from us and thus exposes us to the full force of the imagination.' Similarly, the viewer of black paintings exists in an intermediate state between Outside and Inside, a position that determines how the pictures are experienced.

As she argues, this application of a theory, based on Arnold van Gennep's descriptive term of 1909, *Les Rites de Passage* — those ceremonies that mark transitional states in human life — is not identical in all four cases: Reinhardt's later work can be interpreted as the prolongation of a transitional state of 'not-quite', in which the expectation of complete blackness is held in abeyance, whereas Rothko's black-form paintings from 1964 are a cleansing, an end signalling a new beginning. They draw the beholder softly into darkness, their floating weight of blacks on black an intimate envelopment, and whereas the flat transparency of Reinhardt's surfaces reveals little physical trace of the artist, Rothko's presence is constant, paint and brush evident for us to follow. As John Berger wrote of Vermeer, the material is permeated by silence and stillness.

THE UNGRASPABLE PHANTOM

The visible sign of the 'shhh' returns to painting with Odilon Redon's *Silence*, c. 1911, the face of a woman framed in an oval, as if looking absently at a mirror. Two fingers are pressed to her lips. What kind of silence is this; what cannot be said? We have no way of knowing.

Contemporary artists working with sound tend to be preoccupied with auditory absence not as an isolating, spiritual or pious silence, or the silence of purity, but as a haunting, a memory of sound that is pulled back by various techniques of technological invocation, reconstruction or allusion into the present world of forms. I am thinking, to give some examples, of the following: Christina Kubisch's *Electrical Walks*, which use special headphones that can pick up and amplify the normally inaudible electromagnetic fields that proliferate in urban environments — 'absurd cartographies', Christoph Metzger has called them, '[that] arise out of cash machines, security barriers, neon advertisements, antennas, WLAN, and electrical cables'; Zoe Irvine's retrieval and re-assemblage of thrown-away cassette tapes scavenged from city streets; and Louise K. Wilson's *A Record of Fear* project, developed at Orford Ness, Suffolk, in 2005. Between 1913 and the early 1980s, Orford Ness served as a highly secret military testing site and listening station. At various times in its existence, its activities included the invention of radar, drop tests to determine the ballistic shape of bombs, destructive tests on enemy aircraft, atomic bomb environmental testing and Cold War surveillance. 'The wish to incorporate audio and ideas of "aurality" was key,' wrote Wilson in her description of the project, 'since fictions, anecdotes and stories readily circulate around Orford Ness. Aside from the sonic "fallout" from its military testing past, numerous tales of ghost sightings, unexplained nocturnal noises and proximity to an infamous UFO visitation created a desire to privilege sound, and make audible what is absent or intangible.' The present dereliction of the site, stripped of materials that might have saleable value, means that little is left other than empty structures, associations and atmospheres. To draw sound out of this absence, Wilson collaborated with sound recordists to capture the ambient sounds of the abandoned buildings, and with composer Yannis Kyriakides, the hand bells of the Suffolk Guild of Ringers, and a choral group, the Exmoor Singers, who performed John Bennet's late sixteenth-century madrigal, *Weep, O Mine Eyes* in the centrifuge pit once used to test missile components.

In this way, a residue is collected from a ruin, suggestive of its secret past as an eavesdropper listening on a global scale, yet constructing a future from the relevance of the site for contemporary concerns. Piece by piece, fragment by whisper, all these pieces build an emotional relationship with realities that would otherwise escape apprehension.

The elusive nature of silence is best approached obliquely, by stealth. Akio Suzuki's *Pyramid*, created for *Playing John Cage* at Bristol's Arnolfini Gallery in 2005, began as a flat four-metre square of glassine paper sheets. Successive sheets of paper were laid precisely over each other on the floor of the gallery, with each square being one width smaller than the one underneath. So, this perfect pyramid was constructed to a height of perhaps a few millimetres, and in the centre Suzuki placed a small birdcage, and in the birdcage he placed a clay replica of an ear-shaped stone he had found by the sea. This was the mummy inside the pyramid. Completed, *Pyramid* lay like a milky tartan skin of carpet rolled out on the gallery floor. This was beautiful, but where was the sound? Suzuki explained: if somebody felt the desire to walk over *Pyramid*, they should be allowed to do so. Some people, he said, would take off their shoes and step carefully, and these people would hear the faint, sighing, friction sound of paper on paper. Others, particularly small children, would be more uninhibited, or less sensitive, and so the piece would be destroyed during the course of the exhibition, in the way that pyramids gradually erode and empty over centuries, either from weathering, plunder by robbers, or excavation by scholars. To discover the meaning of *Pyramid*, its sound and process, required the courage or insensitivity to walk through, to go beyond ways of seeing in order to be a part of the process of making and unmaking, to hear sound within the apparent silence of the piece. At regular intervals beginning with its pristine state, the evolution of the work was recorded with a Polaroid photograph, and at the close of the exhibition, this sequence gave the impression that ghosts had moved across the paper floor each night, leaving fresh footsteps in the snow for the morning: 'Silence but for the imaginary murmur of flakes beating on the roof,' wrote Samuel Beckett in *Ill Seen Ill Said*, 'And every now and then a real creak.' Who knows what it is that we hear; who knows what it means?

Time passes; fixity gives way to destruction; visual perfection is relinquished within the faintest of sound fields. As for the work, this ceremony returns us to nothing, 'to the feeling of not knowing exactly what is before us', so to the uncanny, to the shell-like ear found by the sea, the 'ungraspable phantom of life', the record of a haunting, time regained.

Coda: Distant Music

Appropriately, it was a famous old Dublin pub in which I struggled to hear a three-way conversation that sank and rose again from beneath the din of surrounding chatter. Inevitably, talk turned to James Joyce and so to 'The Dead', a short story I may have read as a teenager, but then lost any memory of so doing. Back in London, I bought a copy of *Dubliners* but other books demanded my attention more forcefully. In the pub, artist Susan Philipsz had spoken with passion about Joyce's story. At the end of the evening she gave me a catalogue published for her 2007 exhibition in Santiago de Compostela. Contained within was an account of the work she made in 2000 for the Irish Museum of Modern Art, *The Dead*, inspired by Joyce's story and John Huston's filmed adaptation of the story, shot as he was dying from cancer. Her work is a film, a dark monochromatic frame, and so I think of it as another framing of nothingness within the branch of black works, but like Nam June Paik's *Zen for Film*, it gathers scratches over time so connects with the closely related branch of white silences. For the soundtrack, she sings 'The Lass Of Aughrim' at irregular intervals, over and over, each version different to the last. 'The work is recorded in real time' she wrote in her catalogue, 'where all the ambient sounds in the room can be heard, creating a sense of solitude and time passing.'

To fully understand the singing of this song, and the flickering scratches of the black film, it is necessary to read 'The Dead', so this is what I did. The beginning is a Christmas party in Dublin, a lively affair of actions and language, pleasures and tensions, which bowls along at a terrific pace until the moment of leaving. Coming hard on the heels of a passage of absurdity and without warning, Joyce applies the brakes sharply for a moment of looking and a moment of listening. Gabriel, the central male character of the story, is gazing up the stairway to see a woman in shadow, a still life caught in the pose of listening to whatever sound comes from the room above. He realizes the woman is his wife, Gretta, strains his ear to listen also, but hears little except for laughter on the front steps, 'a few chords on the piano and a few notes of a man's voice singing.' Trying to catch more of this song, he frames the scene and the moment more completely through the language of art: 'There was grace and mystery in her attitude as if she were a symbol of something. He asked himself what is a woman standing on the stairs in the shadow, listening to distant music, a symbol of. If he were a painter he would paint her in that attitude. . . . *Distant Music* he would call the picture if he were a painter.' She has been listening to the singing of an old Irish song, 'The Lass of Aughrim', and when she turns in her husband's direction her cheeks are full of colour and her eyes are shining.

The joy that fills him, drinking in her radiance, grows into a desire so wild that he can barely contain himself when they return to their hotel. What happens then is one of those misapprehensions that litter relationships and are only salvaged by the strongest love. His lust goes unnoticed, slips away in the gulf of misunderstanding that opens suddenly between them as his wife explains her rapture at the song, last heard sung by a young man long ago, a man she might have married but whose life was cut short by tuberculosis. The story ends with Gabriel turned to the window, his attention caught by the tapping of flakes on the pane, perhaps falling asleep as he looks out at the falling snow. The passage is mesmeric in its repetitions and quiet beauty, snow on snow: 'His soul swooned slowly as he heard the snow falling faintly through the universe and faintly falling, like the descent of their last end, upon all the living and the dead.'

Still in Dublin, the day after the pub, I visited the National Gallery on Merrion Square, conscious of treading the boards that Samuel Beckett had passed over so often, looking at paintings that he may have studied: *Vertumnus and Pomona* by Nicolaes Maes, a beautiful gathered atmosphere out of which small details shine, like the key that hangs from Pomona's dress; Rembrandt's wonderfully atmospheric *Interior with figures playing the game 'La Main Chaude'*; Gerrit Dou's *An Old Hermit Praying*; Metsu's *A Man Writing a Letter* and *A Woman Reading a Letter*, Cornelis Bega's *Two Men Singing*, a gloriously abject scene, the room full of junk, a bass viol propped up with all the other rubbish; Chardin's elegant *Card Tricks*, which made me think again of Muñoz, and Goya's mysterious, erotic, sepulchral, silent *Sleep*. As a counterpoint to looking at all this silence and noise, the sound of my boots echoed in these resonant spaces, just as Beckett's footsteps had echoed so often in the 1920s. His pacing play of 1975, *Footfalls*, may have been influenced by this sound: 'Ruby Cohn remembered Beckett stopping at this time in the Neue Nationalgalerie in Berlin,' wrote James Knowlson, 'and asking her to listen to the sounds of the footsteps on the hard polished floor. But we do not know whether this happened before or after the image captured his interest.'

'Were you asleep?' asks May in *Footfalls*. 'I heard you in my deep sleep', replies V, the woman's voice. 'There is no sleep so deep I would not hear you there.'

Acknowledgements

First of all, I want to thank Henry Cowell. He is no longer alive, of course, so I doubt that he cares, but he wrote the composition that gave me my title: *Sinister Resonance*. After much deliberation I felt it worked as well as any two words could to cover what I've been trying to say in these pages. Now for the living, their support and encouragement, without which this book would not have been what it is (though I don't blame them for its shortcomings). In particular, I would like to thank Angus Carlyle for reading the manuscript at various stages and responding with invaluable feedback, useful source material and welcome indications of how the book might be improved. I am also grateful to John Heymans, Danny McCarthy, Alasdair Roberts, Louise Stern, Hans Smit, John Butcher, Louise K. Wilson, Lawrence English, Aleks Kolkowski, Marie Yates, Christian Marclay and Steve Roden for their suggestions, inspiring conversations and warm reassurance. Steve Roden, in particular, has been particularly open and enthusiastic. Since the conversations we had in Marfa in 2008, he has supplied me with an incredible treasure trove of ideas. I can't recommend his work or his website — www.inbetweennoise.com — highly enough. Nic Collins, Patricia Bentson and Christoph Cox were generous with their support when it was most needed. My colleagues in Research, Sound Arts & Design, and CRISAP at London College of Communication's School of Media have been consistently supportive and always a source of stimulating ideas: Janice Hart, Eve Waring, Julian Rodriguez, Cathy Lane, Angus Carlyle, Chris Petter, John Wynne, Salome Voegelin, Peter Cusack, Ciaran Hart and the LCC Sound Arts & Design and postgraduate students. As always, I am profoundly thankful for the love and encouragement of

Eileen and Juliette.

For allowing me access to paintings within their collections, I am grateful to the curators of the Royal Collection, Buckingham Palace; the Harold Samuel Collection at Mansion House; the National Gallery, London; Dordrecht Museum, the Netherlands.

The curators, organizers and administrators of the following conferences and events have been generous in inviting me to present papers which have contributed to the development of this book: *Music and Postmodern Cultures*, Melbourne University; *Isolation*, School of Art, Hobart, Tasmania; *Sonic Focus*, Brown University, Providence; *The School of Sound* at the 2005 Korean Film Festival, Seoul; *Punkt Festival*, Kristiansand; *Sound and Image*, the 27th Annual Conference in Visual Anthropology, University of Trondheim; *Sound and Silence*, Kunsthogskolen, Bergen; *Sound Body*, London College of Communication; *On the Sensation of Sound*, Veenfabriek, Leiden; *The Architecture Programme*, Royal Academy of Arts, London; *The Long Weekend* at Tate Modern; *Sound Art*, 11-Art.com, Beijing; *Sound and Anthropology: Body, Environment and Human Sound Making*, The University of St. Andrews, *Re-enchantment and Reclamation*, Lancaster University; *Open Archive*, Argos Centre for Art & Media, Brussels; *Music, Sound and the Reconfiguration of Public and Private Space*, the Centre for Research in the Arts, Social Sciences and Humanities, Cambridge University; *Centrematic*, Palma; *The Marfa Sessions*, Marfa, Texas. I have also read extracts from the book as a work in progress at the *Quiet Music Festival* in Cork, and the *Noise/Silence* NIVAL Symposium at the National College of Art & Design, Dublin. I am indebted to the feedback and encouragement so generously given after these last two sessions by John Godfrey, Sarah O'Halloran, Danny McCarthy, Mick O'Shea, Pauline Oliveros, Alvin Lucier, Declan Long, Fergus Kelly and others whose names, regrettably, I don't recall.

Early versions of some sections of the book have appeared in the following publications: *Playing John Cage*, exhibition catalogue edited by David Toop and Martin Clark, Bristol Arnolfini Gallery, 2005; *Sound Out* exhibition catalogue, edited by David Toop and Danny McCarthy, National Sculpture Factory, Cork, 2005; *Soundworks*, edited by Julie Forrester and Danny McCarthy, *Art Trail*, Cork, 2005; *Sound and the City*, British Council China SATC Anthology, 2008; *Autumn Leaves*, edited by Angus Carlyle, Double Entendre/CRISAP, 2007; *Soundwaves*, exhibition catalogue, Kinetica/Cybersonica, 2007; *Jem Finer: Score for a Hole In the Ground*, Stour Valley Arts, 2008; *Tim Wainwright and John Wynne: Transplant*, edited by Victoria

ACKNOWLEDGEMENTS

Hume, Royal Brompton and Harefield NHS Trust, 2008; *João Paulo Feliciano: The Blues Quartet*, Lois & Richard Rosenthal Center for Contemporary Art, Cincinnati, Ohio, 2007; *Sounding: Nordic Sound Art*, edited by Mads Kullberg and Rune Sochting, The Museum of Contemporary Art, Roskilde, 2009; *Voids*, edited by Mathieu Copeland with John Armleder, Laurent Le Bon, Gustav Metzger, Mai-Thu Perret, Clive Phillpot, and Philippe Pirotte, JRP Ringier, Zurich, 2009.

Notes

Numbers in right hand column denote corresponding page in the volume

Prelude

James Fenimore Cooper, *The Last of the Mohicans*, Oxford University
Press, Oxford, 1998, p. 72.   viii

Walter Murch, 'Sound Design: The Dancing Shadow' in *Projections 4*, ed
John Boorman, Tom Luddy, David Thomson and Walter Donohue,
Faber & Faber, London, 1995, p. 239.   ix

Harold Pinter, 'The Echoing Silence', *Guardian*, London, 31.12.2008, p. 22.   ix

Virginia Woolf, 'Street Haunting: A London Adventure', in *The Death of
the Moth*, The Hogarth Press, London, 1942, p. 20.   ix–x

Animal Collective, interviewed by Killian Fox, *Guardian*, London,
09.01.2009, p. 6   xii

Paul Auster, *The Invention of Solitude*, Faber & Faber, London and Boston,
1988, p. 140.   xiii

Samuel Beckett, notebook entry, 19 Nov. 1936, quoted in James
Knowlson, *Damned to Fame: The Life of Samuel Beckett*, Bloomsbury,
London, 1997, p. 235.   xiii

Eugene Delacroix, *The Journal of Eugene Delacroix*, trans. Lucy Norton,
Phaidon Press, London, 2004, pp. 276–7.   xiv

Sigmund Freud, *The Uncanny*, trans. David McLintock, Penguin Books,
London, 2003, pp. 123–162.   xiv

Virginia Woolf, *Jacob's Room*, Penguin, London, 1992, pp. 78–79.   xiv–xv

Odilon Redon, *Confessions of an Artist*, quoted in Jodi Hauptman, *Beyond
the Visible: The Art of Odilon Redon*, The Museum of Modern Art, New
York, 2005, p. 31.   xv

Marcel Duchamp, 'The 1914 Box', in *The Essential Writings of Marcel
Ducham: Salt Seller = Marchand du Sel*, ed. Michel Sanouillet and Elmer
Peterson, Thames & Hudson, London, 1975, p. 23.   xv

1. Drowned by voices

Rainer Maria Rilke, *Duino Elegies*, quoted in Michael Tanner, introduction
to Friedrich Nietzsche, *The Birth of Tragedy*, Penguin, London, 2003,
p. xxviii.   3

NOTES

Herman Melville, *Moby Dick*, Oxford University Press, 1998, p. 3.   3
James Joyce, *Ulysses*, Picador, London, 1998, p. 244.   4
P. W. Joyce, *Old Celtic Romances*, The Talbot Press, Dublin, 1966, pp. 79–122.   5
Lady Gregory, *A Book of Saints and Wonders*, Colin Smythe, Gerrards
Cross, Bucks, 1971, pp. 62–63.   5
Virginia Woolf, *The Waves*, Penguin, London, 2000, p. 152.   7
T. S. Eliot, 'The Waste Land', in *Selected Poems*, Faber, 1965, p. 66.   7
Thomas Hardy, *Selected Poems*, Penguin, London, 1993, p. 74.   7
Arthur Machen, *Holy Terrors*, Penguin, Middlesex, 1946, pp. 96–98.   7
Franz Kafka, *The Castle*, trans. Willa and Edwin Muir, Penguin, London,
1957, p. 26.   8
Mladen Dolar, *A Voice and Nothing More*, The MIT Press, Cambridge, MA,
2006, p. 170.   8
Ibid., p. 61.   9
Vladimir Jankélévitch, *Music and the Ineffable*, trans. Carolyn Abbate,
Princeton University Press, Princeton and Oxford, 2003, p. 37.   9
Dante, *The Divine Comedy, Volume 1: Inferno*, trans. Mark Musa, Penguin,
London, 2003, p. 187.   9
Ovid, *Metamorphoses*, Book 1, trans. Arthur Golding, Penguin, 2002, p. 56.   9
James Merrill, 'Syrinx', in *Selected Poems*, Carcanet, Manchester, 1996, p. 88.   9
Robert Graves, *The White Goddess*, Faber & Faber, 1988, p. 355.   10
Stéphane Mallarmé, 'L'Après-Midi d'un Faune', in *Mallarmé*, Penguin,
1970, p. 52.   11
Arthur Machen, *The Hill of Dreams*, Corgi Books, London, 1967, pp. 18–21.   11
Arthur Machen, 'The Rose Garden', in *Holy Terrors*, Penguin, London,
1946, pp. 85–86.   11–12
Kenneth Grahame, *Pagan Papers*, The Echo Library, 2006, p. 16.   12
Aleister Crowley, 'Hymn To Pan', in Lawrence Sutin, *Do What Thou Wilt:
A Life of Aleister Crowley*, St. Martin's Griffin, New York, 2000.   12
Alex Owen, *The Place of Enchantment: British Occultism and the Culture of the
Modern*, University of Chicago Press, Chicago and London, 2004,
p. 216.   12–13
E. M. Forster, *Collected Short Stories*, Penguin, London, 2002, p. 14.   13
J. M. Barrie, *Peter Pan in Kensington Gardens*, Penguin, London, 2004,
p. 174.   13
William Burroughs, *The Soft Machine*, Corgi Books, 1970, p. 153.   14
William Burroughs, *Nova Express*, Panther, 1968, p. 41.   14
Kenneth Grahame, *The Wind In the Willows*, Penguin, 1994, p. 111–13.   15
Rosamund Marriott-Watson, *Two Songs: The Isle of Voices, The Yellow Book*,
London, 1895, p. 72.   15
Kenneth Grahame, 'The Inner Ear', in *The Yellow Book*, London, 1895,
p. 73.   15–16
E. M. Forster, op cit., p. 90.   16
Robert Louis Stevenson, *The Strange Case of Dr Jekyll and Mr Hyde*,
Penguin Classics, London, 2003, p. 66.   16
Thom Gunn, *Ezra Pound: Poems selected by Thom Gunn*, Faber & Faber,
London, 2000, p. xiv.   17
Bruno Schulz, 'Pan', in *The Fictions of Bruno Schulz*, trans. Celina
Wieniewska, Picador, London, 1988, p. 55.   18
Knut Hamsun, *Pan*, Norilana Books, Winnetka, CA, 2007, pp. 40–41.   18

John Boardman, *The Great God Pan: The Survival of an Image*, Thames & Hudson, 1997, pp. 42–43. 19
Ernst Vegelin van Claerbergen (ed.), *David Teniers and the Theatre of Painting*, Courtauld Institute of Art Gallery, London, 2006, pp. 90–91. 19
Thomas Hardy, *Selected Poems*, Penguin, London, 1993, p. 102. 19
Sigmund Freud, *Civilization and Its Discontents*, Vintage, London, 2001, p. 64. 20
Lady Gregory, *A Book of Saints and Wonders*, Colin Smythe, 1971, p. 63–64. 20
Alfred Lord Tennyson, 'The Voyage of Maeldune', in Tennyson: *Selected Poetry*, Penguin, London, 1985, pp. 223–30. 20
Picker, John M., *Victorian Soundscapes*, Oxford University Press, Oxford, 2003, p. 55. 21
Giorgio Agamben, *The Open: Man and Animal*, trans. Kevin Attell, Stanford University Press, Stanford California, 2004, p. 40. 22
J. A. Baker, *The Peregrine*, New York Review Books, New York, 2005, p. 78. 22
Ibid., p. 181. 22
Ibid., p. 180. 22
Seamus Heaney, 'A Dog Was Crying Tonight in Wicklow Also', in *The Spirit Level*, Faber & Faber, London, 1996, p. 55. 22
Mircea Eliade, *Shamanism: Archaic Techniques of Ecstasy*, Routledge and Kegan Paul, London, 1964, p. 479. 22
Anne Ross, *Pagan Celtic Britain*, Cardinal, London, 1974, p. 309. 23
Walter de la Mare, 'A Song of Enchantment', in *Selected Poems*, ed. Matthew Sweeney, Faber & Faber, 2006, London, p. 49. 24
Joseph Conrad, *A Personal Record*, Oxford University Press, 1988, p. xi 25
Homer, *The Odyssey*, trans. E. V. Rieu, Penguin, 2003, pp. 140–54. 25
Virgil, *The Aeneid*, trans. David West, Penguin, 1991, pp. 115–36. 25–26
T. S. Eliot, 'The Hollow Men', in *Selected Poems*, Faber, 1965, p. 78. 26
Robert MacFarlane, *The Wild Places*, Granta Books, London, 2007, pp. 22–23. 26

2. Each echoing opening; each muffled closure

John Berger, *Ways of Seeing*, BBC/Penguin, London, 1972, p. 7. 27
Geoff Dyer, *Ways of Telling*, Pluto Press, London, 1986, p. 99. 27
Hannah Merker, *Listening: Ways of Hearing in a Silent World*, Southern Methodist University Press, Dallas, TX, p. 104. 28
Jenny Diski, *On Trying to Keep Still*, Little Brown, London, 2006, p. 106. 28–29
Anna Karpf, *The Human Voice*, Bloomsbury, London, 2006, pp. 65–66. 29
Yi-Fu Tuan, *Space and Place: The Perspective of Experience*, University of Minnesota Press, Minneapolis, MN, 1977, p. 23. 30
John Berger, op. cit., p. 31. 31
Bernard Berenson, *Italian Painters of the Renaissance*, Phaidon, London, 1952, p. 109. 32
John Berger, preface to Timothy O'Grady, *I Could Read the Sky*, The Harvill Press, London, 1998. 32
John Berger, *The Shape of a Pocket*, Vintage, London, 2003, p. 21. 32
lliers de l'Isle-Adam, *Tomorrow's Eve*, trans. Robert Martin Adams, University of Illinois Press, Urbana, Chicago and London, 2001, p. 10. 33
Virginia Woolf, 'A Sketch of the Past', from *Moments of Being*, ed. Jeanne Schulkind, Sussex University Press, 1985, pp. 75–76. 34

NOTES

Helen E. Ross, *Behaviour and Perception in Strange Environments*, Allen & Unwin, London, 1974, p. 84.   35
Villiers de l'Isle-Adam, *Tomorrow's Eve*, op. cit., pp. 14–15.   36
Tim Ingold, 'Against Soundscape', in *Autumn Leaves*, ed. Angus Carlyle, Double Entendre/CRiSAP, Paris, 2007, p. 11.   37

3. Dark senses

Bernard Weinraub, 'Enticed by Bright Light; From David Hockney, a Show of Photocollages in Los Angeles', *The New York Times*, 15.08.2001.   39–40
Oliver Sacks, *Musicophilia*, Picador, London, 2007, pp. 33–34.   40
Louise Stern, *Silence*, unpublished manuscript, 2007, pp. 1–2.   41
T. S. Eliot, *Four Quartets*, Faber & Faber, 1974, p. 19.   42
Virginia Woolf, *Between the Acts*, Oxford University Press, 1998, pp. 33–34.   42
John Keats, 'Ode On a Grecian Urn', in *John Keats: Selected Poems*, Penguin, London, 2007, p. 191.   42
James Joyce, *A Portrait of the Artist as a Young Man*, Penguin Books, London, 1996, p. 190.   43
Lewis Hyde, *Trickster Makes This World*, Canongate, Edinburgh, 2008, p. 163.   45
Casey O' Callaghan, *Sounds*, Oxford University Press, Oxford, 2007, p. 11.   45–46
José Saramago, *Blindness*, Harcourt, 1997, p. 157.   46
Casey O'Callaghan, op. cit., p. 6.   46
Robert Pasnau, 'What Is Sound?', *The Philosophical Quarterly*, vol. 49, no. 196 (July 1999), p. 309.   46
Ibid., p. 313.   46
Ibid., p. 312.   47
David Bodanis, *Electric Universe*, Abacus, London, 2006, p. 33.   47
Leonardo da Vinci, *Notebooks*, Oxford University Press, Oxford, 2008, p. 37.   48
Anton Ehrenzweig, *The Hidden Order of Art*, Phoenix Press, London, 2000, pp. 30–31.   49
Jonathan Rée, *I See a Voice*, Metropolitan Books, New York, 1999, p. 352.   50
Tim Ingold, op. cit., p. 10.   50
Robert Walser, 'Looking out into the landscape', in *Speaking to the Rose: Writings, 1912–1932*, trans. Christopher Middleton, University of Nebraska Press, 2005, p. 83.   51
Kathleen Jamie, *Findings*, Sort of Books, London, 2005, p. 54.   51
Roger Deakin, *Wildwood: A Journey Through Trees*, Penguin, 2008, pp. 51–53.   51
Lorenzo Langstroth, *On the Hive and the Honey Bee*, Dadant & Songs, Hamilton, IL, 1919, p. 10   52

4. Writhing sigla

Dylan Thomas, *Under Milk Wood*, Penguin Classics, London, 2000, pp. 28–39.   53–54
Walford Davies, introduction to, ibid., p. xxi.   54
Evan Parker, interview by Philip Clark, *The Wire*, Issue 279 (May 2007), p. 36.   55

5. The jagged dog

Carson McCullers, *The Heart is a Lonely Hunter*, Penguin, London, 2000,
p. 240.   58
Curtis Roads, *Microsound*, The MIT Press, Cambridge, MA, 2004, p. 21.   60
Bart Kosko, *Noise*, Viking, New York, 2006, pp. 24–25.   61
Vladimir Jankélévitch, *Music and the Ineffable*, trans. Carolyn Abbate,
Princeton University Press, Princeton and Oxford, 2003, p. 90.   62
Roland Barthes, *Image Music Text*, trans. Stephen Heath, Fontana Press,
1977, p. 185.   62–63
Walter Benjamin, *On Hashish*, Belknap Press of Harvard University Press,
2006, p. 72.   63
Joseph Conrad, *The Shadow-Line*, Oxford University Press, Oxford, 1985,
p. 74.   63
Herman Melville, *Moby Dick*, op. cit., p. 502.   63

6. Act of silence

Hilary Taylor, *James McNeill Whistler*, New Orchard Editions, London,
1989, p. 22.   67
Sacheverell Sitwell, *Conversation Pieces: A Survey of English Domestic
Portraits and their Painters*, B. T. Batsford, London, 1969, p. 3.   68
Sitwell, ibid., p. 84.   69
Calvin Tomkins, *Duchamp: A Biography*, Henry Holt, New York, 1996,
p. 19.   69
Marcel Duchamp, *The Essential Writings of Marcel Ducham: Salt Seller =
Marchand du Sel*, ed. Michel Sanouillet and Elmer Peterson, Thames &
Hudson, London, 1975, p. 23.   69
Ibid., p. 195.   70
Ibid., p. 23.   70
Ibid., p. 194.   70
Ibid., p. 31.   70
Caroline Tisdall and Angelo Bozzolla, *Futurism*, Thames & Hudson,
London, 1993, p. 140.   71
Henri Bergson, *Creative Evolution*, Dover, 1998, p. 4.   71

7. Art of silence

William Shakespeare, *Hamlet* (I.1.129).   73
John Ingamells, *The Wallace Collection: Collection of Pictures, IV, Dutch and
Flemish*, The Trustees of the Wallace Collection, London, 1992, p. 190.   74
León Krempel, *Nicolaes Maes*, Michael Imhof Verlag, Petersberg, 2000,
plates 241, 244, 299.   74
Bruce R. Smith, *The Acoustic World of Early Modern England*, The
University of Chicago Press, Chicago and London, 1999, p. 8.   77
Henry James, *Ghost Stories of Henry James*, Wordsworth Editions, Ware,
2001, pp. 40–41.   78
Georgina Cole, "Wavering Between Two Worlds': The Doorway in
Seventeenth-Century Dutch Genre Painting', *Philament*, Issue 9
(December 2006), p. 30. http://www.arts.usyd.edu.au/publications/
philament/issue9_pdfs/COLE_Doorways.pdf (accessed 05.08.2008).   79
Victor I. Stoichita, *The Self-Aware Image: An Insight into Early Modern Meta-
Painting*, Cambridge University Press, Cambridge, MA, 1997, p. 63.   79

NOTES

Martha Hollander, *An Entrance for the Eyes: Space and Meaning in Seventeenth-Century Dutch Art*, University of California Press, 2002, p. 111. 79

Ovid, *Metamorphoses*, Book 1, trans. Arthur Golding, Penguin, 2002, p. 290. 80

Catullus, trans. Reney Myers and Robert J. Ormsby, Unwin Books, London, 1972, p. 101. 80

Martha Hollander, op. cit., pp. 110–11. 82–83

Rick Altman, 'The Silence of the Silents', in *The Musical Quarterly*, vol. 80, no. 4, Winter 1996, p. 648. 83

William Shakespeare, *King Lear* (IV.6.152). 84

William Shakespeare, *Hamlet* (III.4.4; III.4.33; III.2.266). 84

William Shakespeare. *Othello* (II.1.397; II.1.194; II.3.346). 84

Georges Perec, *Species of Spaces and Other Pieces*, Penguin Books, 1999, p. 38. 84

Simon Schama, 'Wives and Wantons: Versions of Womanhood in 17th Century Dutch Art', *Oxford Art Journal*, vol. 3, no. 1, Oxford University Press, April, 1980, p. 12. 87

Erving Goffman, *The Presentation of Self in Everyday Life*, Penguin, London, 1990, p. 122. 88

Sigmund Freud, 'Fragment of an Analysis of a Case of Hysteria', in *A Case of Hysteria, Three Essays on Sexuality and Other Works*, Vintage, London, 2001, pp. 79–80. 89

Mladen Dolar, *A Voice and Nothing More*, The MIT Press, Cambridge, MA, 2006, p. 133. 89

Ann Gaylin, *Eavesdropping in the Novel from Austen to Proust*, Cambridge University Press, 2007, p. 141. 90

Leonard Barkan, 'The Beholder's Tale: Ancient Sculpture, Renaissance Narratives', *Representations*, no. 44 (Autumn 2003), pp. 147–50. 93

Michael Liebmann, 'On the Iconography of the Nymph of the Fountain by Lucas Cranach the Elder', *Journal of the Warburg and Courtauld Institutes*, vol. 31, 1968, p. 435. 93

Michael Taylor, *Rembrandt's Nose*, Distributed Art Publishers, New York, 2007, p. 124. 93–94

Robert Flaceliere, *Greek Oracles*, Elek Books, London, 1965, pp. 8–16. 95

Svetlana Alpers, *The Art of Describing*, The University of Chicago Press, Chicago, 1983, p. 220. 95–96

Nanette Salomon, *Shifting Priorities: Gender and Genre in Seventeenth-Century Dutch Painting*, Stanford University Press, Stanford, CA, 2004, p. 97. 96

Bootsy Collins, 'Vanish In Our Sleep', from *Stretchin' Out In Bootsy's Rubber Band*, Warner Bros., 1976. 96

Haruki Murakami, *After Dark*, trans. Jay Rubin, Harvill Secker, London, 2007, p. 90. 96

Jonas Mekas, 'Warhol's Sleep', in *Movies*, ed. Gilbert Adair, Penguin, London, 1999, p. 50. 96

Peter Gidal, *Andy Warhol: Films and Paintings*, Studio Vista/Dutton, London, 1971, p. 90. 97

Simon Schama, *The Embarrassment of Riches: An Interpretation of Dutch Culture in the Golden Age*, Fontana Press, 1987, p. 559. 98

Garrett Stewart, *The Look of Reading: Book, Painting, Text*, The University of Chicago Press, Chicago, 2006, p. 171. 99

Svetlana Alpers, op. cit., p. 202. 99

NOTES

Lawrence Gowing, *Vermeer*, University of California Press, Berkeley and
Los Angeles, 1997, p. 26.   99
T. S. Eliot, 'The Love Song of J. Alfred Prufrock', *Selected Poems*, Faber,
London, 1965, p. 12.   99
Louis Andriessen in conversation with Maja Trochimczyk, *Writing To
Vermeer*, booklet, Nonesuch CD 79887-2, 2006, p. 12.   100
Lawrence Gowing, op. cit., p. 39.   100
Timothy Brook, *Vermeer's Hat: The Seventeenth Century and the Dawn of the
Global World*, Profile Books, London, 2008, caption to plate 3.   100
Lawrence Gowing, op. cit., p. 18.   100
John Berger, *And Our Faces, My Heart, Brief as Photos*, Bloomsbury,
London, 2005, p. 25.   101
Richard Leppert, *The Sight of Sound*, University of California Press,
Berkeley, 1993, p. 60.   102
Emily Cockayne, *Hubbub: Filth, Noise and Stench in England*, Yale
University Press, New Haven and London, 2007, p. 123.   103
James Knowlson, *Damned to Fame: The Life of Samuel Beckett*, Bloomsbury,
London, 1997, p. 235.   103
Juhani Pallasmaa, *The Eyes of the Skin: Architecture and the Senses*, Wiley,
Chichester, 2008, pp. 50–51.   103–104
Martha Hollander, op. cit., p. 128.   105
James Elkins, *The Object Stares Back: On the Nature of Seeing*, Harcourt, 1996,
p. 137.   105
Mariët Westermann, *Art and Home: Dutch Interiors in the Age of Rembrandt*,
Denver Art Museum and the Newark Museum, Waanders Publishers,
Zwolle, 2001, p. 18.   105

8. A conversation piece

Mukai Kyorai, 'Which Is Tail? Which Head', in *The Penguin Book
of Japanese Verse*, trans. Geoffrey Bownas and Anthony Thwaite,
Penguin, London, 1966, p. 113.   108
Juan Muñoz and James Lingwood, 'A Conversation', in *Juan Muñoz: A
Retrospective*, Tate Publishing, 2008, p. 145.   108
Homer, *The Odyssey*, Penguin Books, London, 2003, p. 158.   108
Franz Kafka, 'The Silence of the Sirens', in *The Complete Short Stories*,
Vintage, 1999, p. 431.   108–109
James Blades, *Percussion Instruments and Their History*, Faber & Faber,
London, 1975, pp. 214–15.   109
Ibid., p. 46.   109
James Blades and Jeremy Montagu, *Early Percussion Instruments from the
Middle Ages to the Baroque*, Oxford University Press, London, 1976,
pp. 8–11.   110
Jean-Luc Nancy, *Listening*, trans. Charlotte Mandell, Fordham University
Press, New York, 2007, pp. 42–43.   111
Sheena Wagstaff, 'A Mirror of Consciousness', in *Juan Muñoz: A
Retrospective*, Tate Publishing, 2008, p. 102.   111
Jodi Hauptmann, introduction to *Georges Seurat: The Drawings*, The
Museum of Modern Art, New York, 2007, p. 13.   112
Adrian Searle, 'Misdirection: Juan Muñoz and Third Ear', in *Juan Muñoz:
The Voice Alone*, La Casa Encentida, Madrid, 2005, p. 122.   113

Samuel Beckett, 'Not I', in *Collected Shorter Plays*, Faber & Faber, London, 2006, pp. 215–16.   113

James Knowlson, *Damned to Fame*, Bloomsbury, London, 1997, pp. 588–89.   113–114

Catherine Puglisi, *Caravaggio*, Phaidon, London, 2007, pp. 303–304.   114

David Lynch, *Lynch on Lynch*, ed. Chris Rodley, Faber & Faber, London, 1997, pp. 72–73.   115

Steven Connor, *Dumbstruck: A Cultural History of Ventriloquism*, Oxford University Press, Oxford, 2000, p. 276.   115

Victor I. Stoichita, *A Short History of the Shadow*, Reaktion Books, London, 1999, p. 144.   116

Sigmund Freud, *The Uncanny*, trans. David McLintock, Penguin, 2003, p. 135.   116

John Berger, 'Will It Be a Likeness?', from *Juan Muñoz: The Voice Alone*, op. cit., pp. 87–97.   117

Simon Schama, *The Embarrassment of Riches*, Fontana Press, 1987, p. 413.   118

Ivy Compton-Burnett, *The Last and the First*, Penguin, London, 1986, p. 37.   119

Ivy Compton-Burnett, *Parents and Children*, Penguin, London, 1970, p. 133.   119

Andy Warhol, *a: A Novel*, Grove Press, New York, 1968, p. 1.   119

Hélène Prigent and Pierre Rosenberg, *Chardin: An Intimate Art*, Thames & Hudson, London, pp. 68–69.   120

Martin Riches, *Maskinerne/The Machines*, Kunsthallen Brandts Klaedefabrik, Odense, 2004, pp. 88–89.   120

Aleksander Kolkowski, notes to *Recording Angels presents Mechanical Landscape with Bird*, limited edition DVD, 2004.   120

Jodi Hauptman, op. cit., p. 13.   120

Felix Kramer, *Vilhelm Hammershoi: The Poetry of Silence*, gallery guide, Royal Academy of Arts, London, 2008,   121

9. Chair creaks, but no one sits there

Charles Dickens, *The Chimes: A Goblin Story*, Chapman & Hall, London, 1845, pp. 2–3.   125

Charles Dickens, *The Haunted House*, Hesperus Press, London, 2002, p. 13.   126

Hans Anderson, 'The Sandman', in *Anderson's Fairy Tales*, Blackie & Son, London and Glasgow, p. 77.   126

Nicholas Royle, *The Uncanny*, Manchester University Press, Manchester, 2003, p. 136.   127

Sigmund Freud, *The Uncanny*, op. cit., p. 141.   127

E. T. A. Hoffmann, *Tales of Hoffmann*, Penguin, London, 2004, pp. 85–125.   127

Hélène Cixous, 'Fiction and Its Phantoms: A Reading of Freud's *Das Unheimliche* (The "Uncanny")', *New Literary History*, vol. 7, no. 3 (Spring 1976), pp. 525–48, 619–45.   130

Bram Stoker, 'Dracula', in *The Annotated Dracula*, ed. Leonard Wolf, New English Library, London, 1975, p. 79.   131

Robert Louis Stevenson, *Treasure Island*, Oxford University Press, Oxford, 2008, p. 177.   131

John Tyndall, *Sound*, Longmans, Green, and Co., London and Bombay, 1898, p. 286.   132

Shirley Jackson, 'The Haunting of Hill House', in *The Masterpieces of Shirley Jackson*, Raven Books, London, 1996, p. 229.   132

Ibid., p. 253.   132
Ibid., p. 313.   132–133
Ibid., p. 315.   133
Ibid., p. 364.   133
Ibid., p. 373.   133
Ibid., p. 379.   133
Ibid., p. 395.   134
Seamus Heaney, 'Person Helicon', in *Death of a Naturalist*, Faber & Faber,
London, 1991, p.46.   134
Klaus P. Wachsmann, 'The Primitive Musical Instruments', in *Musical
Instruments Through the Ages*, ed. Anthony Baines, Penguin, London,
1961, p. 29.   134
Karl Gustav Izikowitz, *Musical Instruments of the South American Indians*,
S. R. Publishers, Wakefield, 1970, pp. 14–16.   135
Hugo Zemp, *Musique Dan: La musique dans la pensée et la vie sociale d'une
societé africaine*, Mouton, La Haye, 1971, pp. 52–53.   135
Seamus Heaney, *Death of a Naturalist*, op. cit. p. 6.   135
Jules Verne, *Journey to the Centre of the Earth*, Modern Library, New York,
2003, pp. 119–21.   136
Ueda Akinari, *Tales of Moonlight and Rain*, trans. Anthony H. Chambers,
Columbia University Press, New York, 2007, pp. 140–43.   136
J. Meade Falkner, *The Lost Stradivarius*, Penguin, England, 1946,
p. 20.   137
Patricia Pulham, *Art and the Transitional Object in Vernon Lee's Supernatural
Tales*, Ashgate, Hampshire, 2008, p. 7.   138
Charles Patrick, 'Sex-siren Plot to Lure Victim to Slaughterhouse', *Irish
Independent*, 29.02.08. http://www.independent.ie/national-news/
sexsiren-plot-to-lure-victim-to-slaughterhouse-1302168.html
(accessed 26.2.2009).   138
Homer, *The Odyssey*, Penguin Books, London, 2003, p. 158, lines 44–46.   138
James Joyce, *Ulysses, A Reader's Edition*, Picador, London, 1998, p. 263.   138
James Joyce, *Ulysses*, op cit., p. 258.   138
Mladen Dolar, 'If Music Be the Food of Love', in Slavoj Žižek and
Mladen Dolar, *Opera's Second Death*, Routledge, London and New York,
2002, p. 10.   139
James Joyce, *Chamber Music*, Jonathan Cape, London, 1950, p. 28.   139
Vladimir Jankélévitch, *Music and the Ineffable*, trans. Carolyn Abbate,
Princeton University Press, Princeton and Oxford, 2003, p. 148.   140
Jankélévitch, op cit., p. 3.   140
Ibid., p. 37.   140
James Joyce, *Ulysses*, op cit., p. 269.   140
Ibid., p. 269.   141
Ibid., p. 268.   141
Ibid., p. 272.   141
Ibid., pp. 265–266.   142
Vladimir Jankélévitch, *Music and the Ineffable*, op. cit., p. 1.   143
Calvin Tomkins, *Ahead of the Game: Four Versions of Avant-garde*, Penguin,
London, 1968, pp. 170–71.   144
Po Chü-i, 'The Five-String', in *Chinese Poems*, trans. Arthur Waley,
George Allen & Unwin, 1946, pp. 131–32.   144–145

NOTES

R. H. van Gulik, *The Lore of the Chinese Lute*, Sophia University, Tokyo/
The Charles E. Tuttle Company, Tokyo, 1968, p. 158.   145
Georges Rodenbach, *Bruges-la-Morte*, trans. Mike Mitchell, Dedalus,
Sawtry, 2007, pp. 27–28.   145
Ibid., p. 131.   145
Mario Caroli, notes to Salvatore Sciarrino, *Fauno che Fischia*, Attacca CD,
Italy, 2007.   147
Eric Abrahamson and David H. Freedman, *A Perfect Mess: The hidden
benefits of disorder*, Weidenfeld & Nicolson, London, 2007, p. 51.   147–148
James Knowlson, op. cit., p. 17.   148
Ibid., p. 614.   148
Meirion and Susie Harries, *A Pilgrim Soul: The Life and Work of Elisabeth
Lutyens*, Michael Joseph, London, 1989, p.25.   148
George Plimpton, *Shadow Box: An Amateur in the Ring*, The Lyons Press,
Connecticut, 2003, p. 17.   148–149
Cormac McCarthy, 'The Crossing', in *The Border Trilogy*, Picador,
London, 2002, p. 326.   149
Gaston Bachelard, *The Poetics of Space*, trans. Maria Jolas, Beacon Press,
Boston, 1969, pp. 60–61.   150
James Agee, *Let Us Now Praise Famous Men*, Picador, London, 1988,
p. 188.   150
Gaston Bachelard, op. cit., p. 178.   151
Friedrich Jürgenson, *Voice Transmissions with the Deceased*, ed. Carl Michael
von Hausswolff and Leif Elggren, Firework Edition, Stockholm, 2004,
p. 78.   152
J. G. Ballard, 'The Sound-Sweep', in *The Voices of Time*, Indigo, London,
1997, pp. 41–79.   152–153
Lian Hearn, *Across the Nightingale Floor: Tales of the Otori, Book 1*,
Macmillan, London, 2002, p. 21.   154
Michael Cox, introduction to M. R. James, *Casting the Runes and Other
Ghost Stories*, Oxford University Press, Oxford, 1987, p. xvii.   155
M. R. James, 'A Neighbour's Landmark', in ibid., pp. 248–49.   155
M. R. James, 'Canon Alberic's Scrap-book', in ibid., p. 3.   155
M. R. James, 'Oh, Whistle, and I'll Come to You, My Lad', in ibid.,
pp. 55–57.   156
Sir Arthur Conan Doyle, 'The Japanned Box', in *Tales of Terror and
Mystery*, Pan Books, London, 1978, p. 166.   156
Ibid., p. 170.   157
John M. Picker, op. cit. p. 133.   157
Fernando Pessoa, *The Book of Disquiet*, trans. Richard Zenith, Penguin,
London, 2002, p. 34.   158
Virginia Woolf, *Jacob's Room*, op. cit., p. 85.   158
Virginia Woolf, *Mrs. Dalloway*, Penguin, London, 1996, pp. 2–3.   158
Virginia Woolf, quoted in Hermione Lee, op. cit. p. 462.   159
Virginia Woolf, *Mrs. Dalloway*, op. cit., pp. 48–49.   159
Georges Rodenbach, op. cit., p. 61.   159–160
Georges Perec, *Life: A User's Manual*, trans. David Bellos, Vintage,
London, 2003, p. 32.   160
Antonio Damasio, *Descartes' Error: Emotion, Reason and the Human Brain*,
Penguin, London, 2005, pp. 150–51.   160–161

Vladimir Nabokov, 'Sounds', in *Collected Stories*, Penguin, London, 2001,
p. 20.   161
Herman Melville, *Moby Dick*, op. cit., p. 111.   161
Ibid., pp. 132–33.   161
Edgar Allan Poe, 'Notes to Al Aaraaf', in *The Poems of Edgar Allan Poe*,
George Bell, London, 1974, p. 146.   162
Peter Ackroyd, *Poe: A Life Cut Short*, Chatto & Windus, London, 2008,
p. 137.   162
Ibid., p. 137.   162
Edgar Allan Poe, 'The Colloquy of Monos and Una', in *Poe's Tales of
Mystery and Imagination*, J. M. Dent, London, 1959, p. 119.   163
Edgar Allan Poe, 'Silence', in ibid., pp. 111–14.   163
Edgar Allan Poe, 'The Fall of the House of Usher', in ibid.,
pp. 128–44.   163–164
Edgar Allan Poe, *The Narrative of Arthur Gordon Pym of Nantucket*,
Penguin, London, 1980, p. 79.   164
Edgar Allan Poe, 'The Oblong Box', in *Poe's Tales of Mystery and
Imagination*, op. cit., pp. 323–33.   164–165
Sheridan Le Fanu, 'Green Tea', in *In a Glass Darkly*, Wordsworth
Editions, Ware, 1995, p. 17.   165
Daily Mail, 'How Napper was raped as a boy, disowned by family and
inspired by a Victoria horror story'. http://www.dailymail.co.uk/news/
article-1097937/How-Napper-raped-boy-disowned-family-inspired-
Victorian-horror-story.html (accessed 21.12.08).   166
Edgar Allan Poe, 'The Tell-Tale Heart', in *Poe's Tales of Mystery and
Imagination*, op. cit., pp. 289–93.   166
John E. Reilly, 'The Lesser Death Watch and "The Tell-Tale Heart"', The
Edgar Allan Poe Society of Baltimore. Letters and Articles on Edgar
Allan Poe, http://www.eapoe.org/papers/misc1990/jer19691.htm
(accessed 21.12.08).   167
Marcel Proust, *The Guermantes Way*, trans. Mark Treharne, Penguin,
London, 2003, pp. 71–75.   169
Samuel Beckett, *Embers*, Faber & Faber, London, 1965, p. 24.   169
Fernando Pessoa, op. cit., p. 42.   169–170
Tom Raworth, 'Blue Pig', in *Collected Poems*, Carcanet, Manchester,
2003, p. 71.   170
Algernon Blackwood, 'A Case of Eavesdropping', in *Ancient Sorceries and
Other Weird Stories*, Penguin, London, 1968, pp. 59–74.   170–171
Algernon Blackwood, 'The Empty House', in ibid., p. 20.   171
Algernon Blackwood, 'The Listener', in *Three Supernatural Classics*, Dover,
Mineola, NY, 2008, 103–31.   171
Algernon Blackwood, 'A Psychical Invasion', in *John Silence*, The
Richards Press, London, 1943, pp. 1–71.   172–173
Algernon Blackwood, 'The Wendigo', in *Tales of the Supernatural*, The
Boydell Press, Woodbridge, 1983, p. 92.   173
Algernon Blackwood, *The Touch of Pan*, in ibid., p. 233.   173
Algernon Blackwood, *The Willows*, in ibid., pp. 14–15.   173
Thomas De Quincey, *Suspiria de Profundis*, University of Michigan
University Library reprints, pp. 175–76.   174
Thomas Hardy, *Tess of the D'Urbervilles*, Macmillan, London, 1970, p. 440. 174

NOTES

Samuel Taylor Coleridge, *The Major Works*, Oxford University Press,
Oxford and New York, 1985, p. 27.   175
Algernon Blackwood, 'Ancient Sorceries', op. cit., pp. 83–84.   175
Anton Chekhov, *The Cherry Orchard*, trans. Michael Frayn, Methuen
Drama, London, 1990, p. 33.   175
Yasunari Kawabata, *The Sound of the Mountain*, trans. Edward M.
Seidensticker, Penguin, London, 1974, pp. 10–12.   175–176
William Shakespeare, *Macbeth*, (II.2.3).   176
E. M. Forster, *A Passage To India*, Penguin, London, 2005, p. 137.   176
Ibid., p. 139.   176
Ibid., p. 157.   176
E. M Forster, 'The Eternal Moment', in *Collected Short Stories*, Penguin,
London, p. 209.   176–177
Elizabeth Grosz, *Chaos, Territory, Art: Deleuze and the Framing of the Earth*,
Columbia University Press, New York, 2008, p. 26.   177
John Cowper Powys, *A Glastonbury Romance*, Picador, London, 1975,
p. 216.   177

10. Snow falling on snow

John Cowper Powys, *A Glastonbury Romance*, op. cit., pp. 65–66.   181
John Cowper Powys, *Wolf Solent*, Penguin, London, 2000, p. 433.   181
Ibid., p. 105.   181
Ibid., p. 537.   182
William Shakespeare, *Troilus and Cressida*, (V.9.1).   184
Henri Lefebvre, *The Production of Space*, trans. Donald Nicholson-Smith,
Blackwell, Oxford, 1991, p. 286.   184
Leonardo da Vinci, *Notebooks*, Oxford University Press, Oxford, 2008,
p. 106.   185
William Shakespeare, *King Lear* (III.7.82–84).   185
James Joyce, *A Portrait of the Artist as a Young Man*, op. cit., pp. 12–14. 186
Tom Rice, 'The Doctor', *The Erotic Review*, Issue 86, February 2008,
pp. 74–78.   186–187
Vladimir Nabokov, *Laughter in the Dark*, Penguin, London, 2001,
p. 103.   187
Wilkie Collins, *The Haunted Hotel*, Oxford University Press, Oxford,
1999, p. 230.   187–188
Leonora Carrington, *The Hearing Trumpet*, Penguin, London, 2005,
p. 6.   189
Bruno Schulz, 'The Night of the Great Season', in Schulz, op. cit., p. 91. 189
Barbara E. Weinstein, *Geriatric Audiology*, Thieme, NY, 2000, p. 86.   189
William Shakespeare, *Julius Caesar* (III.2.78–79).   189
Martin Gayford, *The Yellow House*, Fig Tree, London, 2006, p. 293.   191
David Sweetman, *Paul Gauguin: A Complete Life*, Hodder & Stoughton,
London, 1995, pp. 213–15.   191
Siegfried Wiemann, *Japonisme*, Thames & Hudson, London, 1999, p. 42.   191
Georges Bataille, 'Sacrificial Mutilation and the Severed Ear of Vincent
Van Gogh', in *Visions of Excess: Selected Writings, 1927–1939*, Theory
and History of Literature, Volume 14, ed. Allan Stoekl, University of
Minnesota Press, Minneapolis, 1985, pp. 67–70.   191
Zbigniew Herbert, *Still Life with a Bridle*, Vintage, London, 1991, p. 84. 192

NOTES

Lafcadio Hearn, 'The Story of Mimi-Nashi-Hoichi', in *Writings From Japan*, Penguin, London, 1984, pp. 319–28. 192
Poul Erik Tojner, *Munch: In his Own Words*, Prestel, Munich, London, New York, 2003, p. 21. 193
Ibid. p. 91. 193
Ibid. p. 122–23. 193–194
David Anfam, 'The World in a Frame', in *Rothko*, ed. Achim Borchardt-Hume, Tate Publishing, London, 2008, p. 55. 194
Henri Lefebvre, *Rhythmanalysis: Space, Time and Everyday Life*, trans. Stuart Elden and Gerald Moore, Continuum, London, 2005, pp. 10–11. 195–196
Harry Martinson, *Views from a Tuft of Grass*, Green Integer, Copenhagen and Los Angeles, 2005, p. 34. 196
Henri Lefebvre, *Rhythmanalysis*, op. cit., p. 19. 196
Joseph Conrad, 'The Secret Sharer', in *'Twixt Land and Sea*, Penguin, 1990, pp. 81–124. 196–198
Albert J. Guerard, *Conrad: The Novelist*, Oxford University Press, London, 1958, 24–25. 198
Georges Bataille, 'The Sacred Conspiracy', in *Visions of Excess*, op. cit., p. 180. 199
Joseph Conrad, *Heart of Darkness*, Penguin, London, 1978, p. 48. 199
Joseph Conrad, *The Lagoon*, Oxford University Press, Oxford, 1997, p. 27. 199
Joseph Conrad, *The Shadow-Line*, op. cit., pp. 108–14. 199
William Shakespeare, *Hamlet* (III.1.75). 200
John Cage, *Silence*, Marion Boyars, London, 1987, p. 8. 200
William Faulkner, *The Sound and the Fury*, Vintage, London, 1995, p. 122. 200
Virginia Woolf, *Jacob's Room*, op. cit., p. 49. 200
Virginia Woolf, *To the Lighthouse*, Penguin, 1970, p. 161. 200–201
Po Chü-i, 'After Getting Drunk, Becoming Sober in the Night', in *Chinese Poems*, trans. Arthur Waley, op. cit., p. 176. 201
Philip Gröning, *Into Great Silence*, Soda Pictures DVD, UK, 2006. 201
Wilkie Collins, *The Woman in White*, Oxford University Press, Oxford, 1998, p. 43. 202
Ibid., p. 313. 202
Ibid., p. 363. 202
Ibid., p. 268. 202
Ibid., pp. 580–81. 202–203
Mark Godfrey, *The Last Silent Movie*, exhibition catalogue to accompany *The Last Silent Movie* by Susan Hiller, Matt's Gallery, London, 2008, p. 2. 203
Jenny Diski, Little Brown, London, 2006, p. 66. 204
Samuel Beckett, quoted in James Knowlson, *Damned to Fame*, op. cit., p. 233. 204
Michel Chion, *The Films of Jacques Tati*, trans. Antonio D'Alfonso, Guernica, Toronto, 2003, p. 79. 205
Angelique Chrisafis, 'Marceau, last master of mime, dies at 84', *Guardian*, 24.09.2007, p. 1. 205
Peter Eisenman, quoted in Luke Harding, '60 years on, Berlin honours Hitler's victims', *Guardian*, 11.05.2005. http://www.guardian.co.uk/world/2005/may/11/secondworldwar.germany (accessed 30.12.2008). 206
Susan Sontag, 'The Aesthetics of Silence', in *Aspen: The Minimalism Issue*,

249

NOTES

ed. Brian O'Doherty, Fall/Winter 1967, Roaring Fork Press, NYC, no. 5–6, p. 18.   206

Franz Kafka, 'Great Noise', trans. Michael Hoffmann, in *Metamorphosis and Other Stories*, Penguin, London, 2007, p. 296.   206

Franz Kafka, 'The Burrow', trans. Willa and Edwin Muir, in *The Complete Short Stories*, Vintage, London, 1999, pp. 325–59.   206–207

Franz Kafka, *The Blue Octavo Notebooks*, ed. Max Brod, Exact Change, Cambridge, MA, 1991, p. 1.   207

Anthony Vidler, *The Architectural Uncanny: Essays in the Modern Unhomely*, The MIT Press, Cambridge, MA, 1992, p. 167.   207

Lawrence Weschler, *Seeing is Forgetting the Name of the Thing One Sees: A life of Contemporary Artist Robert Irwin*, University of California Press, Berkeley, 1982, pp. 128–30.   208

Adrian Kohn, *See Like Irwin*, Chinati Foundation newsletter, volume 12, October 2007, p. 26.   208

Emily Cockayne, op. cit., pp. 127–28.   209

Francois Rabelais, *Gargantua and Pantagruel*, trans. J. M. Cohen, Penguin, London, 1974, p. 322.   209

William Seabrook, *Witchcraft*, Sphere Books, London, 1970, p. 244.   210

William Seabrook, *No Hiding Place*, J. B. Lippincott Company, Philadelphia/London and New York, 1942, p. 9.   210

Man Ray, *Self Portrait*, Andre Deutsch, London, 1963, p. 194.   210

William Seabrook, *Witchcraft*, op. cit., pp. 198–99.   210

Georges Rodenbach, *The Bells of Bruges*, trans. Mike Mitchell, Dedalus, Sawtry, 2007, p. 35.   211

Ibid., p. 34.   211

Knut Hamsun, *Pan*, op. cit. pp. 131–32.   211

Virginia Woolf, *Jacob's Room*, op. cit., p. 31.   211

Mark Rothko, *The Artist's Reality: Philosophies of Art*, Yale University Press, New Haven and London, 2004, p. 56.   212

Herman Melville, *The Enchanted Isles*, Hesperus Press, London, 2002, p. 6.   212

Edward S. Casey, *The Fate of Place: A Philosophical History*, University of California Press, Berkeley, 1998, p. 343.   212

David Lynch, *Lynch on Lynch*, op. cit., p. 102.   212

Jacob Kirkegaard, *4 Rooms*, Touch CD, Tone 26, UK, 2006.   213

Tōru Takemitsu, 'A Single Sound' (1971), in *Confronting Silence*, Fallen Leaf Press, Berkeley, 1995, p. 52.   213

Tom Johnson, notes to *Organ And Silence*, Ants CD, Italy, 2003.   213

Vladimir Jankélévitch, *Music and the Ineffable*, op. cit., pp. 140–41.   213–214

Herbert Henck, notes to Federico Mompou, *Música Callada*, ECM CD, ECM 1523, 1995.   214

Vladimir Jankélévitch, op. cit., p. 142.   214

Morton Feldman, 'The Future of Local Music', in *Give My Regards to Eighth Street*, Exact Change, Cambridge, 2000, p. 194.   214

Yasunari Kawabata, *The Old Capital*, trans. J. Martin Holman, Shoemaker & Hoard, USA, 2006, p. 42.   214–215

Stuart Sim, *Manifesto For Silence: Confronting the Politics and Culture of Noise*, Edinburgh University Press, 2007, p. 122.   215

John Lane, *The Spirit of Silence: Making Space for Creativity*, Green Books, Devon, 2006, p. 55.   215

Lavinia Greenlaw, *The Importance of Music to Girls*, Faber & Faber, London, 2007, p. 90.   216
Virginia Woolf, *The Voyage Out*, Oxford University Press, Oxford, 2001, p. 249.   217
Sara Maitland, *A Book of Silence*, Granta, London, 2008, p. 41.   217
Ibid., p. 276.   217
Fernando Pessoa, *The Book of Disquiet*, op. cit., p. 65.   218
Alberto Manguel, *A History of Reading*, Flamingo, London, 1997, p. 51.   218
Thomas Merton, *Dialogues with Silence: Prayers & Drawings*, ed. Jonathan Montaldo, HarperSanFrancisco, New York, 2001, p. 145.   218
Patrick Leigh Fermor, *A Time to Keep Silence*, John Murray, 2004, p. 37.   219
Ibid., pp. 7–8.   219
George Eliot, *Silas Marner*, Penguin, London, 1996, p. 6.   219
Sylvia Plath, *The Bell Jar*, Faber & Faber, London, 1966, p. 17.   220
Tsuboi Shigeji, 'Silent, but . . .', in *The Penguin Book of Japanese Verse*, op. cit., p. 191.   220
'Magic Mountain: A conversation between Ilya and Emilia Kabakov and Cheryl Kaplan', *DB ArtMag*, Issue 19. http://www.db-artmag. de//2004/4/e/1/218.php (accessed 31.10.2008).   220
Yasunari Kawabata, 'Gleanings from Snow Country', in *Palm-of-the-Hand Stories*, trans. Lane Dunlop and J. Martin Holman, North Point Press, New York, p. 236.   221
Yasunari Kawabata, 'Raindrops', in *First Snow on Fuji*, trans. Michael Emmerich, Counterpoint, Washington DC, 1999, p. 97.   221
Yasunari Kawabata, 'Love Suicides', in *Palm-of-the-Hand Stories*, op. cit., pp. 53–54.   221–222
Yasunari Kawabata, 'Silence', in *First Snow on Fuji*, op. cit., 153–73.   222–223
Ad Reinhardt, *Art As Art: The Selected Writings of Ad Reinhardt*, ed. Barbara Rose, The Viking Press, New York, 1975, pp. 206–7.   223
Matthew Gale, 'From Alphabet to Zone', in *Beyond Painting: Burri, Fontana, Manzoni*, Tate Publishing in association with Mazzotta, London, 2005, p. 83.   224
Robert Ryman, quoted in Robert Storr, *Robert Ryman*, Tate Gallery, London, 1993, p. 12.   224
Henri Michaux, 'With Mescaline', in *Darkness Moves: An Henri Michaux Anthology 1927–1984*, trans. D. Ball, Berkeley and London, 1994, p. 198.   224–225
Hannah Weitemeier, *Klein*, Taschen, Cologne, 2001, p. 11.   225
Ad Reinhardt, op. cit., p. 113.   226
Ibid., p. 99.   226
Robert Lax, 'On Poetry and Language', in Robert Garlitz, Nicholas Zurbrugg, Robert Lax and Rupert Loydell, *Robert Lax: Speaking into Silence*, Stride, Exeter, 2001, p. 49.   226
Robert Lax, *Psalm*, Stride, Exeter, 1991.   226
Robert Lax, *Journal F: Kalymnos Journal*, ed. John Beer, Pendo, Switzerland, 1997, p. 118.   226
Robert Lax, *Speaking into Silence*, op. cit., p. 26.   227
Novalis, *Hymns to the Night*, trans. Dick Higgins, McPherson & Company, New York, 1988, p. 49.   227

NOTES

Stephanie Rosenthal, *Black Paintings*, Haus der Kunst, Hatje Cantz
Verlag, Munich, 2007, p. 73.   227 228

Christoph Metzher, 'Mapping — Contexts: The Electrical Walks of
Christina Kubisch — Cartographies Through Sound', in Christina
Kubisch, *Stromzeichnungen/Electrical Drawings*, Kehrer Verlag,
Heidelberg, 2008, p. 81.   228–229

Louise K. Wilson, *A Record of Fear*, National Trust and Commissions
East, Cambridge, 2005, pp. 8–9.   229

Akio Suzuki, *Pyramid 2005 for John Cage, Playing John Cage*, exhibition
catalogue ed. David Toop and Martin Clark, Arnolfini Gallery,
Bristol, 2005.   229–230

Samuel Beckett, *Ill Seen Ill Said*, John Calder, London, 1997, p. 34.   230

Coda: Distant Music

Susan Philipsz, *There Is Nothing Left Here*, Centro Galego de Arte
Contemporánea, Santiago de Compostela, 2007, p. 101.   231

James Joyce, 'The Dead', in *Dubliners*, Penguin, London, 2000, p. 211.   232

Ibid., p. 225.   232

James Knowlson, *Damned to Fame*, op. cit., p. 614.   233

Samuel Beckett, 'Footfalls', in *Collected Shorter Plays*, op. cit., p. 239.   233

Index